Headlines in Women's Health 1997

Headlines in Women's Health 1997

Essential News You Can Use to Shape Up, Energize, and Outsmart Disease

Edited by Sarí Harrar

Rodale Press, Inc.
Emmaus, Pennsylvania

This book is being published simultaneously by Rodale Press as *Health Hints for Women*.

Copyright © 1997 by Rodale Press, Inc.

Illustrations copyright © 1997 by Janet Hamlin
Illustrations copyright © 1997 by Michael Gellatly
Cover photographs copyright © 1997 by Mitch Mandel

The credits for this book begin on page 295.

ISBN 0–87596–392–7 hardcover

Distributed in the book trade by St. Martin's Press

2 4 6 8 10 9 7 5 3 1 hardcover

───── OUR PURPOSE ─────

*"We inspire and enable people to improve
their lives and the world around them."*

Headlines in Women's Health 1997

Editorial Staff

Editor: Sarí Harrar
Managing Editor: Sharon Faelten
Contributing Writers: Betsy Bates, Jan Bresnick, Tara Cranmer, Mark Golin, JoAnn Greco, Toby Hanlon, Carla Kallan, Linda Konner, Denise Lanctot, Laura Flynn McCarthy, Holly McCord, Peggy Morgan, Marty Munson, Kristine Napier, Emrika Padus, Cathy Perlmutter, Linda Rao, Cheryl Sacra, Susan Telingator, Elisabeth Torg, Margo Trott
Permissions Coordinator: Joely Johnson
Book Researcher: Valerie Edwards-Paulik
Fact-Checkers: Susan E. Burdick, Christine Dreisbach, Carol J. Gilmore, Joely Johnson, Nicole A. Kelly, Kathryn Piff, Sandra Salera-Lloyd, Michelle M. Szulborski
Associate Art Director: Faith Hague
Book and Cover Designer: Christopher R. Neyen
Studio Manager: Stefano Carbini
Technical Artist: William L. Allen
Photo Editor: Susan Pollack
Copy Editor: Karen Neely
Production Manager: Helen Clogston
Manufacturing Coordinator: Melinda B. Rizzo
Office Staff: Roberta Mulliner, Julie Kehs, Bernadette Sauerwine, Mary Lou Stephen

Rodale Health and Fitness Books

Vice-President and Editorial Director: Debora T. Yost
Art Director: Jane Colby Knutila
Research Manager: Ann Gossy Yermish
Copy Manager: Lisa D. Andruscavage

Contents

INTRODUCTION   ix

PART 1: NEW CHOICES IN WOMEN'S HEALTH

Female Advantage: Making the Most of Your Longevity Edge   2

1   Perimenopause: The New "In" Condition   3
2   Birth Control: New Facts That Calm the Fears   9
3   Saying No to Hysterectomy: The Controversy Continues   16
4   The New Prescription for Passion   22
5   Custom-Tailor Your Hormone Therapy   28
6   Call the Shots with Your 40-Something Pregnancy   36

PART 2: FOOD AND YOU

Female Advantage: The Wisdom behind Food Cravings   44

7   Slash the Fat, Keep the Flavor   45
8   The Healing Power of Phytomins   52
9   Soy: Savor the New, White-Hot Superfood   58
10   Trans-fat: The Big, Bad, Sneaky Fat   63
11   Olestra: Olé or Oh No?   67
12   Brave New Breakfast   71

PART 3: NATURAL HEALING

Female Advantage: Alternative Healing Pioneers   78

13   Alternative Healing: New Options for Women   79
14   The Mind-Body Connection: Stronger Than Ever   86
15   Uncommon Relief from the Common Cold   92
16   New Thinking That Outsmarts the Blues   98

PART 4: OUTSMARTING DISEASE

Female Advantage: Estrogen—A Woman's Healthy Hormone   108

17   Build Stronger Bones at Any Age   109
18   Get Heart Smart   116
19   Good, Better, Best Breast Care   123
20   Take Control of Your Checkup   130
21   Smoking: Why Women Need to Quit   134
22   Diabetes: Avoid It Now   140
23   Eating Clear of Cancer   146

24 Arthritis, at Your Age? 152
25 At Last, Relief for That Splitting Headache 157
26 The New Tune-Up for Stress Incontinence 162

Part 5: Your Perfect Weight

Female Advantage: Why Big Hips Are Less Risky for Your Health **170**
27 Fill Up to Slim Down 171
28 New Lessons from the *Real* Weight-Loss Experts 176
29 The New Obesity Drugs: Are They Right for You? 182
30 Break the Emotional Eating Cycle 186
31 The Seven-Meals-a-Day Diet 192

Part 6: Body Sculpting

Female Advantage: That's Not Vacuuming, It's Aerobics **200**
32 Walking: Everybody's Doing It! 201
33 A Routine to Shed a Size 206
34 The New Strategy for a Flat Stomach 225
35 Stop Making Excuses! 233
36 The Stairway to Weight-Loss Heaven 237

Part 7: Nurturing Yourself

Female Advantage: The Healing Power of Sex **244**
37 The New Fatigue Fighters 245
38 The Perfect De-Stressors 251
39 Sizzling Secrets for More and Better Sex 256
40 Take Five to Make Love Last 261
41 Good News That Can Jolt Your Marriage 266

Part 8: Age-Defying Beauty Secrets

Female Advantage: Turn Back the Clock **272**
42 The Year's 20 Top Natural Beauty Solutions 273
43 How Will You Look Ten Years from Now? 279
44 Sleep: Nature's New Beauty Secret 286
45 The Inside Story on Thick, Lustrous Hair 290

Credits 295

Index 296

Introduction

Once, news about women's health was a scarce commodity. Researchers barely studied us. Our doctors knew little about our unique needs. And so we were left with lots of unanswered questions.

Today, it's a far different story. Urgent reports demand our attention daily, courtesy of screaming newspaper headlines and breathless television announcers: Breast Cancer Gene Discovered! New Diet Pill on the Market! New Tools for Pap Smears! Fake Fat Hits Supermarket Shelves! New Benefits of Hormone Replacement Therapy! Obesity Gene Found! Menopause Breakthrough! Diabetes Alert! Arthritis Epidemic!

Whew. Once a drought, women's health news is now a thundering deluge. With it come new questions: How do we sort it all out? What's really important? And what, in this information overload, is useful?

That is where *Headlines in Women's Health 1997* comes in. For while women's health research has skyrocketed into exciting, new territory—thanks in part to a huge financial commitment from the federal government and its Women's Health Initiative—this is territory without a guidebook. Sure, more is known today than ever before about how to eat for good health; keep fit and firm despite a busy schedule; protect your body from disease in gentle, natural ways and look—and feel—young, but you have to know where to look to get the latest, most practical information—the news you can really use. You need a guide. And that's just what this book is.

From weight-loss strategies that really work to the latest on breast cancer, from natural cosmetics to women's most surprising, overlooked health threats, this is the only almanac that translates the year's most significant medical breakthroughs into expert advice you can put to use right now.

That's not all. At *Prevention* Magazine Health Books, we haven't forgotten that being a woman is something to be celebrated and enjoyed. Look inside for our special reports on the unique advantages of being female—from the hormone that promotes radiant health to the real reasons why women live longer, from the food cravings that enhance a woman's well-being to the unique ways we sidestep the aging process.

There has never been a more exciting time to learn about our bodies, minds and spirits. We believe that the information inside this book can help you enhance your life. Use it in good health.

—Sarí Harrar
Editor

NEW CHOICES IN WOMEN'S HEALTH

Part **1**

We have to protect our bodies, preserve our health. It's exhilarating, if we really take charge.

—gynecologist Anita L. Nelson, M.D.

Female Advantage

Making the Most of Your Longevity Edge

Next time someone claims that women are the weaker sex, play this card: On the average, life expectancy at birth for women is seven years longer than for men.

Why? For starters, we can thank our health care habits—women between 15 and 44 years of age go to the doctor's office about four times a year, compared to 2.1 visits by men.

"Women see doctors more than men do, and I think that contributes to their overall well-being," says Mary Lake Polan, M.D., Ph.D., chairman of obstetrics and gynecology at Stanford University Medical Center in California.

Women have lower rates of heart disease prior to menopause, have a lower rate of cigarette smoking and also have somewhat lower death rates from trauma, accidents and injuries than men do, says JoAnn E. Manson, M.D., associate professor of medicine at Harvard Medical School and co-director of women's health at Brigham and Women's Hospital, both in Boston.

Finally, women are relationship-oriented, and relationships seem to extend life. "It's quite clear that people with no social contact don't do well," Dr. Polan says.

Yet, while women tend to live longer, the quality of those last years can be compromised by disease and disability, experts say. Happily, they needn't be. Here are steps that you can take to maintain your longevity advantage and enjoy that extra time.

▶ Censure cigarettes. If you're not a smoker, don't begin, says Dr. Manson. And if you are, do your best to quit, she says.

▶ Eat right and exercise. Do your best to eat a low-fat, high-fiber diet that is rich in fruits, vegetables, whole grains and calcium. Also, be sure to get at least 30 minutes of exercise daily, Dr. Manson says.

▶ Know your history. Take a really good look at your family's health history, says Jean L. Fourcroy, M.D., Ph.D., past president of the American Medical Women's Association in Alexandria, Virginia. Did anyone have heart disease, osteoporosis, cancer or other health problems? If so, you're at higher risk, too, and should take preventive steps now.

▶ Go for those routine doctor visits and ask lots of questions, says Dr. Polan.

▶ Try hormone replacement therapy. Women who use HRT at menopause live about seven years longer than women who don't, says Dr. Polan.

▶ Connect. Maintain strong social support networks, says Dr. Polan.

Perimenopause: The New "In"Condition

Jane was fit, fine and 42 when she went to the gynecologist for her yearly checkup. It was a medical ritual she had followed every year since her first pregnancy. She expected no news but the same news: All systems go.

But this time, lab tests showed that Jane was in something called perimenopause. Jane was startled. So soon? She thought menopause was years away.

She wasn't alone. This year, an estimated 21 million American women will find themselves in perimenopause—the transition years between fertility and menopause. For many, it will come as a surprise—as it did for Jane. For while perimenopause is a natural, normal experience that nearly every woman will experience, few have known about it.

Prelude to the Change

Menopause signals that you're done with the 900,000 or so eggs that you were born with. The supply source, your ovaries, shuts down hormone production.

But it doesn't happen all at once. Before fertility is officially over, the ovaries make noises about retirement and get ready to hang out the sign, "Gone fishin'." It's this stage of limbo that doctors call perimenopause.

During perimenopause, a woman's supply of the hormone estrogen starts to waver. The hormone supply doesn't stop suddenly, but it declines enough to cause irregular periods. And the hormone has an influence on so many of our bodies' functions that all sorts of changes occur when there's a shortage.

Perimenopause is a stage that can last anywhere from two to ten years or so. For each woman, the symptoms and signs of approaching menopause are different—and so is the time frame.

Falling levels of estrogen usually cause irregular periods—and often this is the first clue of menopause. Also, some women experience vaginal dryness and frequent urination.

About 85 percent of American women have hot flashes when they're in perimenopause. But hot flashes come in different forms. You may start sweating furiously even when the weather is cool. Or you'll suddenly feel the merest flicker of heat at the back of the neck. Night sweats are another common form of hot flashes, which may in turn be responsible for some of the many other symptoms often blamed on menopause: insomnia, fatigue, irritability, mood swings, depression and forgetfulness, says Jennifer Prouty, clinical faculty at Northeastern University College of Nursing in Boston and a menopause consultant.

Estrogen affects the body in other ways as well. "Every place you turn in a woman's body there are estrogen receptors. They're in her heart, her bones, her arteries and her brain—not just in her reproductive organs and her breasts," notes Bernadine Healy, M.D., a cardiologist at the Cleveland Clinic Foundation in Ohio and former director of the National Institutes of Health in Bethesda, Maryland.

A woman's risk of osteoporosis and heart disease begins to soar when estrogen is depleted. Since estrogen protects your bones and is believed to also protect your heart, when it recedes, you have to consciously work to compensate for its loss—with diet, exercise and possibly hormone replacement therapy.

Listen to Your Body Clock

Think of perimenopause as a little wake-up call. Your body's saying, "Hey, big changes are just ahead. Now's the perfect time to start protecting your health, your energy, even your figure."

Knowing that someday your body will stop producing estrogen, you can help reduce your risks of bone loss and heart disease if you prepare for that change in advance. "We have to prepare for what's coming—protect our bodies, preserve our health. Menopause is sobering, but it's exhilarating, too, if we plan ahead and really take charge of our health," says Anita L. Nelson, M.D., associate professor of obstetrics and gynecology at the University of California, Los Angeles.

The two best ways to prepare for menopause sound awfully familiar. They're the one-two combo of diet and exercise. But even if you already pay attention to both, you may need to revise them a little to get ready for the changes that menopause brings.

Bear some weight. If your diet is low in calcium and your life is low in exercise, you may actually start losing bone in your thirties. That loss accelerates as you approach menopause. But you can slow the rate of bone loss with weight-bearing exercise. "Exercise that bears the full weight of the body is what's important," says Prouty.

For many women, the most convenient forms of weight-bearing exercise are walking, running or low-impact aerobic dancing. Try to get at least 20 to 30 minutes of nonstop moderate aerobic exercise three times a week.

Be upwardly mobile. While walking and running will help build the bones below the waist, you need strength training to build bone in the upper part of your body. Experts recommend resistance exercise three times a week (preferably on nonconsecutive days), using dumbbells, weight machines or

---

Baby Boomers Tell Doctors: Pay Attention!

HEALTH FLASH

Finally, doctors are taking seriously the hot flashes, irregular menstrual cycles, sleep problems, lethargy and roller-coaster moods reported by women as early as their mid-thirties and into their late forties—the years before falling hormone levels place them in "official" menopause.

"The big news is that physicians are now recognizing that most symptoms actually peak in perimenopause, not in menopause," says Carolyn Coker Ross, M.D., president of Women's Health Specialists of San Diego.

For so long, women thought that the symptoms of perimenopause were all in their heads; since their hormone levels were completely normal, there was no "proof" to support their symptoms, says Dr. Ross. But no longer—doctors now know that as many as 90 percent of all women go through perimenopause, which can last four to five years before menopause occurs.

Why has this long-overlooked phase of life suddenly come to light? Thank the baby boomers, experts say. With their health savvy and financial clout, female baby boomers are demanding more information about perimenopause from their doctors so that they can sail through this time with confidence and comfort—rather than be controlled by it.

When should you take perimenopause seriously? Once your symptoms begin to interfere with the quality of your life, Dr. Ross suggests.

Start with self-care techniques, including exercise to boost your mood and fight weight gain. Load up on foods rich in natural estrogen, which may help offset falling levels of estrogen in your body, and energy-boosting protein, such as soy and split peas, Dr. Ross says.

exercise bands to target specific muscles or muscle groups in the body.

Attack fat. Since your risk of heart disease shoots up when your body needs estrogen, the less artery-clogging fat in your diet, the better. A diet that is low in saturated animal fat and high in fiber, fruits and vegetables is your best heart-healthy bet.

The Big Decision

If you're in your forties or even late thirties, your eye has probably been caught by the latest article on menopause and hormone replacement therapy. Every day, it seems, new research on hormone replacement's risks and benefits hits the journals and newspapers.

As soon as you approach perimenopause, your gynecologist will most likely raise the issue of hormone therapy for you to consider. She may believe deeply in its benefits, because it does chill out hot flashes and may relieve other symptoms such as irritability and sleep disturbances. Hormone replacement will also improve the ratio of "good" cholesterol to "bad" cholesterol in your blood, and it helps put the brakes on bone loss. There are even some studies linking this therapy to a lower incidence of Alzheimer's disease.

One factor to consider is how long you may be on hormone replacement. Originally, the hormones were prescribed to quell hot flashes and other menopause symptoms. "But that's a relatively short-term consideration—five years or so," says Irma L. Mebane-Sims, Ph.D., an epidemiologist and program administrator of the groundbreaking Postmenopausal Estrogen/Progestin Interventions Trial at the National Institutes of Health.

A woman who is taking hormones for its two greatest benefits—to reduce heart disease risk or osteoporosis risk—is using it as a preventive medication for the long term. "Osteoporosis specialists give a women at least 10 to 15 years on hormone replacement therapy, and then they re-evaluate her. A cardiologist knows that only current users of hormone replacement enjoy the reduction from heart attack risks," says Dr. Nelson.

Despite the benefits, some doctors are reluctant to prescribe it, relying instead on exercise and diet to treat symptoms and lessen risk.

A number of doctors, like JoAnn E. Manson, M.D., associate professor of medicine at Harvard Medical School, co-director of women's health at Brigham and Women's Hospital in Boston and the co-principal investigator of the cardiovascular component of the Harvard University Nurses' Health Study, agree with the conclusion of a mega-study that reviewed all the data on hormone therapy since 1970: "Hormone therapy should probably be recommended for women who have had a hysterectomy and for those with coronary heart disease or at high risk for coronary heart disease. For other women, the best course of action is unclear."

Whether you choose to take hormones or not, doctors agree that you shouldn't neglect diet and exercise.

"You shouldn't rely on pills to do things a good lifestyle should be doing," says Rena Vassilopoulou-Sellin, M.D., associate professor of endocrinology at the University of Texas M. D. Anderson Cancer Center in Houston.

The American Medical Women's Association has declared that "for a woman entering or past the age of menopause, exercise may be the single best thing she can do for her emotional and physical health."

Cooling the Hot Flashes

One of the benefits of hormone replacement therapy is that it eliminates hot flashes. But there are also specific techniques that you can use to help control the hot flashes—or night sweats—that are so uncomfortable for women in perimenopause. Here's what Diana L. Dell, M.D., assistant professor of obstetrics and gynecology at Duke University Medical Center in Durham, North Carolina, recommends.

Deep breathe. Hot flashes can hit unexpectedly, whether you're lying in bed about to doze off or on the brink of a very important meeting with a very big client. What to do? Start breathing.

Here's how: Expel as much breath as you can, then fill your lungs again by expanding your diaphragm—the area between your rib cage and abdomen. Release that breath fully. Repeat with a steady rhythm, and you may be able to squelch a hot flash before the sweating begins.

Douse that sizzle. Sizzling foods—either high temperature or fired with chili peppers—are notorious hot-flash provocateurs, so stick with cooler fare.

Check your drinks. Alcohol and caffeine can make you flush. Watch your reaction to coffee, tea and colas—and give them up if they lead to hot flashes. And remember, chocolate also has caffeine, too.

Hydro Power

Some women report a lack of sexual desire that comes with menopause—which may be partly due to vaginal discomfort. Loss of estrogen has a general drying effect on tissues and organs in the body, particularly in the pelvic region. And if your vagina is dry, sexual activity may be uncomfortable.

Happily, simple solutions exist. Here's what experts recommend.

Make it moister. "There are a variety of lubricants and moisturizers on the market now," says Prouty. K-Y Jelly is the classic. But that has been joined by Astroglide and moisturizers like Replens. "They have chemicals in them that create a little bit of penetration into the vaginal walls, so they're longer lasting," says Prouty.

Some women like evening primrose or vitamin E oils—and saliva works, too, adds Prouty. But avoid perfumed oils and petroleum jelly that may contain irritating substances.

Do a dab of estrogen. A topical estrogen cream, available by prescription,

The Perimenopause Diet

With just a little tweaking, a good diet can turn into a menu that counters some of the effects of estrogen's fall during perimenopause and into menopause.

For starters, you'll need more calcium—1,500 milligrams daily (or 1,000 milligrams if you're on hormone replacement therapy). Ideally, you should get all this calcium from food, because the mineral is best absorbed when it comes from food sources. Low-fat and fat-free dairy products, canned fish with bones such as sardines, and calcium-fortified orange juice are good places to start.

But calcium isn't the only nutrient that you need at menopause. Here are some other foods that Diana L. Dell, M.D., assistant professor of obstetrics and gynecology at Duke University Medical Center in Durham, North Carolina, recommends to help you through this time.

▶ Eight eight-ounce glasses of water a day help keep that pelvic area moist.
▶ Foods with fatty acids, like sunflower seeds, salmon, soybeans and leafy green vegetables, moisturize the body, too.
▶ Potassium salt (such as Morton Salt Substitute) instead of table salt can reduce menopausal bloating and water retention.
▶ Foods with beta-carotene and vitamins C and E—the antioxidants—have been found to help reduce the risk of heart disease.
▶ Onions and garlic lower cholesterol.
▶ Foods with fiber, like whole-wheat breads, fruits and vegetables, also help lower cholesterol and may be useful in colon cancer prevention.
▶ Chamomile and ginger are herbs that soothe symptoms. Both make good tea.

thickens the tissues around the vagina. But talk to your doctor before using it long term; since estrogen is very efficiently absorbed by the body, using it for a long time can have side effects, according to Dr. Dell.

Go orgasmic. Regular orgasms—either with a partner or through masturbation—help to maintain healthy tissues, according to Prouty.

Controlling Factors

After menopause, tissues in the pelvic area get thinner and weaker, which can cause an increase of urinary tract infections and vaginal infections in some women. Lacking estrogen, muscles in the pelvis also start to slacken. And when the bladder loses the support of surrounding tissues, you'll probably urinate more often. And a sudden laugh or cough may produce the unsettling sensation that you're wetting yourself.

To help prevent urinary tract and vaginal infections, Dr. Dell advises wearing cotton underpants, even under panty hose. Avoid underwear that's made of nylon, rayon and other synthetic fibers. Those fabrics trap moisture, air and bacteria—three ingredients that help increase the opportunities for infection.

If you're having problems with stress incontinence or frequent urination, you can train your pelvic floor muscles to help control yourself. Kegel exercises will strengthen the muscles and tissues of the urinary tract and vagina. Next time you urinate, stop the flow, then release it again. The muscles you use to stop your urinary stream are the pelvic floor muscles. That's the movement to practice when tuning them up for action.

Birth Control: New Facts That Calm the Fears

Q uestion: What do you call a couple who uses the rhythm method for birth control?

Answer: Parents!

Okay, so the joke's not Seinfeld material. And you realize that the rhythm method is not much of a method at all.

But let's take stock. Are you up-to-date on current forms of birth control? Do you know as much as you need to know? And is what you think you know really accurate?

There's a chance that the answer for each is no.

Surprised? Quite a few myths and misperceptions about birth control still persist, doctors say. For example, once women pass age 35, they often think that they don't need to worry about birth control as much. The reality is, they do.

Some women view sterilization as the only effective long-term method of birth control. The truth of the matter is, it's not.

Still other women may fear that the Pill is unsafe. Yet for the right women, doctors say, it's very safe.

Many women probably think that the intrauterine device (IUD) isn't really an option for them. But it's one that some women should consider more, doctors say.

When it comes to birth control, clearing up rumors and misconceptions is a full-time job for myth-busters. Here are some of those myths—and what experts say about them.

Myth #1: I'm Too Old to Get Pregnant

When women reach their late thirties and early forties, they often perceive that their chances of conceiving are less likely, agrees Paul Blumenthal, M.D., assistant professor of obstetrics and gynecology at Johns Hopkins Bayview Medical Center in Baltimore. But it's not always true.

Thirtysomething and fortysomething women can accidentally get pregnant when their birth control methods fail, when they choose less effective methods with high failure rates or when they forget and don't use anything, says Dr. Blumenthal.

How can you decide what method to use at this point in your life? Here's what doctors recommend.

Start with the kid question. For women over 30, the first question to ask is, "Do I want to preserve my future fertility?" says Margaret Dooley, nurse practitioner at Thomas Jefferson University in Philadelphia. The answer to that question will help you decide between reversible and irreversible methods and between long-term and short-term methods.

If you think that you may want to get pregnant within the next year, for instance, you'll want to go with the methods that can be easily reversed—such as the diaphragm, condoms or the Pill. If you want to wait between two and five years, you may want to consider Depo-Provera, the birth control shot, says Dr. Blumenthal. If you don't want children for five years or more, then the Norplant implant device and IUD are additional options.

Talk it over. "The most important thing—for any method—is to talk it over with your partner," says Dr. Blumenthal. Try to arrive at a mutually agreeable decision.

Ask questions. Don't be afraid to ask your doctor for her opinion on what methods might be good for you to consider. If you don't ask questions, your doctor may assume that you are satisfied with your current method and may not offer suggestions.

Myth #2: Only One Method Is Sure

Sterilization is a very popular means of birth control in the United States among women in the 30- to 45-year-old age group, says Dr. Blumenthal. An estimated 14 million women rely on it for contraception—but, of course, it's not just women who request the procedure.

About 9.6 million women have been sterilized, which means the fallopian tubes are closed off so that sperm can't reach the egg. Another 4.1 million women are relying on their partners' vasectomies—the sterilization procedure for males—to ensure that they don't have children.

Once a woman has her tubes tied, her chances of getting pregnant during the first year are lower than the failure rates of most temporary methods. But should you have it done?

While the procedure is superb for women who have decided that they definitely don't want to have any more children, says Andrew Kaunitz, M.D., professor in the Department of Obstetrics and Gynecology at the University of Florida Health Science Center in Jacksonville, the idea that it is the only effective long-term method is a myth. The IUD, Depo-Provera and Norplant can provide long-term protection and can be just as effective as sterilization, and yet they're reversible, he says.

The only good reason to choose sterilization, says Dr. Kaunitz, is if you

Tubes Tied? Unwanted Pregnancy Still Possible

In a large study from the Centers for Disease Control and Prevention (CDC) in Atlanta, women who had their tubes tied as a form of "permanent" contraception were five times more likely to get pregnant than what was usually expected by doctors.

When researchers reviewed the histories of 10,685 women who had undergone tubal ligation surgery, they discovered that there had been 143 pregnancies—about 100 more than expected. They calculated that the lifetime risk of pregnancy among women studied was close to 1 in 50, a much higher rate than the 1 in 250 commonly recognized by experts, says lead researcher Herbert B. Peterson, M.D., clinical professor of obstetrics-gynecology at Emory University School of Medicine in Atlanta and chief of the Women's Health and Fertility Branch at the CDC.

Age plays a role, according to Dr. Peterson. "We found that women sterilized at younger ages had higher pregnancy rates," he says.

How could it happen? Investigators remain uncertain. It is clear to doctors that sometimes an egg is fertilized in the fallopian tube and remains there. Such a tubal pregnancy can endanger a mother's life—so it's important for anyone who suspects that she is pregnant after previously having this procedure to be diagnosed and treated immediately, Dr. Peterson says.

Despite the pregnancy risk, sterilization remains the best option for some women who want long-term contraception, Dr. Peterson notes. All decisions regarding contraception should take both risks and benefits into account and be made on an individual basis, he adds.

HEALTH FLASH

decide that you *never, ever* want to be pregnant—or you have children and you know that you don't want to get pregnant again. There's a misconception that tubal ligation is easily reversible. The truth is, it's not.

Myth #3: The Pill Isn't Safe

After sterilization, the Pill is the contraception method women choose most. The Pill prevents pregnancy by interfering with ovulation, among other things. It also thickens the cervical mucus—the layer of slippery cells lining the cervix that makes a slick passageway for sperm. Thicker mucus means that sperm have a tougher time swimming their way toward the uterus.

Even though the Pill remains popular, doctors say that misperceptions and myths abound. One prevailing myth, says Dr. Kaunitz, is the assumption

The New Hormonal Methods

Before 1990 the Pill was the only form of hormonal birth control available in the United States. But since 1992, American women have had two new hormone-powered choices: Norplant and Depo-Provera.

This year, more than one million American women will step into this brave, new world of modern birth control.

Both Norplant and Depo-Provera contain forms of the hormone progesterone and prevent pregnancy three ways: by inhibiting ovulation, thickening the cervical mucus and thinning out the lining of the uterus. This one-two-three combination interferes with egg production, makes it harder for sperm to reach the uterus and, by thinning the uterine lining, makes a less friendly "nest" for the fertilized egg.

Beyond that, the two methods are radically different. Here's how.

Norplant:
For Five Years of Protection

Norplant consists of six matchstick-size capsules that are inserted under the skin on the inside of your upper arm. Protection lasts for five years, with few failures. Fewer than 1 out of every 100 women experience an accidental pregnancy during the first year of use.

Long-acting and convenient, Norplant is also easily reversible. Once it's re-moved, protection against pregnancy is gone immediately.

The downside? Some women have experienced disruptions to their menstrual cycles, from lighter bleeding or missed periods to increased days of heavier bleeding. And some women have reported complications when getting Norplant removed.

Depo-Provera:
The Shot in the Arm

If you opt for Depo-Provera, you'll have to see your doctor for a shot every three months.

During the first year you may see some spotting, and after that you may stop having periods. A significant advantage of the shot, doctors say, is that it is a totally private method of birth control. If you're getting the quarterly shots, your doctor is the only other person who needs to know about it.

But Depo-Provera is not a good choice for women who are ready to become pregnant right away, cautions Andrew Kaunitz, M.D., professor in the Department of Obstetrics and Gynecology at the University of Florida Health Science Center in Jacksonville. It can take women six months or more to get pregnant after they stop receiving the shot.

that it is too risky to take the Pill after age 30. Yet both the Food and Drug Administration and the American College of Obstetricians and Gynecologists have found the Pill to be safe for nonsmoking, healthy women of any age, he says. "Nonsmoking" and "healthy" are the operative words when it comes to the Pill and women over 30.

The concern over the safety of the Pill hails primarily from the days when oral contraceptives contained higher doses of estrogen. Researchers sounded the alarm when they suspected that women taking higher estrogen levels were at higher risk for heart attacks and strokes. Over the 30 years since the Pill was introduced, however, the dosage of estrogen in the Pill has been reduced to one-quarter of what it originally was. The lower dosage of estrogen has not reduced the Pill's effectiveness, yet it's safer, Dr. Blumenthal says.

In women who don't smoke, Pill takers have no significant increase in cardiovascular complications over non–Pill takers, agrees Alan Rosenfield, M.D., dean of the School of Public Health at Columbia University in New York City.

In addition to being safe, the Pill has a number of noncontraceptive benefits—but women aren't always aware of them. "Clearly, one of the biggest fears women have regarding taking hormones is the fear of cancer, particularly breast cancer," says Dr. Kaunitz. "Many women are not aware that by taking oral contraceptives they can substantially reduce the risk of ovarian cancer."

While ovarian cancer is rare, it's the leading cause of gynecological cancer death. A woman who takes the Pill for only a year or so can decrease her risk for the deadly cancer by as much as 50 percent, he says.

If a woman takes the Pill longer than a year, she cuts the risk of ovarian cancer even more. A woman who takes it for a decade or longer can reduce her risk by as much as 80 percent, says Dr. Kaunitz. This protective effect persists for years after she stops taking the Pill.

Not only that, the Pill will also slash your risk of getting endometrial cancer—cancer of the lining of the uterus, says Dr. Kaunitz.

But what about the risk of breast cancer? The message is somewhat less clear on this topic, according to Dr. Kaunitz. Studies are contradictory. Some show that the Pill increases breast cancer risk; others indicate a decreased risk. Overall, though, when you look at all the studies on oral contraceptives and breast cancer combined, researchers conclude that the Pill does not increase breast cancer risk.

In addition, the Pill offers protection against ectopic pregnancy, a sometimes life-threatening form of pregnancy in which the fertilized egg implants outside the uterus—usually in the fallopian tubes. The Pill can also help make menstrual periods more regular and relieve menstrual cramping. If you're considering the Pill, you should discuss it with your doctor. Here are some considerations.

Look at your medical history. The Pill is appropriate for healthy, nonsmoking women, says Dr. Kaunitz. It may be a less desirable option if you have a history of blood clots, high blood pressure, diabetes or other medical conditions. Also, your doctor may advise against the Pill if you're a regular smoker over age 30.

Look at the calendar. The effects of the Pill can be reversed fairly quickly, says Dr. Kaunitz. While it may take you a little longer to get pregnant when you stop taking the Pill than it would have if you hadn't taken it, the delay appears to be two to three months at most. Nearly 1 out of 50 women, however, will not menstruate for six months or more after coming off the Pill.

Look at your habits. "Sexually active women who miss more than two or three pills in a row will increase their risk of pregnancy," says Dr. Kaunitz. Ask yourself, in all honesty, whether you are a good pill taker. If you aren't, then you may want to consider another method.

Myth #4: The IUD Is Out of the Question

According to doctors, the IUD currently suffers from an identity problem in the United States. "American women need to rethink the IUD," says Dr. Kaunitz.

The IUD is a little plastic device that is inserted into your uterus by your doctor. A string connected to the IUD hangs down through the cervix and serves as a telltale sign for detecting whether the device is placed properly.

In the 1970s and 1980s the IUD became synonymous with risk and danger. Most of the unfavorable publicity was the result of lawsuits over the Dalkon Shield, an IUD whose use was associated with an increased risk of pelvic infection. "That publicity really killed the IUD in this country," says Dr. Kaunitz.

Studies have shown that the IUD is a safe and effective method of birth control for women who are at low risk for sexually transmitted diseases (STDs), says Dr. Kaunitz. If you have one partner and you know that your partner is monogamous and disease-free, the IUD can be a very practical form of birth control, offering protection for as long as ten years. So it is a good alternative to sterilization if you're finished with childbearing but have yet to reach menopause.

If you're comparing the IUD with the Pill, the IUD may be preferable if you can't use hormonal methods of birth control—if you're a smoker, for instance, or if you're breastfeeding, says Dr. Blumenthal. But some doctors won't recommend the device unless you've had a child.

There are two types of IUDs currently available. The first is the copper-T 380A, also known as ParaGard in the United States. "While we used to think that this device prevented pregnancy by preventing a fertilized egg from implanting in the uterus, we now have learned more about how it

Emergency Contraception

Forget something?

If the cold light of day finds you worrying about what happened last night—and the possible consequences—you may still have an option.

"I think one thing that women in this country should be aware of is emergency contraception," says Paul Blumenthal, M.D., assistant professor of obstetrics and gynecology at Johns Hopkins Bayview Medical Center in Baltimore. This is a form of contraception that women can access within three days after they have had unprotected intercourse.

If taken within 72 hours of unprotected intercourse, low-dose birth control pills are 97 percent effective in preventing pregnancy, says Dr. Blumenthal. If your doctor recommends this route, you'll get a prescription for eight pills: four to take immediately, with another four to be taken 12 hours later.

If conception hasn't occurred yet, the pills will interfere with the movement of sperm toward the egg by thickening the cervical mucus and changing the rate at which the sperm move through the fallopian tube, if they make it that far. Even if a sperm has fertilized an egg, pregnancy may be blocked, because the pills change the lining of the uterus so that the fertilized egg cannot implant in most cases.

While birth control pills are not approved by the Food and Drug Administration as emergency contraceptives, doctors are free to prescribe them for this kind of use.

Women who have unprotected sex can also use the intrauterine device, or IUD, as an emergency form of birth control, says Dr. Blumenthal. If your doctor inserts it within three to five days of unprotected sex, it can prevent a fertilized egg from implanting.

works," says Dr. Blumenthal. Research indicates that the device actually interferes with conception. That is, it appears to interfere with the ability of sperm to navigate up through the uterus and into the fallopian tubes.

The second type of IUD is called the Progestasert, an IUD that is medicated with progesterone. Progestasert works by changing the cervical mucus so that sperm have a harder time swimming north and, if conception occurs, a fertilized egg is less likely to implant in the uterine lining.

Myth #5: Barrier Methods Are Old-Fashioned

If you've dismissed condoms, the cervical cap and the diaphragm as too clumsy, out-of-date and unreliable, maybe you should reconsider. Condoms, for instance, are the most commonly used barrier method. Not only are they effective birth control devices, they're also insurance against STDs, including HIV and AIDS.

So if you're not in a monogamous relationship, or you're sleeping with someone who you're not positive is disease-free, it makes sense to use condoms.

In fact, Dr. Kaunitz says that women who are not in monogamous relationships should use condoms even if they're already using an effective birth control method such as the Pill or sterilization.

Saying No to Hysterectomy: The Controversy Continues

T he statistic is shocking: One American woman in three will have a hysterectomy in her lifetime. It is estimated that doctors will perform a record 800,000 of these procedures this year—that is, more than one hysterectomy every minute.

Yet the reality is that few hysterectomies are truly necessary. It's been this way for years. And it's still true that whether or not you have one may depend on how much you—and your doctor—know about the alternatives.

Nancy, a Colorado teacher, had known for several years that she had a benign fibroid tumor on her uterus. Although it was about the size of a grapefruit—larger than the uterus itself—it caused her no discomfort. Then, during a routine exam, Nancy's gynecologist told her that she needed an immediate hysterectomy. Otherwise, he said, the growth would press against her ureter, the tube connecting the kidney and bladder, and could damage her kidney.

"I think he felt that a fibroid larger than a certain size just has to be taken out," says Nancy, "and, if it's necessary, you have to scare the patient into having the surgery."

Nancy was scared enough to seek a second opinion. Rather than confirm the recommendation, though, the second gynecologist said the fibroid wasn't in a position to damage her kidney and that the only benefit she could expect to gain from a hysterectomy would be a flatter stomach.

A Hasty Prescription

Hysterectomy, the second most commonly performed surgery in the United States (after cesarean section), is routinely—some say hastily—prescribed for problems ranging from fibroids and endometriosis to abnormal bleeding, a displaced uterus and certain cancers.

In the operation, the uterus is removed. As a result, a woman no longer menstruates, and she is unable to bear children. Since women born during the postwar baby boom are now in their thirties and forties—the peak age range for hysterectomies—the total number of operations is expected to hit record numbers. In many of the cases, however, these radical surgeries could be avoided.

"If you look at the reasons for hysterectomy, only about 15 percent of the time is the operation the only choice—that is, there are no viable alternatives," says Robert Reiter, M.D., associate professor of obstetrics and gynecology at the University of Iowa College of Medicine in Iowa City. These situations include emergencies during and after childbirth, life-threatening cases of pelvic inflammatory disease, cancer and some pre-cancers.

Why, then, are so many women subjected to such a drastic and costly procedure? The financial incentive cannot be overlooked, especially in this era of proliferating high-tech (and high-cost) medical equipment.

Another reason for the frequency of unnecessary hysterectomies is that many doctors subscribe to outmoded thinking about common gynecological problems.

Furthermore, so the thinking goes, there is always the chance that the growth isn't a fibroid at all, but an ovarian cancer that just feels like a fibroid. Thanks to ultrasound, however, surgery is no longer necessary to rule out ovarian cancer, says Andrew E. Friedman, M.D., chief of the Division of Reproductive Endocrinology at Brigham and Women's Hospital in Boston.

"Now that we have a way to look inside without operating," he says, "we can challenge the guidelines." And recent studies show no correlation between the size of a fibroid and the number or severity of symptoms it produces.

When You Need One, When You Don't

In addition to questioning long-held beliefs about fibroids, researchers are rethinking the other reasons why doctors traditionally perform hysterectomies. They have concluded that some conditions once thought to be dangerous actually pose little, if any, health threat. Therefore, a hysterectomy should be considered only if a woman has a significant amount of pain or other symptoms that interfere with her ability to function and carry out her usual activities.

The bottom line is that if you have a gynecological condition, you should first find out whether it's as serious as it seems; you may not need any treatment. If therapy is necessary, consider all your options—medication or surgery that spares the uterus may work as well as hysterectomy.

Below are the conditions that account for about 85 percent of hysterectomies, and some alternatives to consider. (In most of the remaining 15 percent of cases, there are no viable alternatives.) Realize that these options are not risk-free, nor are they always permanent solutions. Thoroughly discuss the risks and benefits of each approach with your physician.

Fibroids

About 30 percent of hysterectomies in this country are performed because of fibroids. A woman may have one fibroid or many.

Why you may not need any treatment: If you don't have any symptoms (such as heavy bleeding, urinary urgency or frequency, constipation or backache), the best plan is regular monitoring by your gynecologist. Also, do keep in mind that fibroids usually shrink on their own as a woman approaches menopause, even if she takes hormone replacement therapy.

When to consider treatment: If your fibroids are causing symptoms that are significantly bothering you, you should think about treatment. But first make sure the growths are the true culprits. Something else may be responsible—an irritable bowel, for instance, or a bladder infection. "In most cases your

Younger Doctors Are More Cautious about Hysterectomy

H E A L T H F L A S H

If your doctor prescribes a hysterectomy, get a second opinion—but watch who you ask. According to a recent study, older gynecologists are more likely to suggest this often-unnecessary procedure than younger doctors.

"Doctors who had trained more recently were less likely to do hysterectomies than the doctors who got their training in the more distant past," says study leader Nina Bickell, M.D., assistant professor of health policy and medicine at Mount Sinai School of Medicine of the City University of New York.

Women doctors also had lower rates of performing hysterectomies. But this may simply reflect the fact that most women doctors are younger and have more recent medical-school training, she notes. Regardless of your doctor's age, though, Dr. Bickell found that gynecologists were less likely to recommend a hysterectomy for women who expressed qualms about surgery.

When may alternative treatment be a good option? While hysterectomy is necessary for cancer, it may not be necessary if you have endometriosis, fibroids or even a precancerous condition called cervical dysplasia, she says.

"The take-home message is, if you have concerns about hysterectomy, you should express them," Dr. Bickell says.

doctor will be able to determine the true cause of the symptoms by taking a very careful history," says Dr. Reiter.

Alternatives to hysterectomy: Frequently, women whose fibroids are causing bothersome symptoms can opt for a myomectomy—a procedure in which the doctor removes only the growths, leaving the uterus intact.

Although standard myomectomy involves opening the abdomen, the surgeon may be able to use one of the newer, less invasive techniques, depending on the number, size and location of the fibroids. During these procedures, the doctor extracts the growth through a hysteroscope (a lighted tube that is inserted into the uterus through the vagina) or a laparoscope (a lighted tube that is passed into the pelvis through a tiny abdominal incision).

Abnormal Bleeding

As women approach menopause, their periods often become heavier or irregular. (As mentioned, fibroids can also cause heavy periods.) About 20 percent of hysterectomies are performed in order to relieve this symptom.

Why you may not need any treatment: Though you should always report abnormal bleeding to your physician, since it can signal a serious condition such as uterine cancer, the symptom itself is usually not dangerous. Many women assume that they're losing too much blood because their periods are heavier than they used to be, says Dr. Reiter. In fact, when researchers evaluated women seeking medical care for bleeding problems, they found that only 40 percent were experiencing an abnormal amount of blood loss (more than a third of a cup during an entire period).

When to consider treatment: Discuss treatment options with your doctor if your periods are so heavy that they interfere with your lifestyle or cause anemia.

Alternatives to hysterectomy: Nonsteroidal anti-inflammatory drugs (NSAIDs), such as naproxen and ibuprofen, taken throughout your period can reduce menstrual blood loss by about half. Check with your doctor before you use NSAIDs on a regular basis and ask her what dose to take. Iron supplements, which should also be taken under a doctor's direction, can help relieve anemia. (Again, be sure to check with your doctor before taking iron supplements.)

In addition, heavy bleeding can be treated with a relatively new surgical technique known as endometrial resection, in which a laser or electrocautery is used to eliminate the inner lining of the uterus to decrease or stop monthly bleeding. Like hysterectomy, however, the procedure leaves women infertile. In one British study women who underwent this operation recovered four times more quickly than those who had a hysterectomy.

Uterine Prolapse

In this condition, which accounts for about 15 percent of hysterectomies, the uterus drops from its normal position. Prolapse occurs when the pelvic floor muscles and ligaments, which hold the uterus in place, are stretched such as during childbirth.

Why you may not need any treatment: Uterine prolapse isn't dangerous, though it can be very uncomfortable.

When to consider treatment: If the condition is so pronounced that it interferes with daily functioning, you should make a doctor's appointment. In severe cases the uterus drops to the point where it can be seen outside the vagina.

Alternatives to hysterectomy: Some women can avoid having a hysterectomy by using a removable ringlike device known as a pessary, which holds the uterus in place. In fact, says Dr. Reiter, a contraceptive diaphragm makes a very simple and effective alternative. You should also know that a special surgical technique that resuspends the uterus can be used to correct prolapse, though this treatment is not widely available.

Five Crucial Questions

Hysterectomy is rarely an emergency, so if your doctor suggests it, you have time to think about your options. Asking these questions can be a good way to start gathering information.

1. Is the surgery necessary to save my life, or to improve its quality?

"With hysterectomy you're usually trying to improve the quality of life," says Karen J. Carlson, M.D., director of women's health at Massachusetts General Hospital in Boston. If that's the case for you, it's up to you to decide whether your discomfort warrants surgery.

2. What type of hysterectomy would you perform?

While hysterectomies have traditionally involved cutting into the abdomen, they can sometimes be performed through the vagina, which usually results in fewer complications.

3. What are the side effects?

This will vary depending on the type of surgery you have. With traditional hysterectomy, up to 30 percent will have some type of complications. (Most of these are minor.) Realize, though, that in addition to the side effects associated with the surgery itself, you may also ex-

perience problems later on. Some women report diminished sexual responsiveness. Also, some scientists have found that hysterectomy increases the rate of heart disease. This may be because the uterus produces a protective chemical known as prostacyclin.

4. Will my ovaries also be removed?

Many doctors remove the ovaries during a hysterectomy—a procedure known as oophorectomy—particularly in women approaching menopause, to reduce the risk of ovarian cancer (which affects about 1 percent of women). But be aware that if a woman does not take hormone replacement therapy, removing her ovaries may increase her heart disease risk. What's more, the ovaries also produce small amounts of male hormones, which contribute to energy and libido.

5. Are there any alternatives to hysterectomy?

Ask about your options and let your doctor know if you want to avoid hysterectomy. Expressing this preference is one of the best ways to avoid the operation, according to a new study from the University of North Carolina at Chapel Hill.

Endometriosis

About 10 percent of hysterectomies are performed to treat endometriosis—a condition in which parts of the uterine lining spread and implant on tissue outside the uterus.

Why you may not need any treatment: Though endometriosis can cause severe menstrual cramps and may interfere with conception and pregnancy, in the vast majority of cases the endometrial implants are small and generally produce no symptoms, says Dr. Reiter. As more and more women have been examined with the laparoscope, either for diagnostic purposes or while getting their tubes tied, doctors have found that about 10 percent of these women have endometrial implants, in many cases causing no pain or fertility problems.

When to consider treatment: This is controversial. Some physicians maintain that endometriosis should always be treated to keep it from progressing. Others advise against treatment unless you're having severe cramps or fertility problems and the condition is extensive. If your endometriosis is mild, your pain is likely due to something else, says Dr. Reiter.

Alternatives to hysterectomy: Medications that alter the body's hormonal balance and suppress ovulation can help reduce endometriosis. These include birth control pills (often progesterone-only pills are used); danazol, an oral medication taken for three to six months at a time; and drugs called Gn-RH agonists—available in a nasal spray, an injection or as an implant beneath the skin—which can be used for six months at a time. Each of these drugs provides some pain relief in about 90 percent of cases, according to a recent literature review. Dr. Reiter adds that NSAIDs can relieve some of the discomfort of endometriosis in most cases.

Another option is having surgery to remove the endometrial growths, which can often be destroyed with a laser used in conjunction with a laparoscope.

Pre-cancer

About 10 percent of hysterectomies are performed for pre-cancers of the uterus, cervix or ovaries.

Why you may not need any treatment: Researchers are rethinking the classification of one type of pre-cancer. Some doctors consider all cases of endometrial hyperplasia—a thickening of the uterine lining—to be precancerous. The latest studies, however, show that there are several types of hyperplasia, and only the kind known as atypical carries a significant risk of cancer. If your doctor diagnoses atypical endometrial hyperplasia, consider a second opinion. Pathologists often disagree on the diagnosis.

When to consider treatment: Treatment is essential for confirmed cancer and most pre-cancers of the uterus, cervix or ovaries.

Alternatives to hysterectomy: Atypical endometrial hyperplasia can often be treated with monitoring and hormone therapy. Most precancerous conditions of the cervix are treatable with cryosurgery (freezing) or a new technique called loop electrosurgical excision.

The New Prescription for Passion

Judith hit menopause eight years ago, and it was as bad as everyone had said it would be. Like other women experiencing changes prompted by hormone shifts, she experienced hot flashes and a drop in sexual desire. "You're sitting there, and all of a sudden you feel like it's 120 degrees," says the Washington, D.C., businesswoman, now in her sixties. "You cope by layering clothes, and then once an hour or so you literally tear everything off."

Such behavior may have been interesting for her boyfriend of 14 years, but there was nothing sexual about Judith's frequent desire to strip. "My libido went from ten down to none. Zip. Zero," she says. "It was interfering with my life."

Then, when Judith complained to her gynecologist one day that even the estrogen tablets he had prescribed were not easing her hot flashes and loss of libido, the doctor interrupted. "Let's try an experiment," he said. He gave her a six-week supply of green, oblong tablets that contained a combination of estrogen and the male hormone testosterone. That's when Judith's life turned around.

"It kicked in within a couple of weeks," she says. "Suddenly, I felt normal. In fact, I felt very good."

And, she adds with obvious delight, "I got sexy again. This was no placebo effect. This was physical."

Sexy Again

Judith is part of a growing chorus of women singing the praises of testosterone. Across the United States, Canada and Europe, physicians are increasingly prescribing the quintessential male hormone to menopausal women who still feel "not right" after taking estrogen, the primary female hormone and standard drug treatment for menopause.

It's still rare to find testosterone in U.S. medicine cabinets. Only about 20 percent of American menopausal and postmenopausal women even take estrogen, despite the hormone's well-documented ability to relieve the hot flashes, sleeplessness and mood swings of menopause and to lower the risk of heart disease and osteoporosis significantly. With testosterone's benefits still a matter of debate, only 3 to 4 percent of these women today take testosterone along with their estrogen, experts estimate.

While these numbers aren't high, interest in testosterone is steadily growing. In the United States, sales of testosterone for menopausal women have more than doubled in the past five years. And they are expected to expand even more as female baby boomers pass into the change of life—and as word gets out about recent studies showing that some women do benefit from the treatments.

"People used to say, 'You can't give testosterone to women. You'll turn them into men,'" says Barbara Sherwin, Ph.D., the McGill University psychologist whose pioneering research 15 years ago first gave credence to the concept of testosterone replacement therapy. "Now, in the face of scientific evidence, you hear very little of this kind of talk."

Not for Men Only

Dr. Sherwin's groundbreaking work grew out of a simple fact of life well-known to physiologists but classically ignored by women's doctors: Women's ovaries produce not only female hormones, like estrogen and progesterone, but also testosterone, and the production of all three declines around menopause.

Midlife shutdown is not total. But Dr. Sherwin had a hunch that given the brain's exquisite sensitivity to even small concentrations of sex hormones, a 50 percent drop in testosterone levels at menopause may have physiological and psychological consequences.

Testosterone is not ignored by a woman's body. It builds muscles, burns fat cells and works directly on the limbic system—the ancient "reptilian" part of the brain—and other emotional centers of the brain in ways that seem to foster a can-do attitude. At high concentrations it can cause sexual desire in both men and women, and even blatantly aggressive behavior.

So, doctors questioned, why shouldn't regular supplemental doses provide a physical, emotional and sexual boost to women whose personal production of the hormone has begun to drop from mini to micro?

To test her hypothesis, Dr. Sherwin and another researcher tracked 65 women who had entered menopause as a result of getting total hysterectomies, in which the uterus and ovaries are completely removed. One-third of the women received no hormone replacement at all, one-third got estrogen and one-third received an estrogen-testosterone combination.

The results: Compared to the women in the first two groups, those who took the hormone combination reported higher levels of sexual desire and arousal and more sexual fantasies. At the highest testosterone levels, they also reported having more sex and significantly more orgasms per sexual encounter.

Well-Being and Better Bones, Too

Later studies by Dr. Sherwin and others backed up these findings. In one two-year study, researchers at the Women's Medical and Diagnostic Center, a large, private clinic in Gainesville, Florida, specializing in menopause research and treatment, showed that among women whose ovaries had been surgically removed, those given the two-hormone regimen scored significantly higher on tests that measured overall psychological well-being.

A similar study at Baylor College of Medicine in Houston found that

Testosterone May Not Hurt Heart Health

HEALTH FLASH

A new laboratory study suggests that adding testosterone to hormone replacement therapy may not diminish the therapy's important, heart-healthy benefits for women.

"We saw the same positive effects whether testosterone was included or estrogen was alone in the hormone treatments," says Janice Wagner, Ph.D., assistant professor of comparative medicine at Bowman Gray School of Medicine of Wake Forest University in Winston-Salem, North Carolina.

The study, performed on laboratory animals, is a step toward allaying fears that testosterone would work against estrogen, a hormone that helps keep blood cholesterol levels low. Heart disease is the number one killer of postmenopausal women, and so the issue of heart health has overshadowed testosterone's unique benefits.

Dr. Wagner says she feels confident that testosterone, which is naturally produced by women's bodies in small amounts, will prove to be a safe, effective way to help a postmenopausal woman revive her sex drive, lift low moods and lessen concentration problems as well as hot flashes.

women getting testosterone with their estrogen reported having enhanced libidos, more frequent sex and greater sexual satisfaction.

Adding to the case for testosterone, a recently published study from Emory University in Atlanta showed that 12 months of estrogen and testosterone in combination actually increased the density of bone in the spine in postmenopausal women, while women who took estrogen alone merely maintained their bone density.

The Case against Testosterone

When taking the lower doses of testosterone more commonly prescribed today, 20 to 30 percent of menopausal women still experience side effects including oily skin, acne, facial hair and even a deeper voice. Many women are forced by such symptoms to lower their doses, leading some scientists to wonder whether testosterone doses low enough to cause no side effects can really have a noticeable effect on mood, and on libido in particular.

As it turns out, the handful of definitive studies on female libido do not suggest a major influence from normal levels of testosterone. Research has mostly found that women are not more interested in sex as their testosterone level peaks around ovulation. In fact, several studies have discovered a surge in libido at testosterone's low points, just before or after menstruation.

The Food and Drug Administration (FDA) is not convinced of testosterone's benefits, either. Among the FDA's concerns are testosterone's effects on cholesterol levels and its potential to raise the risk of heart disease, already the leading cause of death among women.

The FDA is not alone in this concern. Testosterone therapy was great, says Isobelle, a 54-year-old former director of special events at the University of Florida in Gainesville, whose energy level and libido perked up soon after she started taking the pills. "It changed my life," she said. "Until I had a heart attack."

Isobelle landed in the hospital less than a year after increasing her dosage and is convinced the timing was no coincidence. And she has since learned that several studies have found that testosterone tablets can lower high-density lipoprotein (HDL), the "good" cholesterol that protects against heart disease. After her attack, she went back through her medical records and charted her cholesterol levels over a six-year period; her HDL levels, normal for years, dropped precipitously in 1993, when she and her doctor decided to up her dosage of testosterone. At the same time, her levels of "bad" low-density lipoprotein (LDL) cholesterol climbed, as did her ratio of total cholesterol to HDL—a signal of potential heart attack risk that her doctor at first attributed to her "eating too many chocolates."

"I cannot stress more the need for each individual to be her own detective," Isobelle says, "to do the research and find a physician who will be an interested partner in her health care."

Hormone How-To

Should you try testosterone replacement therapy? Here's what the experts say that you should consider first.

Are you a good candidate? The best candidates are menopausal women who, after taking estrogen prescribed by their doctors, still suffer from hot flashes, lack of energy and—assuming sex drive was healthy before menopause—lack of libido. Benefits are especially likely in women whose menopause is due to their ovaries having been removed as part of a hysterectomy.

Are you willing to risk side effects? Testosterone replacement therapy is controversial. Consult with a doctor and carefully consider the side effects: oily skin, acne, facial hair growth and a possible increased risk of heart disease. If you're still not sure, get a second opinion. If you go ahead, make sure that your blood cholesterol levels are checked every six months.

Are you simply looking for a sexual boost? Healthy premenopausal women should not turn to testosterone for a sexual boost. Women who menstruate already produce plenty of testosterone, and extra doses can cause not only facial hair growth but also a potentially permanent lowering of the voice, irritability and aggressive behavior.

Do you have a hormone imbalance? Testosterone may help premenopausal women with abnormal or absent menstrual periods, a possible indication of hormone imbalance.

Do you feel blue? Depression can cause exactly the same symptoms as menopause—fatigue, loss of libido and generally feeling lousy.

If a woman is depressed, counseling and antidepressants are the more appropriate approach, despite the attraction of a quick hormone fix, explains Helen Singer Kaplan, M.D., Ph.D., director of the human sexuality program at New York Hospital–Cornell Medical Center in New York City. She advocates blood tests, imperfect as they

A Trio of Options

Testosterone can be obtained by prescription in three forms: pills, shots or implants. Costs and coverage by insurance companies can vary, so check your policy before making a decision.

Pills. Easiest to take, testosterone pills contain the hormone in a variety of doses, often in combination with estrogen. But unlike other forms, oral testosterone, once absorbed, goes directly to the liver, where it can affect the body's processing of cholesterol and can cause a drop in high-density lipoprotein (HDL), the "good" cholesterol, raising the risk of heart disease.

Shots. Lasting about a month, testosterone shots provide a quick hit of testosterone. The downside is that levels fall off gradually, rather than offering a slow, steady dose.

Implants. Small "seeds" the size of rice grains, testosterone implants are embedded under the skin, in the hip or below the bikini line. They dissolve slowly, releasing a steady dose of testosterone over a four- to six-month period. They require a visit to the doctor's office, a shot of local anesthetic and a small incision that can leave a tiny scar.

Drug-Free Alternatives

Natural remedies are not as scientifically proven as Food and Drug Administration–approved drugs, but some women swear by them for the relief of menopause symptoms, particularly failing sex drive. Among the most popular are foods high in natural estrogens, like soybeans and alfalfa sprouts.

Herbalists also recommend dong quai, sarsaparilla, red clover and damiana. And some claim that supplements of evening primrose oil, vitamin E and zinc chelate can increase sex hormone production in the adrenal glands.

Sex counseling has a high success rate among menopausal women who are unsatisfied with their sex lives. A range of behavioral therapies are available, including psychological and physical exercises. For referrals, write to the American Board of Sexology, 1929 18th Street N.W., Washington, DC 20009 or have your physician contact the American Association of Sex Educators, Counselors and Therapists, P.O. Box 238, Mount Vernon, IA 52314.

are, to see if a woman really is low in testosterone before jumping on the hormone replacement bandwagon.

Ditch the Desire Drainers

Sleeping pills, tranquilizers, anti-seizure medications or blood pressure medication can also numb sexual desire. Disorders such as hormonal imbalances caused by an underactive thyroid or overactive segment of pituitary gland can block your sex drive as well.

Don't discount psychological ties to lovemaking. Current sexual relationships are directly tied to past ones and the messages we got when we were in those past relationships, notes Gina Ogden, Ph.D., licensed marriage and family therapist in Cambridge, Massachusetts, and author of *Women Who Love Sex*.

"If a woman has experienced some kind of sexual abuse or terror or control in the past, she'll take that into the bedroom with her, even if her partner is the most gentle person in the world," Dr. Ogden notes. "She needs to work on those issues before she can fully let go into sexual pleasure. In addition, her partner needs to be a part of this working out. A couple may find that with extra sensitivity they can deepen their relationship.

"However, many couples find it helpful to seek counseling for these issues," Dr. Ogden adds. She recommends that couples look for a counselor who is trained in both sex therapy and abuse counseling.

5

Custom-Tailor Your Hormone Therapy

T his year, half the women who opt for hormone replacement therapy will quit within 12 months. That's a discouraging statistic, given the important heart-protecting, bone-building, mood-lifting benefits of hormone therapy after menopause.

But it doesn't have to be that way. More and more doctors are helping women to custom-fit their hormone regimens, warding off unpleasant side effects such as menstrual bleeding or spotting and other aches and pains that mimic premenstrual syndrome.

"I've been able to find a symptomless side-effect-free regimen for nearly all my patients," says R. Don Gambrell, M.D., clinical professor of endocrinology and gynecology at the Medical College of Georgia in Augusta.

Today, there are dozens of options available to you and your physician—thanks to the wide variety of pills, patches, creams, implants, suppositories and different brands, forms and dosages of estrogen and progestin (the major hormones used in hormone replacement therapy).

Still, Dr. Gambrell cautions that the process of customizing hormone therapy to a woman's individual needs is complex. It requires open and ongoing communication between a woman and her doctor—and lots of patience. It's not uncommon to make course corrections several times before settling in with a comfortable regimen.

Your Unique Needs

Why customize? James Simon, M.D., chief of reproductive endocrinology at Georgetown University School of Medicine in Washington, D.C., contends that every woman's response to hormone replacement is highly individual.

Some women are especially sensitive to synthetic progesterone preparations, called progestins, which are responsible for most side effects.

"In some women, symptoms are dose-dependent, meaning that they do well when lower progestin dosages are given," Dr. Simon says. "Other women are duration-dependent. They do better on higher doses of progestin given over fewer days of the month."

As a last resort, a progestin-sensitive woman can opt for an estrogen-only regimen.

Other women may want to lower the amount of estrogen in their therapy to decrease side effects such as spotting and breast pain.

Flexible Hormones

Ten to 15 years ago, the idea was for hormone replacement therapy to mimic the menstrual cycle as closely as possible. Today, there's more flexibility. Doctors commonly prescribe variations on one of two basic regimens to replace the body's hormones.

- On continuous regimens, estrogen alone or estrogen and progestin are taken every day.
- On cyclic regimens (also called sequential), estrogen is taken either every day or nearly every day of the month and progestin for part of the month— 10 to 14 days.

In women taking hormones, it's normal to have some symptoms that feel like premenstrual syndrome. Women with a uterus may experience menstrual bleeding and associated symptoms, at least temporarily. Most symptoms resolve after two to four months, although for some women it may take longer. Sometimes, you can also make lifestyle changes—read on for some suggested changes—to help ease the side effects and enhance your therapy's effectiveness.

Another option is to use lower doses of the hormones estrogen and/or progestin. But be aware of the trade-offs that you're making.

While the lower limits for all brands of estrogen have not been firmly established, studies do show benchmark dosages for certain forms of estrogen. Below those levels, the bone- and heart-protecting benefits of estrogen are questionable.

Yet others argue that taking some estrogen may be better than taking none at all. Talk with your doctor.

If you reduce or eliminate progestin, you can lose protection against endometrial cancer. In that case, your doctor may recommend yearly biopsies of endometrial tissue from the lining of your uterus to monitor for cancer. (Of course, if you have had a hysterectomy, you needn't take progestin at all.)

Easing the Side Effects

If you and your doctor are working to customize your hormone therapy, give your treatment time—and keep a record of your symptoms. If they still plague you long after the adjustment period, consider the following sampling of suggestions from the experts.

Bloating

Fluid retention apparently is a natural physiological response to rising levels of progestin, says gynecologist Brian Walsh, M.D., assistant professor of obstetrics and gynecology at Harvard Medical School and director of the Menopause Clinic at Brigham and Women's Hospital in Boston. Progestin relaxes smooth muscle tissue, including blood vessels. This has a blood pressure–lowering effect, which the body responds to by holding on to water and salt to maintain blood pressure.

Some of the retained fluid goes into the body's tissues, because it has nowhere else to go. At the same time, progestin relaxes the muscles of the in-

---

New Protection against Fatal Colon Cancer

There's a new reason to consider hormone replacement therapy: New research shows that it provides protection against colon cancer, women's third most prevalent fatal cancer.

In a study of 422,373 postmenopausal women, researchers saw that those currently using hormone replacement therapy had a 45 percent lower risk of fatal colon cancer than did women who never used estrogen. The more years on the therapy, the lower the risk.

The hormone estrogen seems to reduce the amount of bile acids—compounds that are believed to promote colon cancer tumors—found in the gut, the researchers surmise.

"If this research stands the test of time, this is a very exciting association," says Eugenia E. Calle, Ph.D., director of analytic epidemiology for the American Cancer Society. "Colon cancer is a very important cancer," she says. In terms of incidence and deaths, "it's right there behind lung cancer and breast cancer in women."

While it's too early in the research process for doctors to prescribe estrogen for women concerned about colon cancer, a reduced risk may be an extra benefit for women already taking the therapy.

---

testines, slowing them down and allowing gas to accumulate. Hence, the bloated sensation.

If you're feeling uncomfortable, try one of these short-term solutions.

Restrict your salt intake. The body retains water in proportion to salt. So if you restrict salt, your body won't want to retain as much water.

Try a diuretic. Dr. Gambrell prescribes a mild diuretic for four to six months. Taken seven to ten days before menses or during the days of added progestin, it brings relief to about half of all sufferers in his practice, he says.

If your bloating hasn't subsided after four months, consider these strategies.

Lower the dose. Talk with your doctor about reducing your progestin dose to a level that still protects your uterus. You may be better able to tolerate it.

Switch. Try a different progestin or a natural form of progesterone. You may be experiencing some side effects that are specific to one progestin. So you may do better, for example, with norethindrone, norethindrone acetate or norgestrel. Oral micronized progesterone, a natural form of the hormone, may provoke fewer side effects than its synthetic cousins.

Food Cravings

Has your hormone therapy prompted raving cravings for sweet and salty foods? Experts have long recognized that being exposed to higher levels of progesterone (during pregnancy or premenstrually) or progestin (during hormone replacement therapy), could act on your appetite centers to cause cravings or an increased appetite. The strategies outlined above for bloating may help you.

Weight Gain

The hormone replacement therapy/weight-gain controversy still simmers. According to one large, nationwide menopause survey, weight gain was the number one complaint of postmenopausal women, whether or not they took hormones.

The real culprits, then, may be a sluggish lifestyle and slower metabolism. To counter their effect, try this option.

Turn up your metabolism. Aerobic exercise can help burn calorie and fat. But workouts that build muscle, like resistance training, turn up your body's metabolic rate so that you can burn more calories even in your sleep.

Unpredictable Bleeding or Spotting

Have panty liners become your constant companions? Unpredictable bleeding or spotting, called breakthrough bleeding, often occurs during the first few months on a continuous hormone regimen. Talk with your doctor about trying these coping strategies.

Lower your estrogen dose. The more estrogen that your body has, the more the uterine lining is being stimulated to grow and, consequently, the more likely breakthrough bleeding is to occur.

Side Effects? Consider This

It's possible that some women who are sensitive to synthetic progestin may be able to tolerate a natural form of progesterone called micronized progesterone.

Derived from soybeans and yams, this natural hormone may cause fewer side effects. It also does not appear to diminish estrogen's ability to raise high-density lipoprotein (HDL) cholesterol (the good kind) and lower low-density lipoprotein (LDL) cholesterol (the bad kind) as synthetic progestin may do.

Micronized progesterone is made by extracting certain substances in the yams or soybeans, which are then converted into progesterone. To enhance absorption, it is crushed into a fine powder, or micronized. The powder can be compounded into various forms: oil- or wax-based capsules, loose-filled capsules, tablets or suppositories. Absorption may vary, depending on which of these you decide to take.

Ordinarily, it is taken cyclically for 12 to 14 days. Since it is quickly metabolized, the 200- to 300-milligram dose that your doctor prescribes (the minimum dose to protect the uterus) must be divided over the day to maintain adequate blood levels.

Some women may experience transient lightheadedness or drowsiness when they take oral micronized progesterone, so the dose may be divided as 100 milligrams in the morning and 200 milligrams at night before bedtime. It is also available from some compounding pharmacies in a timed-release tablet.

Widely used in Europe, oral micronized progesterone has yet to receive approval from the Food and Drug Administration in this country. As a result, you cannot buy it prepackaged here. With a doctor's prescription, however, you can obtain it through select pharmacies that specialize in compounding. If your local pharmacy cannot fill your prescription, here are four pharmacies (recommended by the experts) that can.

Bajamar Women's Healthcare
 Pharmacy
9609 Dielman Rock Island Drive
St. Louis, MO 63132
1-800-255-8025
(314) 997-3414 (in St. Louis)

Belmar Pharmacy
12860 West Cedar Drive, Suite
 210
Lakewood, CO 80228
1-800-525-9473

Madison Pharmacy Associates
429 Gammon Place, P.O. Box 9641
Madison, WI 53715
PMS access lines:
1-800-222-4767
(608) 833-5916

Women's International Pharmacy
1-800-279-5708

Take more progestin. An alternative (if you need to maintain a higher level of estrogen to maximize hormone therapy benefits) is to take more progestin.

Switch to a cyclic regimen. Studies show that after six months on a continuous regimen, about two-thirds of women stop bleeding; unscheduled spotting can continue for the other one-third of women for as long as three years, however. A cyclic regimen produces a scheduled period.

Note: Report unusually heavy and/or prolonged bleeding to your physician. While such symptoms can result from hormone replacement therapy, other causes, including endometrial cancer, must be ruled out.

Unwanted Periods

So you thought you could toss your tampons? Surprise, surprise. On a cyclic regimen, you take progestin for two weeks but then stop for two weeks. That withdrawal triggers periods every month until the endometrium thins.

If you're not happy with what nature intended, consider these strategies.

Switch to a continuous regimen. Since there's no withdrawal of progestin, you won't have a monthly period. And because these hormones are spread over the entire month, you can take the same amount of medication (especially progestin) in smaller doses than with the cyclic regimens.

Lower the dose. Try a form of progestin that protects your uterus at a lower dose. This won't eliminate monthly periods. But certain compounds, including norethindrone, norethindrone acetate and norgestrel, may cause less withdrawal bleeding than medroxyprogesterone acetate.

Take progestin four times a year. A quarterly regimen of progestin (given for 14 consecutive days) allows you to bleed only once every three months instead of every month.

A downside: Your bleeding can last longer than on other regimens and will be somewhat heavier. This approach is new and not as well studied as the continuous and cyclic regimens, however. So discuss it carefully with your doctor.

Note: Unless you're on a quarterly regimen of progestin, heavy and/or prolonged bleeding should be reported to your physician.

Breast Pain and Tenderness

Achy, tender breasts, even fibrocystic changes, can be aggravated by estrogen or progestin or both, Dr. Simon explains. If the pain occurs cyclically, progestin is probably the culprit, fluid retention the cause. The suggested strategies mentioned above for relief of bloating may help you, too.

If pain persists throughout your hormone replacement therapy cycle, it may be that your breasts are too sensitive to the dose of estrogen being given. If breast problems persist longer than four months, consider the following strategies.

Reduce your dose of estrogen. Your breasts may be less sensitive with a lower dose. Discuss this strategy with your doctor.

Try androgens. The ovary normally makes a lot of estrogen and a small amount of androgen. The androgen counteracts the estrogen's stimulation of the breast tissue. Oral estrogen combined with a little bit of androgen is available.

Change progestins. If you're not taking medroxyprogesterone acetate, try it. Women who have trouble, however, on medroxyprogesterone acetate sometimes do very well on megestrol acetate, says Dr. Walsh.

Opt for a natural form. If these alternatives fail, try oral micronized pro-

Prescription for Menopause

Enhance the effectiveness of your hormone regimen by following this good advice—advice that experts say should be given to all women in menopause but is often overlooked by their doctors.

▶ Maintain a trim and well-toned body.
▶ Aim for 60 minutes of activity every day, including at least 30 minutes of nonstop moderate aerobics such as fitness walking. As part of the 60 minutes, also include 20 minutes of resistance training three times a week.
▶ Adhere to a very low-fat, high-fiber, practically vegetarian diet.
▶ Supplement with calcium to ensure that you're getting 1,000 milligrams a day if you're on estrogen, 1,500 milligrams if you're not. Maximize benefits by getting 400 international units of vitamin D.

gesterone. While it is less commonly available than synthetic forms of progestin, this natural progesterone seems to be well-tolerated.

Cut down on caffeine. That includes coffee, tea, colas, some pain relievers (read labels) and chocolate.

Headaches

Estrogen and progestin can trigger biochemical changes that cause migraine headaches. Fluid retention appears to be one culprit and may be eased by the strategies for bloating.

Women on some oral regimens may also respond poorly to the rapid rise and fall of estrogen in their bloodstreams, says Dr. Simon. One reason may be that estrogen taken by mouth is quickly metabolized by the liver, changing the amount and makeup of the estrogen reaching your bloodstream. But if your occasional headaches persist for longer than four months, consider these strategies.

Take less. Reduce your dose of oral estrogen—check with your doctor about how low you can go.

Change to a continuous regimen. Headaches that occur when estrogen levels drop quickly may be controlled on a regimen where you don't stop taking it for part of the month.

Put on the patch. If you're on oral estrogen, switch to the estrogen patch. Patches have the advantage of providing constant level of estrogen to the blood, says Dr. Simon. Also, when estrogen is delivered through the skin, a one-to-one ratio can be maintained between estradiol and estrone.

Try taking androgens. Doctors sometimes use this as a last resort. Talk with your doctor about the proper dose.

Depression and Anxiety

Depression and anxiety may be among the premenstrual-like symptoms that women develop on cyclic regimens, in which progestin levels ebb and flow. Fluid buildup may contribute to these symptoms.

Use the strategies for controlling bloating first. If depression or anxiety persist for longer than four months, consider the following action plans as well.

Alter your exposure to progestin. Dr. Simon says that some women do better on low doses of progestin given continuously, while others do better on higher doses over a shorter period. Each woman has to determine this by trial and error.

Stop, briefly. If you're not sure whether your depression is due to progestin, ask your doctor if you can stop it for a while. Then resume dosage to see if the depression recurs. This can help determine whether a situation or the medication is getting you down.

Add a low dose of androgen. While doctors don't know how androgens act to relieve depression and anxiety, they find adding it to be clinically effective for some women.

Nausea

Even though it's rare on the low doses of estrogen given today, if nausea does occur, you may be sensitive to the form and dosage of estrogen that you are taking. To reduce this effect, consider the following strategies.

Take estrogen pills at bedtime. This will allow you to sleep through any nausea, says Dr. Walsh.

Switch to the patch. That way, you're not putting anything in your stomach, in case you're sensitive to the pills.

Mix and drink. Crush progestin tablets and take them in juice. Sometimes nausea keeps a woman from being able to swallow a pill and keep it down.

Call the Shots with Your 40-Something Pregnancy

When Mary K. got pregnant for the first time, at age 31, she didn't worry much about prenatal tests. "I was still four years away from the age when doctors suggest the tests," she says. "I decided to forgo them, and my daughter was fine."

But with her second pregnancy, at age 40, Mary found herself in a whole new world. "Older moms are considered high-risk pregnancies," she says. "I was healthy, but I wanted to make sure my baby was, too. So I underwent the tests and had the peace of mind of knowing that my son was going to be just fine."

Like Mary, more and more baby-boomer women are opting for motherhood later in life. Between 1970 and the present, births to over-40 moms increased by more than 50 percent. In years to come, experts estimate the numbers will grow still higher.

Yet as the sight of older mothers-to-be becomes commonplace at work, in the supermarkets and in shopping malls, doctors still say these "twilight pregnancies" carry greater risks for both mother and child.

That's the reason why they still recommend a battery of prenatal tests for older mothers—and the reason why words like amniocentesis, chorionic villus sampling and maternal serum alpha-fetoprotein are as much a part of 40-something pregnancy these days as are pre-baby preparations such as decorating the nursery, choosing a diaper service and finding suitable day care.

Weighing the Odds

Prenatal tests search for a staggering array of conditions—everything from chromosomal abnormalities (like Down syndrome) to fetal abnormalities (such as spina bifida) to genetic disorders (like cystic fibrosis). Yet the results you get can be far from conclusive. In fact, there are two distinct types of prenatal tests, and it's important that you know how they differ.

Screening tests deal in probabilities, not in certainties. In other words, they show the chance that your baby will be born with a chromosomal abnormality or genetic disease, not whether the baby you're carrying actually has a specific problem.

Diagnostic tests, on the other hand, detect specific abnormalities (such as spina bifida) with virtually 100 percent accuracy. The two most widely used diagnostic tests—amniocentesis and chorionic villus sampling—are sometimes ordered as follow-ups to screening tests. For instance, when a maternal serum alpha-fetoprotein (AFP) screening test (a blood test that checks the mother's blood for the presence of AFP, a protein produced by the fetus) comes back abnormal, doctors usually recommend an amnio to find out why.

Why Some Women Say No

How do you know which tests to get and when? It depends on the kinds of abnormalities you want to know about and those you want to ignore. A lot rides on your age, too. And your doctor's another factor— some physicians push certain tests more than others.

Physician, or Midwife?

Compared to physician-assisted births, births attended by certified nurse-midwives are less likely to involve electronic fetal monitoring, episiotomies (an incision between the vagina and rectum to widen the birth canal), a forceps delivery or to result in induced labor or cesarean section.

Study after study suggests that, for women with normal pregnancies, involving a certified nurse-midwife (CNM) in prenatal care and delivery is a good way to minimize surgical intervention. One large study, comparing the outcomes of 8,266 physician-assisted mothers and 529 mothers attended by nurse-midwives at the same Chicago hospital, concluded that care by a certified nurse-midwife is 34 percent less likely to result in a cesarean section. CNM-assisted moms also had fewer interventions and equally good mother-and-baby outcomes as women cared for by doctors.

Not to be confused with a lay midwife who has no formal midwifery education, a CNM is a registered nurse who has completed four semesters of advanced training and graduated from a midwifery program accredited by the American College of Nurse-Midwives. All certified nurse-midwives must also pass a national certification examination and meet strict requirements set by state health regulatory agencies.

Certified nurse-midwives provide primary care to women expecting low-risk pregnancies before, during and after childbirth. If complications arise during pregnancy or labor, the nurse-midwife can consult with or refer the woman to a physician. Their approach is one-on-one care during labor, steeped in a belief in the human body and the payoff of patience, says Teresa Marsico, C.N.M., president of the American College of Nurse-Midwives. "Have faith and trust in the normal process of birth."

All things considered, it's important that you discuss your options and inclinations with your doctor during your preconception visit. Schedule this thorough gynecological exam about a year before you try to conceive; it will help ensure that you have a healthy pregnancy. Discuss them again at your first prenatal visit, which you should schedule as soon as you suspect that you're pregnant.

If tests like amniocentesis are so accurate, why don't all pregnant women have them? One reason is that there are risks involved.

Experts say that the risk of complications from an amnio is 1 in 200; the risk of problems as a result of chorionic villus sampling is about 1 in 100. Before age 35, you're more likely to have complications from an amnio than to be carrying a fetus with a chromosomal abnormality.

At 35, however, your chance of carrying a baby with a chromosomal abnormality increases to 1 in 192. (The older you are, the greater your chances of conceiving a baby with an abnormality.) And your risk of complications from an amnio drops below your risk of having a child with problems.

Like most statistics, however, these numbers can be misleading. For instance, the complications you risk by having an amnio include relatively harmless problems (such as bleeding, cramping and leakage of amniotic fluid) that often resolve naturally. Your risk of miscarrying after an amnio isn't actually 1 in 200; it's more like 1 in 400. The same goes for chorionic villus sampling: Your risk of miscarriage afterward is closer to 1 in 200 than it is to 1 in 100.

Still, some women find the inherent risks—and the issue of age—irrelevant.

"Comparing the different risks is like comparing apples and oranges," says Sarah H., 34, a New York City doctoral student who opted to have an amnio during her second pregnancy, even though she was only 32. "I could recover from a miscarriage, but if my husband and I had a child with a serious abnormality, our family would be reeling from it for the rest of our lives."

Information Overload?

Information can be a double-edged sword—another reason why some women pass on prenatal tests. Kristi P., 40, an advertising researcher in New York City, provides a case in point: Kristi's doctor urged her to have a maternal serum alpha-fetoprotein (AFP) test to check for the possibility of neural tube defects (deformities of the spine or brain).

Kristi and her husband agreed—but only because the doctor told them the test could detect spina bifida. They made it clear that they didn't want to test for chromosomal problems—such as Down syndrome—since they were sure they wouldn't terminate the pregnancy because of them.

Kristi's AFP results came back low, so there was little chance of her baby having neural tube defects. But a low AFP sometimes indicates Down's.

Kristi's doctor then pushed hard for her to have an amnio to rule out Down's. When Kristi refused, her doctor became adamant. "She said, 'I'm telling you, you want to have these tests!'" recalls Kristi.

But Kristi knew she didn't. So she and her husband switched to a midwifery practice, where there was no pressure to have an amnio. Their healthy baby was delivered four months later.

"Almost unavoidably, a physician who does a test will come across information that wasn't asked for and will have to make judgments about whether to reveal it or not," says Norman Fost, M.D., director of the program in medical ethics at the University of Wisconsin Medical School in Madison.

The lesson here? If you decide to test for problems, you must know what kinds of results you could get. "I agreed to the AFP because I thought spina bifida sounded devastating for the baby," says Kristi. "But if I'd been told that the test was for Down's, too, I probably wouldn't have had it done."

Eva S., 37, a computer analyst in Madison, Wisconsin, had a maternal

---

More Evidence: Moms-to-Be Need Folate

Planning a pregnancy? There's strong new proof that moms-to-be should take a multivitamin with folic acid before conception.

In one study, California researchers looked at children born with the common problems of cleft lip and cleft palate. Incidence of these problems was 25 to 50 percent lower for women who took multivitamins containing folic acid anywhere from one month before conception through two months after conception than for women who didn't supplement their diets.

There's no way to be sure whether the folic acid could have been the protector or whether there was something else in the vitamin supplement that may have prevented the birth defects, says study leader Gary Shaw, D.P.H., epidemiologist at the California Birth Defects Monitoring Program. But because of folic acid's ability to help DNA develop normally, it could possibly be the "active ingredient" in this case, says Dr. Shaw.

"The U.S. Public Health Service's recommendation for women of reproductive age to take 400 micrograms of folic acid a day is a good one," says Dr. Shaw. So check the label on your multi to see if it contains enough—keeping in mind that foods such as fortified breakfast cereals can provide as much as 100 micrograms per day.

Researchers already know that folic acid is important in preventing birth deformities called neural tube defects. But prevention of all these birth defects needs to happen as early as two weeks after conception—that's why researchers suggest getting your levels up beforehand.

Assessing Prenatal Tests

Following are five of the most common prenatal tests—and the stats and facts you should know about each.

Amniocentesis. An invasive diagnostic test that detects chromosomal abnormalities (such as Down syndrome) and hundreds of genetic diseases (such as Huntington's chorea), done at 16 to 18 weeks.

A needle is inserted into the uterus through the abdomen and some amniotic fluid is removed for analysis. Pain is minimal to medium. Test takes 45 minutes to an hour; results take two weeks. Accuracy is better than 99 percent.

Risks: Minor cramping is common. There is a 1 in 200 chance of relatively harmless complications such as maternal bleeding, cramping and leakage of amniotic fluid; and approximately a 1 in 400 chance of miscarrying. Very rarely, fetal injury due to the needle may occur.

Chorionic villus sampling. An invasive diagnostic test in which a small piece of the chorion (the fetal side of the placenta later in pregnancy) is removed and analyzed for chromosomal and genetic disorders, done at 9 to 11 weeks.

A needle is inserted into the uterus through the mother's abdomen (or a catheter is inserted into the uterus through the vagina) and guided to the chorion. Some villi (small, fingerlike projections in the chorion) are removed. Pain is minimal to medium. Test takes up to an hour; results take two weeks. Accuracy is better than 99 percent.

Risks: Minor cramping and spotting are common. Studies show chorionic villus sampling may raise your chances of miscarriage by as much as 1 percent—but not all experts agree. Ask for a doctor who's done at least 500. Also, some studies show chorionic villus sampling boosts your baby's risk of limb defects—but most experts say it's very low.

Maternal serum alpha-fetoprotein. A noninvasive screening test that analyzes levels of alpha-fetoprotein (AFP), a protein made by the fetus that spills into the mother's blood, done at 15 to 18 weeks. May help detect Down syndrome and other birth defects.

Blood is drawn from the mother's arm and analyzed. Test takes less than five minutes; results take less than a week. Virtually no pain. Accuracy is 80 percent for neural tube defects; 20 percent for Down's.

Triple screen. A new noninvasive screening test that analyzes AFP and two other chemicals in the mother's blood, done at 15 to 18 weeks. More accurate in detecting chromosomal abnormalities than AFP analysis alone.

The procedure is the same as for maternal serum alpha-fetoprotein. Accuracy is 80 percent for neural tube defects and 60 percent for Down syndrome. Risks: No known physical risks to mother or fetus. But with accuracy relatively low, the AFP often raises anxiety needlessly.

Ultrasound. A noninvasive diagnostic test done to view the fetus and determine its age, usually done at 7 to 12 weeks and sometimes repeated at later stages. Can also detect severe abnormalities such as spina bifida.

A technician inserts a probe into the vagina or moves what's called a transducer back and forth across the mother's belly. Test takes 20 minutes to two hours; results are immediate. Accuracy is high for detecting age of fetus as well as severe birth defects, but low for detecting milder birth defects. Discomfort is minimal.

Risks: No known risks to mother or fetus.

serum alpha-fetoprotein test early in her second trimester. When the results came back at 17 weeks, she was told that her baby "almost certainly" had Down syndrome or another serious abnormality—despite the fact that AFP results can give only probabilities.

She had to wait several weeks to have an amnio and then three more weeks for the results.

"I had already scheduled an abortion," says Eva. "I was going to be almost six months pregnant by the time the results came back."

Fortunately, an amnio showed that Eva's baby was healthy. But she worries that her relationship with her daughter suffered because she felt tentative about the pregnancy for so long. "It has always cost me this feeling of guilt—of detachment from my baby," she says.

The Case for Testing

No matter what you think you might do if your unborn baby is diagnosed with an abnormality, many physicians and genetic counselors argue that it's still better to find out all you can about your child before its birth—for simple reassurance, if nothing else.

"Ninety-five percent of the time, parents get good news," says Wendy Robertson, M.S., a genetic counselor at Dean Medical Center in Madison, Wisconsin. "And that good news can make the rest of your pregnancy tolerable."

During her second pregnancy two years ago, Harriet B. started spotting. In the eleventh week, she had an ultrasound, which showed her baby had stopped developing early on, at around six weeks. This was a fairly sure sign of severe chromosomal abnormalities. Soon after, she had a miscarriage. When Harriet got pregnant again a year later, her obstetrician offered her an ultrasound at eight weeks.

"We wouldn't normally do one now," the obstetrician said, "but it might make you feel better to know that everything's okay."

She was right. Harriet hadn't realized how worried she'd been about this pregnancy until she lay on the examining table and watched a tiny white blip—her baby—on the ultrasound screen. She was infinitely grateful for the reassurance the procedure gave her.

Of course, if you're among the unlucky 3 to 5 percent of women for whom the news is bad, you're not going to be reassured. But there are other factors to consider.

For instance, you cannot change the fact that your baby has Down syndrome, but you might be able to increase her chances of survival. More than 40 percent of babies with Down's also have congenital heart defects. If you know well ahead of time that your baby has Down syndrome, you can arrange to have a pediatric cardiologist present in the delivery room to begin immediate treatment.

What's more, knowing about your baby's condition in advance also gives you and your partner the time you need to prepare emotionally for the birth of a baby with special needs.

"No matter how much you love a baby with any kind of abnormality, you're still going to have to grieve for the 'perfect' baby you had imagined," says Kim Miller, M.D., an obstetrician based in Madison, Wisconsin. "When parents know what's coming, they have the chance to do that—and can feel more positive when their baby finally arrives."

FOOD AND YOU

Part 2

The fact is, you have to eat your veggies.

—nutrition researcher Paul A. Lachance, Ph.D.

Female Advantage

The Wisdom behind Food Cravings

Women are more likely to choose a thick slab of marble cake over a thick slab of marbled steak. Men will often choose meats over sweets.

New "food lust" studies prove what you always suspected: Women and men have a tendency to yearn for different edibles. But did you know that a woman's food cravings also have distinct advantages?

"Women have an inborn food wisdom that men lack," says Debra Waterhouse, R.D., a dietitian in Oakland, California, and author of *Why Women Need Chocolate*. "Our cravings are biological messages to eat a specific food in order to optimize our energy levels, our moods and our general well-being."

In a recent study, researchers at the Monell Chemical Senses Center in Philadelphia found that women lust after combinations of sugar and fat, such as butterfat-rich chocolate ice cream, more often than men. Men are more likely to go for high-protein stuff like meat.

Why? A woman may need the energy and brain-chemical boosts provided by sweets. A man may need more protein because his body carries about 40 pounds more muscle than a woman's, says Waterhouse.

Women may enjoy sensual and feel-good benefits from satisfying food cravings. How? For one thing, women, for the most part, have more acute ability to perceive flavor than men do, says Marcia Pelchat, Ph.D., biological psychologist and cravings researcher at the Monell Chemical Senses Center in Philadelphia. Then there's the well-being factor. Some studies also suggest that just the sensory experience of consuming certain foods, such as chocolate, can cause a release of endorphins (the body's natural pleasure chemicals).

Of course, if you satisfy that chocolate craving with a pound of Godiva truffles every time, weight gain is inevitable.

Waterhouse suggests the following three ways to fulfill a food craving without packing on extra pounds.

▶ Don't settle. Consume the food that you feel is going to satisfy your craving the most. Otherwise, you may end up eating more calories.

▶ Savor every bite. Focus on the first three bites. Smell the food; let it float in your mouth for a bit, chew it slowly then swallow.

▶ Eat only small amounts. When fully appreciated, just a few bites of the food you desire will have the power to satisfy.

Slash the Fat, Keep the Flavor

S alad dressing on the side. Lean cuts of meat trimmed of all visible fat. Sorbet, not ice cream, for dessert. If you've adopted low-fat eating habits like these—or would like to—then consider yourself in good company.

In a new nationwide survey conducted for the American Dietetic Association (ADA), women dieters said that cutting dietary fat is one of their major weight-loss strategies. With up to two-thirds of American women between the ages of 18 and 64 trying to shed excess pounds, that means a lot of us are choosing skim milk over whole milk, eating chicken without the skin and avoiding the butter dish.

Why a leaner cuisine? Women say their motivation goes beyond looking svelte in a swimsuit. While 23 percent of dieters told the ADA they simply wanted a more attractive appearance, nearly twice as many—42 percent— hoped to improve their health. And another 34 percent aimed to accomplish both.

Trimming the fat and calories, experts say, is one of the most effective dietary routes to both goals.

"There are certainly a lot of benefits to a low-fat diet, including weight loss and decreased health risks for heart disease, cancer and diabetes," says Susan Zelitch Yanovski, M.D., an obesity expert with the National Institute of Diabetes and Digestive and Kidney Diseases at the National Institutes of Health in Bethesda, Maryland. Other benefits include higher energy levels, lower odds of developing gallstones and osteoarthritis, lower blood pressure and a reduced risk of stroke.

Eat Lean, Stay Lean

Lowering fat is probably the most important thing that you can do with your diet to achieve and maintain lower body weight, says JoAnn E. Manson, M.D., associate professor of medicine at Harvard Medical School, co-director of women's health at Brigham and Women's Hospital in Boston and co-principal investigator of the cardiovascular component of the Harvard University Nurses' Health Study.

"In terms of health, 50 percent of all chronic diseases in the United States are related to obesity," Dr. Manson says. "Cutting fat and exercising are the best ways to prevent obesity."

As a bonus, you'll feel more energetic. And when your diet shifts from french fries, cheeseburgers and other high-fat fare to fruits, vegetables and whole grains, you're giving yourself more of the nutrients that your body needs, too.

"And you can eat more," says Dr. Yanovski. "You could have a big bowl of fruit salad for the same calories as a few bites of cheesecake."

Of Red Meat and Ranch Dressing

The trouble is, we love fat. The average American woman gets 38 percent of her calories from it, according to the National Cancer Institute. That's a far cry from the 25 to 30 percent that doctors recommend.

And with 9 calories per gram, a little fat packs a big caloric wallop. (In contrast, there are about 5 calories in a gram of protein and 4 in a gram of carbohydrate.) Excess fat calories can easily become excess pounds: Spreading your dinner roll with two teaspoons of butter, for example, would add 68 calories to your daily total. Do it for two months, and you'll put on an extra pound.

But the trouble with excess fat goes beyond mere calories.

Women who eat a lot of fat also tend to eat fewer fruits, vegetables and high-fiber bread and cereal. In a study of 11,758 women, researchers from the National Cancer Institute found that women who consumed the least fat ate nearly 20 servings of fruit and vegetables weekly, while high-fat eaters ate less than 13. This "produce gap" probably explains why the fat-lovers had lower intakes of vitamin C, folate, fiber and beta-carotene, the researchers noted.

"Fruits and vegetables are your best natural sources of antioxidant vitamins and a whole host of micronutrients and phytochemicals that are important for health but can't be found in vitamin pills," says Dr. Manson. "You get them in a low-fat, high-fiber diet."

Just what foods do high-fat aficionados favor? Creamy salad dressings. Red meat. Butter. Whole milk and cheese. Salty snacks and rich desserts. In short, a diet rich in animal fat—a primary source of saturated fats that medical researchers say are linked to a greater risk of heart disease, diabetes and cancer.

Less Fat Means Better Health

Medical research has good news for women: Eating lean can have a powerful and positive impact on your health, reducing the threat of major diseases now and in the future. Here's a sampling of the ways a low-fat diet can boost your health.

- Lowers the risk of coronary heart disease
- Defends against diabetes
- Lowers risk of ovarian and endometrial cancers
- Guards against colon cancer
- Puts a stopper on lung cancer
- Protects against skin cancer

Dietary Fat: How Low Should You Go?

So the consensus seems to be that women are better off curbing their taste for fat. Just how little fat should you aim for? As with calculating your ideal weight, the ideal percentage of calories from fat is not absolute. Rather, the ideal is a range that depends on individual health concerns.

Low-Fat Fans May Be Eating Excess Calories

In a new nationwide survey, more than eight out of ten women said that dietary fat was their top food concern. Sounds good. But are we missing the big picture?

A high percentage of women said that they're choosing more chicken, fish and vegetables at the supermarket—and less beef and other fat-laden foods—according to the 1,200 women surveyed by Hachette Filipacchi Magazine's Research and Marketing Services Department in New York City.

Yet at the same time, less than six out of ten said that calories were an important factor in their buying and cooking choices.

"The good news is that women are clearly getting the message that we need to cut back on the fat in foods," says Gail Frank, R.D., Dr.P.H., director of the Child Nutrition Program at California State University, Long Beach, and spokesperson for the American Dietetic Association. But we may be forgetting that calories add up to weight gain.

"Clearly, we're viewing nutrition in isolated ways," she says. "Fat is just a snapshot of a much bigger weight-management picture."

So put down the fat-free, high-calorie cookies, chips and ice cream and march back to the produce aisle. Dr. Frank suggests that old-fashioned snacks, such as apples, bananas and even precut, prepackaged vegetables are still the best low-fat, low-calorie alternative.

HEALTH FLASH

"The need to limit dietary fat depends on a number of factors," says James J. Kenney, R.D., Ph.D., nutrition research specialist at the Pritikin Longevity Center in Santa Monica, California. "Your family's and your own health history will help determine the relative dangers of the amount and type of fat you're eating."

Is your cholesterol high or borderline high? Is your HDL (high-density lipoprotein) level low? "The higher your cholesterol, the more likely you are to develop blocked arteries," says Dr. Kenney. So if blood tests show that your cholesterol is high, you should talk to your doctor about trying a very low fat diet (10 to 15 percent of calories from fat). Such diets have had tremendous success in reversing heart disease. The same applies if you have high blood triglyceride levels, high blood pressure, diabetes, a family history of heart disease or if you have had a heart attack. Those conditions increase your risk for heart disease.

"If, for example, your cholesterol is high and you're overweight, 30 percent of calories from fat may be too much, and you may need to lower yours to as low as 15 percent," says Georgia G. Kostas, R.D., director of nutrition at the Cooper Clinic in Dallas and author of *The Balancing Act Nutrition and Weight Guide*. Lower your fat calories to 30 percent for starters; if you are already eating 30 percent, try 20 percent, then 15 percent if needed, to lower cholesterol, she says.

Are you overweight? A diet in the 25 to 30 percent range is compatible with weight loss, as long as you include five servings a day of high-fiber fruits and vegetables and couple your diet with regular exercise, says James Anderson, M.D., professor of medicine and clinical nutrition in the Division of Endocrinology and Metabolism at the University of Kentucky College of Medicine in Lexington.

Are you in good health? If you're one of the lucky few with no pressing health concerns—slim and trim, favorable cholesterol, easy-going blood pressure, a healthy insulin level—then up to 30 percent of calories from fat would be fine, say some experts.

"A woman who's slender, fairly active and doesn't have a family history of diabetes or fat-related cancers, like breast or colon cancer, can probably take in more dietary fat than someone who's overweight and has a family history of breast cancer and diabetes," says Dr. Kenney. "If you have good genes, you can probably get away with a little more fat, particularly if it comes from fish, nuts (except coconuts), tofu, avocados and seeds such as pumpkin or sunflower."

"Generally, it's healthy and reasonable if a woman or a man sticks to the 20 to 30 percent range," says Kostas.

A Little Dab Goes a Long Way

A very small amount of dietary fat is essential for good health, says Dr. Kenney. The key is to make sure that when you do eat fat, it's the right kind, say experts.

"Small amounts of omega-3 (found in cold-water fatty fish such as mack-erel and sardines) and omega-6 fatty acids (found in whole grains and most other plant foods) are essential," says Dr. Kenney.

Furthermore, certain kinds of vegetable oils—namely monounsaturated oils (like canola and olive oil) and polyunsaturated oils (like corn and soybean oil)—have been found to lower total blood cholesterol when substi-tuted for saturated fat (animal fat). They also are carriers of fat-soluble vita-mins, which are essential for optimal health.

On the other hand, saturated fat and cholesterol (found primarily in red meats, full-fat dairy products and fatty cream and sauces) are totally expend-able, says Dr. Kenney. Limit calories from saturated fat to no more than 7 percent of calories from fat if you have high cholesterol or heart disease and 10 percent if you don't, says Margo A. Denke, M.D., associate professor of internal medicine at the Center for Human Nutrition at the University of Texas Southwestern Medical Center in Dallas and a member of the Amer-ican Heart Association's Nutrition Committee.

On a 2,000-calorie-a-day diet, that 7 percent adds up to 140 calories from fat—about 15 grams a day (the amount in one hot dog).

Slim Math: The Rule of Thirds

Figuring out your daily allotment of fat is simple: Say that you're eating 2,000 calories a day—the standard allotment from nutrition experts. Say, too, that you're shooting for 25 percent of calories from fat. The idea, then, would be to limit your intake of calories from fat to 500 a day, or about 55 grams total. If you're on a very low fat diet—say, 10 percent of calories from fat—your daily limit is 22 grams of fat total.

Follow the rule of thirds. As for the type of fat that makes up those 55 grams or so, Kostas offers a handy rule of thumb.

"At the Cooper Clinic, we use the rule of thirds recommended by the American Heart Association," says Kostas. "That is, one-third of the fat grams should come from monounsaturates, up to one-third from polyunsat-urates and one-third (at the most) from saturates.

"The easiest way to hit those proportions," says Kostas, "is first, use olive oil and limited amounts of vegetable margarine; second, limit meals featuring red meat to three times week (and stick to lean cuts and three-ounce servings); and third, have fish, chicken, beans and low-fat dairy prod-ucts the rest of the week. Let the rest of your diet consist of nonfat plant foods like fruits, vegetables, beans and whole grains."

More Handy Fat Subtracters

Here are inside ways to trim the fat without sacrificing flavor.

Think substitutions. Low-fat living begins with smart shopping choices—especially when you're most vulnerable, such as when you're ravenous or your only ready source of food is a convenience store. Here are some emergency tactics from Rodman Starke, M.D., senior vice-president in the Office of Scientific Affairs of the American Heart Association.

- Instead of a candy bar, have a banana or an apple.
- Instead of a package of nuts, have ready-to-eat cereal.
- Instead of cookies, have graham crackers.
- Instead of chocolate, have licorice.
- Instead of a hot dog with chili, have a microwaved bean burrito.

Buy low-fat treats. When the Girl Scouts of the U.S.A. (or their moms and dads) peddle their cookies in your neighborhood or office, you don't have to be a Scrooge just because you're trying to cut fat, says Judy E. Marshel, R.D., director of Health Resources in Great Neck, New York, and former senior nutritionist for Weight Watchers International. Ask for their low-fat or nonfat cookies, she advises. Then help yourself to just one or two and leave the rest in the lunchroom for others to share.

Never eat standing up. Follow this rule and you automatically eliminate many places that dispense high-fat foods: pizzerias, hot dog stands and ice cream wagons, to name just three, says Steven Gullo, Ph.D., president of the Institute for Health and Weight Sciences and former chairperson of the National Obesity and Weight Control Education Institute of the American Institute for Life-Threatening Illness at Columbia Medical Center, both in New York City.

Lean toward loin. If you must eat meat at least occasionally, select loin cuts—sirloin, tenderloin and, if you like pork now and then, center-cut loin chops, advises Steven Jonas, M.D., Ph.D., professor of preventive medicine at the School of Medicine at the State University of New York at Stony Brook.

Substitute ground turkey for ground beef. But don't assume that ground turkey is low-fat, warns Jayne Hurley, R.D., senior nutritionist with the Center for Science in the Public Interest in Washington, D.C. Most of the ground turkey sold contains turkey skin, which, like any poultry skin, has fat. "So look for products labeled 'ground turkey breast,'" says Hurley. "You'll get breast meat only, no skin."

Grilling? Try fat-free or low-fat hot dogs. Chicken or turkey franks may not necessarily be the best option for frankfurter fans, says Hurley. Some brands are indeed quite low in fat; others contain as much as 12 grams of fat apiece (compared to 15 or 16 for oversize or jumbo franks). Scrutinize labels and consider one of the fat-free varieties. With a little mustard and ketchup, you'll hardly know the difference.

Sample before you spread. If you tend to go on autopilot when adding butter to your bread or dressing to your salad, forgo added fat as an experiment. "Plain, unadorned rolls and bread taste great without butter," says Dr. Jonas.

Spear and dip. Don't smother your salads in oil or dressing. Spear a piece of salad with your fork, then dip it into the dressing for a lighter, lower-fat lunch or starter, says Dr. Jonas.

Drizzle, don't drench. "If you must use butter or sour cream on your potatoes, for example, use only a fraction of what you'd normally add," says Marshel. "Also, if you're making home fries or french fries, don't fry them in a pan of oil. Instead, bake them on a lightly greased cookie sheet. They'll soak up far less fat."

Nix the fat. In many recipes you can delete the fat or cut it considerably, says Linda Van Horn, Ph.D., professor of preventive medicine at Northwestern University Medical School in Chicago. "Recipes often call for twice as much fat as they really need, especially desserts. I can easily take any recipe for anything and immediately reduce it."

8

The Healing Power of Phytomins

I f you haven't seen them on the shelves of your local health food store or pharmacy, just wait.

Nutraceuticals, the newest type of dietary supplements, are joining the ranks of vitamins and minerals as the latest (and most high-tech) form of preventive medicine. They could spark a supplement controversy this year, as experts debate whether or not they're worthwhile.

Made from compounds called phytomins, nutraceuticals are extracted from fruits and vegetables and concentrated into pills, powders and capsules. The purpose? To provide the disease-fighting power of these plants in an easy-to-swallow form. For example, proponents of nutraceuticals say that you can get the cancer-fighting potential of a plate of broccoli or the cholesterol-reducing benefits of a head of garlic simply by swallowing a few capsules.

Sound too good to be true?

It may be. There is evidence that some of the compounds found in nutraceuticals play an important role in the prevention of disease. But so far, research shows that getting your phytomins from foods rather than from pills may be best.

But no one's debating whether or not phytomins themselves are important. Researchers across the country are now reporting what many natural-health practitioners have known for years—that a diet rich in grains, legumes, fruits and vegetables keeps us healthy by lowering our risk for diseases like cancer, heart disease, diabetes, high blood pressure and obesity. The benefit seems to come from these mysterious phytomins.

A Pepper or a Pill?

Before you trade in your wok for a tablet dispenser, you should know that even the most vocal supporters of nutraceuticals maintain that a whole-foods diet—rich in grains, beans, fruits and vegetables—is still the surest way to meet your nutritional needs.

"When you eat whole foods, you not only get their vitamins and minerals but their phytochemicals as well," says Clara Hasler, Ph.D., director of the Functional Foods for Health program at the University of Illinois in Urbana. "You're reaping the benefits of all the things that haven't been researched. When we pull things out of the matrix, out of the original form, we're not sure how that supplement is going to act in the body—a very complex biological system."

The fact is, too, that these chemical compounds have been found to be a microscopic component that appears in practically every plant, even in parts per million of the entire piece of produce.

"If you drink an eight-ounce glass of orange juice, you're getting 200 milligrams of phytochemicals a day," says Tony Montanari, Ph.D., a research scientist at the State of Florida Department of Citrus. "If you eat a piece of whole fruit, you're getting phytochemicals and a biopolymer called pectin, found to be effective in reducing serum cholesterol."

There is a real complexity to the chemistry of compounds in plants and a danger in trying to get all of these chemicals out of a handful of pills, says Paul A. Lachance, Ph.D., professor of nutrition and food science at Rutgers University in New Brunswick, New Jersey. The secret to tapping the power of phytochemicals, he contends, lies in eating a combination of foods.

"The fact is," he says, "you have to eat your veggies."

Secret Ingredients

Scientists now think they know why a plant-based diet is integral to your health. And the reason lies in phytochemicals—the substances responsible for a plant's color, odor, flavor and natural defense against disease.

Researchers theorize that these same properties allow plants to protect the people who eat them.

Of particular interest is the role phytochemicals seem to play in lowering the risk of cancer. Phytochemicals appear to arrest cancer's development at every stage—from the initial assault by carcinogens to the abnormal cell production that is finally diagnosed as cancer. In test tubes, animal studies and limited human trials, certain phytochemicals have been found to fight cancer in several ways: by reducing tumor production, combating hormone-related cancers and helping the body produce enzymes that flush out carcinogens.

Nearly all plant foods contain these potentially beneficial components, and researchers have identified thousands of different phytochemicals. Of these, scientists have linked hundreds to specific health benefits.

- Consumption of carrots and green leafy vegetables is associated with lung cancer prevention.
- Cruciferous vegetables can combat colon cancer.
- Fruits offer protection from cancers of the larynx, throat, mouth and esophagus.
- Lettuce and onions seem to help prevent stomach cancer.
- Garlic, perhaps the best-known of the vegetable superfoods, has been shown to prevent the development of at least six types of cancer.

On the horizon, phytochemicals such as the indoles found in brussels sprouts and cabbage, the carnosol in rosemary and polyphenols found in red grapes and strawberries have only recently been recognized for their anti-cancer properties.

In addition, phytochemicals appear to have tremendous potential to help

Eating Vegetables Cuts Cancer Risk

The more vegetables women consume, the lower their risk of breast cancer, according to a new study from the State University of New York at Buffalo.

"We found a trend: the more vegetables, the more protection," says researcher Jo L. Freudenheim, R.D., Ph.D., associate professor in the Department of Social and Preventive Medicine at the university where the study was conducted.

Researchers compared the diets of 297 women who have breast cancer and those of 311 cancer-free women. All were premenopausal women over age 39. Those women who ate about five vegetable servings a day had about half the risk of breast cancer, compared with women who ate two servings or less.

Women who consumed more than four daily servings of fruit lowered their breast cancer risk by about 30 percent.

There was no clear evidence that any one nutrient in vegetables could explain the effect. "It may be that you need several nutrients in combination as they are in vegetables," Dr. Freudenheim says. "Or there could be other protective factors in vegetables which we haven't discovered yet."

Does it make sense to eat more vegetables to prevent breast cancer? "Remember that while there seems to be some indication from several studies that vegetables may decrease risk of breast cancer, the cause-and-effect relationship is not at all certain," Dr. Freudenheim notes. "But there's plenty of evidence that a diet high in vegetables and fruit, and also low in fat, is a prudent, healthy diet for many reasons."

HEALTH FLASH

prevent other illness as well. Researchers have found antioxidant benefits in many carotenoids and flavonoids. Other phytochemicals also have been found to lower cholesterol levels and blood pressure, boost the immune system and even prevent tooth decay.

Eating Your Phytomins

The phytochemicals listed here are found in abundance in natural, whole foods—and can be found as supplements in health food stores. Generally, experts recommend whole foods over supplements, as phytochemicals tend to coexist in a number of foods.

Allyl Sulfides

Foods found in: Garlic, onions, leeks, chives, shallots
Benefits: Lower harmful low-density lipoprotein (LDL) cholesterol. Studies also have linked garlic consumption with a decreased risk of stomach and colon cancer.

Alpha-carotene

Foods found in: Carrots, seaweed
Benefits: Increases vitamin A activity; improves immune response: may decrease risk of lung cancer (associated with slowed growth of cancer cells in lab studies); may stave off heart disease and some inflammatory disorders.

Anthocyanins

Foods found in: Cranberry juice
Benefits: May prevent and cure urinary tract infections.

Beta-carotene

Foods found in: Carrots; squash; apricots; peaches; red, yellow and dark green vegetables
Benefits: Beta-carotene has been linked to decreased risk of lung, colon, bladder, gynecological and skin cancer; improved immune response has also been cited.

Capsaicin

Foods found in: Chili peppers
Benefits: Anti-inflammatory agent, useful as a bronchitis or cold treatment.

Carnosol

Foods found in: Rosemary
Benefits: An antioxidant that acts to slow the development of some tumors; seems to alter lipid metabolism, preventing fats in the body from oxidizing and damaging cells.

Genistein

Foods found in: Soybean products
Benefits: A phytoestrogen, genistein may protect against breast cancer, osteoporosis, heart disease and menopausal symptoms. In addition, other components of soybeans may help lower blood cholesterol and slow cancer cell growth or reproduction.

Gingerol

Foods found in: Gingerroot
Benefits: Can reduce nausea caused by motion sickness or pregnancy; anti-inflammatory properties can relieve symptoms of migraine headaches.

Glycyrrhizin and Triterpenoids

Foods found in: Licorice root extract
Benefits: Enhanced immune function. Some cancer-fighting potential (they slow cell mutation and contain anti-tumor properties). Useful in treatment of gastrointestinal ulcers; antibacterial properties help fight tooth decay and gum disease.

Indoles

Foods found in: Brussels sprouts, cabbage, kale, dark green leafy vegetables
Benefits: Increase immune activity; may protect against cancer.

Limonenes

Foods found in: Citrus fruit
Benefits: May help prevent cancer. D-limonene has been shown to protect against breast cancer in lab studies. In addition, the soluble fiber in fruit has been found to ward off gastrointestinal tract cancer and pancreatic cancer.

Lutein and Zeaxanthin

Foods found in: Yellow squash; spinach; collard, mustard and turnip greens
Benefits: Decrease risk of lung cancer; slow onset of age-related macular degeneration (an eye disease that can result in blindness). Chemicals in members of the mustard family strengthen the immune system and are effective against colon, lung, prostate and esophageal cancer.

Lycopene

Foods found in: Tomatoes, red grapefruit, watermelon, apricots
Benefits: Lycopene is an antioxidant. It may decrease risk of colon and bladder cancer (linked to reduced growth of cancer cells in lab studies). It may also reduce risk of cardiovascular disease and protect against cell damage.

Monoterpenes

Foods found in: Basil, carrots, parsley, mint, cabbage, citrus fruits

Benefits: May interfere with carcinogens.

Phenethyl Isothiocyanates

Foods found in: Horseradish, mustard, cabbage, turnips

Benefits: Can suppress tumor growth; inhibit lung cancer; trigger formation of enzymes that can block carcinogens from damaging a cell.

Phytic Acid

Foods found in: Rye, wheat, rice, lima beans, sesame seeds, peanuts

Benefits: Appears to prevent colon cancer and reduce frequency and severity of intestinal cancer.

Polyphenol Catechins and Theaflavin

Foods found in: Green tea, black tea
Benefits: May help fight several types of cancer; may aid immune system and lower cholesterol levels. Phenols have been found to protect body tissue from oxidation.

Pulp Facts

Juice fans, take note: Spare the pulp when you whir your fruits and veggies—you'll retain more of the beneficial compounds, called phytomins, that Mother Nature packs into produce.

Half the fabulous vitamins and phytomins in fruit and vegetables are wasted if you juice and discard that precious pulp, according to a new study. Researchers first measured levels of two phytomins: lycopene (a possible colon cancer fighter) in tomatoes and sulforaphane (a possible breast cancer fighter) in broccoli. They also measured the nutrient beta-carotene (a possible cancer and heart disease fighter) in carrots.

After the vegetables were juiced and strained, levels of beta-carotene and the two phytomins in the remaining juice dropped by 30 to 60 percent. The lost phytomins and beta-carotene were found in the discarded pulp.

Solution: If you want to drink your veggies, use a juicer (such as Vita-Mix) that pulverizes the pulp right into your juice. Otherwise, make it a double when you mix that carrot-juice cocktail. You still won't get all the fiber, but you may get a full measure of vitamins and phytomins by drinking twice as much.

Polyphenols

Foods found in: Red grapes and red wine, artichokes, strawberries, yams
Benefits: May reduce risk of cancer by trapping toxic chemicals and flushing them out of the body; may lower risk of heart disease.

Saponins

Foods found in: Kidney beans, chick-peas, soybeans, lentils
Benefits: May slow the spread of cancer cells in the colon; may prevent cancer cells from multiplying.

Sulforaphane

Foods found in: Broccoli, cauliflower, brussels sprouts, turnips, kale
Benefits: Helps cancer-fighting enzymes remove carcinogens from cells; shown to inhibit the development of breast cancer tumors in lab studies.

9

Soy: Savor the New, White-Hot Superfood

A h, soy. This humble little bean made big headlines last year when, after years of neglect, new studies found that it can help women dodge major health threats like heart disease, breast cancer and maybe even osteoporosis.

Soy may very well be this year's superfood. It's the latest entry in a list of must-eat foods for women, say experts, who are ranking soy with health-promoting good stuff like fruit, vegetables, whole grains and low-fat dairy products.

One little problem, though. Soy foods like tofu and tempeh may be menu staples for women all over Asia. But in the United States, where we grow half of the world's soybeans and then feed them mostly to chickens, the idea of soy for dinner somehow doesn't cut it, does it? Fear of tofu—a white, spongy soybean curd that most of us don't have a clue how to cook with—runs deep.

If this describes you, relax. Lately, soy's disease-defying powers have been matched by new powers to please the palate. Look in your supermarket—soy foods are taking a great leap forward in terms of variety, flavor, texture and culinary possibilities. Think chocolate pudding. Sloppy Joes. Creamy fruit smoothies. All made with soy.

Mind you, no one is claiming that soy makes miracles. "You can't expect to wash down your cheeseburgers and fries with soy milk and come out even," says soy authority Mark Messina, Ph.D., former program director of the Diet and Cancer Branch of the National Cancer Institute. "But when you add it to a healthy diet, one serving of soy a day makes too much sense to ignore."

Inside the Bean

What's so great about soy? Researchers have discovered that it contains hormonelike substances called isoflavones. Your body can mistake them for estrogen, the female hormone that helps protect against heart disease, brittle bone disease and even menopausal discomfort.

When researchers in Australia gave 58 menopausal women soy flour mixed into a drink or cereal or baked into a muffin, they found that the average number of hot flashes fell by 40 percent. Since soybeans are such a good source of isoflavones, you could probably get enough from just three to four ounces a day of tofu—which is made from soybean curd.

How much soy should you deploy to reap this bean's health benefits? Experts don't know precisely yet. What's more, the level of soy protein and protective isoflavones in soy products varies, depending upon where the soy was grown and how it was processed.

For now, Dr. Messina advises eating at least one serving of soy food a day (the average intake in Asia) without worrying over grams of protein or milligrams of isoflavones. Unless, he says, you're using soy to lower your high blood cholesterol.

In that case, you may need 25 to 50 grams a day. But before you try to pack that much soy into your diet, check with your doctor. She may send you to a registered dietitian to determine how much animal protein you should omit. You'll need a concentrated source of soy protein, too, such as a soy breakfast cereal or a high-protein soy powder. Alternatively, you'd need two to three servings of other types of soy foods to get 25 grams of soy protein.

Happily, there are lots of new ways for soybean sissies to experience the joys of soy.

Seven Simple Ways to Serve Soy

Pudding? Sloppy Joes? Creamy, frosty fruit smoothies? There's soy in every one. Here's a week's worth of easy ways to get a little soy into your life.

Pour it on. Use soy milk on your breakfast cereal. This is probably the easiest soy-step of all. Soy milk doesn't taste exactly like cow's milk, and it's sometimes beige in color. Never mind. Chilled and poured on your favorite cereal, it's terrific.

Most soy milk comes in aseptic cartons in supermarkets or health food stores. Look for nonfat or 1% low-fat versions, plain or vanilla-flavored. After opening, you can refrigerate soy milk for about one week if kept in original container.

Note: If you replace cow's milk with soy milk, try to find a calcium-fortified brand. Per one-cup (8-ounce) serving: 80 to 120 calories, 0 to 2.5 grams of fat.

Whir and sip. Whip up tofu blender smoothies by whirring tofu, juice and frozen fruit into healthy shakes so creamy that they seem sinful. Use Mori-Nu Lite Firm Silken Tofu (aseptic pack) or soft tofu packed in water and sealed in plastic (both are in supermarkets).

Breakfast becomes dessert with this Strawberry Banana Smoothie: Combine in a blender one cup unsweetened apple juice, one cup unsweetened frozen strawberries, one small banana, one (10.5-ounce) package Mori-Nu Lite Firm Silken Tofu. Blend till smooth. Makes two (10-ounce) servings. Per serving: 200 calories, 2 grams of fat, 2 grams of fiber.

(Keep unopened aseptic packages of tofu in your cupboard until "best used by" date; after opening, refrigerate in sealed container for two to three days. Keep unopened water-packed tofu refrigerated until "best used by" date; after

Disease-Fighting Powers of Soy Revealed

Ah, the humble soybean. In a flurry of new studies, researchers have uncovered potent disease-battling powers in this superfood that's been a staple of Asian home cooking for 5,000 years.

Here's how it can help women.

▶ Lowers heart disease risk. A soy-rich, low-fat diet dramatically reduced heart-damaging, "bad" low-density lipoprotein (LDL) cholesterol in women at risk for heart disease, according to new research from the University of Kentucky College of Medicine.

▶ May protect against breast cancer. Isoflavones, disease-fighting substances found only in soy, may account for the low rate of fatal breast cancer among Japanese women.

▶ Battles brittle bones. Osteoporosis is far less common in Asian women, possibly because soy causes less calcium excretion than animal protein does.

How can you reap soy's full benefits? "About six ounces a day would have major benefits for lowering cholesterol," says soy researcher James Anderson, M.D., professor of medicine and clinical nutrition in the Division of Endocrinology and Metabolism at the University of Kentucky College of Medicine in Lexington. That amounts to two to three servings, totaling 20 to 25 grams of soy protein daily.

"I eat a soy snack bar every afternoon," Dr. Anderson says. "At home, my granddaughter and I devised a French toast recipe using soy milk that's delicious."

HEALTH FLASH

opening, keep refrigerated and change water daily; use in five to seven days.)

Flavor it with deep, dark chocolate. Make chocolate pudding that no one can resist. You won't believe how easy or how luscious this is: Blend one (10.5-ounce) package Mori-Nu Silken Lite Extra-Firm Tofu with one pack of brand-new Mori-Nu Mates Chocolate Pudding and Pie Mix (sold in health food stores); then chill. Wow! Per half-cup serving: 150 calories, 1.5 grams of fat.

Say beans. Add sweet beans to your repertoire. Possibly this year's star veggie (you heard it here first), these pretty soybeans are about the size of plump baby limas but are brighter green, sweeter and firmer. They're picked before maturity, blanched and sold frozen in 16-ounce poly bags.

Boil sweet beans for two minutes, then serve as a side dish with a squeeze of fat-free liquid margarine, as a main dish with pasta, chopped red bell pepper and Parmesan, or in a salad with tomato and onion. Look for Sun-Rich Sweet Beans in health food stores or Yu Yee Frozen Soy Beans in Asian grocery stores. Per half-cup serving: 60 calories, 2 grams of fat, 8 grams of fiber.

Heat and eat on a bun. Indulge in healthy sloppy joes—a fast-to-fix comfort food that is basically fat-free if you make it with textured soy protein (often called textured vegetable protein—TVP) granules.

How? Rehydrate TVP with hot water for five minutes to resemble the consistency and flavor of ground beef. Add a can of sloppy joe sauce, heat and serve on a bun. Today's TVP will amaze you—it's great. Find it in health food stores and some supermarkets. Per half-cup (reconstituted): 60 calories, 0.1 gram of fat and 11 grams of protein.

Go crunch in the morning. Nutlettes, the only ready-to-eat soy breakfast cereal, has the texture of crunchy nuggets, stays crispy in milk and boasts a wholesome, nutty flavor. Made from a TVP you don't rehydrate, this cereal is a best bet if you are looking for a concentrated source of soy protein (25 grams of soy protein per half-cup).

Order by phone from Dixie USA at 1-800-347-3494 (24 hours a day). Price: about $6 for two pounds (18 half-cup servings) plus shipping. Per half-cup serving: 140 calories, 1.5 grams of fat, 9 grams of fiber.

Drink your protein. Drink soy-protein beverages, that is. They're another best bet for a concentrated source of soy protein. One product, Take Care High Protein Beverage Powder, is the same beverage used in many cholesterol-lowering studies.

Made from isolated soy protein, Take Care High Protein packs 20 grams of soy protein in each serving. It comes plain, chocolate-flavored or strawberry-flavored; you mix with water or juice or use in shakes. Order by phone from Nutritious Foods at 1-800-445-3350. Price: about $8 per 12 to 14 servings, plus shipping. Per serving: 100 to 130 calories, 1.5 grams of fat.

For somewhat less protein, get regular soy-protein isolate powder in health food stores. Blend unflavored varieties with orange juice. Or mix Spiru-Tein Chocolate Peanut Butter Swirl soy protein powder with skim milk—this we

One Serving of Soy

Exactly how much soy is one serving? The answer depends on what form of this versatile bean you're eating. Here are examples of one serving.

▶ one cup (eight ounces) soy milk
▶ one-half cup (two to three ounces) tofu
▶ one-half cup rehydrated textured vegetable protein
▶ one-half cup green soybeans ("Sweet Beans")
▶ one (three-ounce) soy-protein-concentrate burger
▶ one-half cup Nutlettes cereal

loved. Per serving: 179 calories, 0 gram of fat, 1 gram of fiber. Be aware that both Take Care and Spiru-Tein have lots of added vitamins and minerals. You may not want a multi-vitamin and mineral supplement on the days when you drink this.

Soy Considerations

Supermarkets and health food stores carry umpteen good soy products these days, including vegetarian hot dogs, cheese, yogurt and ice cream and, surprisingly, many of them taste just great. So why didn't any of these foods make our shopping list?

Dr. Messina's advice (while you and soy are still making friends): Avoid soy versions of foods you love. A direct comparison between the two is likely to make the soy product seem second-best—just because it's different from what you're used to.

But that caution doesn't apply to scrumptious veggie burgers made from soy-protein concentrate. These really do mimic a beef burger's taste, with jumbo health advantages.

Be aware, too, that many soy products are higher in price. Dr. Messina's advice is to buy in bulk or order by the case if you can. Stock up at sale time, too. "My favorite soy milk," he says, "is whatever is least expensive when I'm shopping."

Trans-fat: The Big, Bad, Sneaky Fat

This year, about three out of four of us will spread margarine on our morning toast. We're abandoning butter: Compared with the 1960s, we eat 43 percent less of it now. Most Americans, it seems, have gotten the message: If you're watching your cholesterol, make the switch to margarine.

Confident that we were doing our hearts a favor, many of us did just that. Then the news . . . well, spreading that margarine might not be so great after all. There's evidence that trans-fatty acids, a type of fat found primarily in margarine as well as in commercially prepared baked goods and fried foods, raise "bad" low-density lipoprotein (LDL) cholesterol, lower "good" high-density lipoprotein (HDL) cholesterol and, therefore, increase the risk of heart attack.

The jury is still out on the health risks posed by trans-fatty acids. Some experts say that women should avoid them at all costs. Others say margarine is still a healthier choice than butter and so has a place in your diet. Even so, choosing varieties with the least trans-fats may be best.

"Studies show that while both trans-fatty acids and saturated fat increase LDL cholesterol, saturated fat has a greater effect on cholesterol," says Alicia Moag-Stahlberg, R.D., a dietitian in Chicago and a spokesperson for the American Dietetic Association. Further, we consume far more saturated fat. "About 3 percent of our total calories come from trans-fatty acids, compared with 12 to 13 percent from saturated fat," says Moag-Stahlberg.

Don't slather margarine over every baked potato or piece of toast, though. Experts advise consuming all fats—margarine included—in moderation.

Barely Better Than Butter?

Like butter, margarine is 100 percent fat. But the fat in margarine is primarily unsaturated, which is normally easier on your coronary arteries

63

than saturated fat. Butter contains about seven grams of saturated fat per tablespoon; margarine, about two grams per tablespoon.

So what's the problem? Trans-fatty acids, a by-product of innovations in food technology. Margarine is made mostly from unsaturated oils—corn, canola and safflower, to name a few. Unsaturated oils are liquid at room temperature. To solidify these unsaturated oils, manufacturers pump them up with hydrogen in a chemical process called hydrogenation. "Hydrogenation makes fats harder," says Sheah Rarback, R.D., director of nutrition at the Mailman Center at the University of Miami School of Medicine. "A stick margarine is more hydrogenated than a soft-tub margarine, for example."

Hydrogenation also creates trans-fatty acids. Ironically, when unsaturated fatty acids are chemically combined with hydrogen, they become more saturated.

The margarine controversy began some years ago, when a Dutch study found that trans-fatty acids elevate cholesterol levels. Some experts noted that the people in the three-week study consumed about four times more trans-fatty acids than the average American. But subsequent studies added fuel to the trans-fat fire, suggesting that smaller levels of trans-fats could add to the clogging of coronary arteries.

Perhaps the most persuasive of these investigations was the Nurses' Health Study at Harvard Medical School, which analyzed the health habits of more than 85,000 women. The study found a strong link between margarine consumption and higher rates of heart disease.

But international studies show that societies that eat the most butter have higher heart attack rates, says William P. Castelli, M.D., medical director of the Framingham Cardiovascular Institute, a wellness program at Metro West Medical Center in Framingham, Massachusetts. On the other hand, he says, a highly regarded clinical trial called the Finnish Hospital Study found that people who ate margarine lowered their cholesterol by about 15 percent and cut their heart attack rates roughly in half over a six-year period compared with people who ate butter.

Select the Healthiest Spread

Ready to get rid of your margarine and renew your love affair with butter? Not so fast. For now, say experts, your best bet is to cut back on saturated fat, including butter. If you're still using butter, switching to margarine can be a good start. "You will dramatically lower your intake of saturated fat and your intake of trans-fatty acids, since many margarines have lower levels of trans-fatty acids than butter," says Dr. Castelli.

But with so many varieties of margarine to choose from, picking a truly heart-healthy product can be tricky. These guidelines can help.

▶ First and foremost, select a margarine that contains no more than two grams of saturated fat per tablespoon, advises the American Heart Association.

"Choose only margarines that list water as the first ingredient," advises Dr. Castelli. These products will be low in trans-fatty acids as well as in saturated fat. "And avoid margarine that lists partially hydrogenated vegetable oil as the first ingredient," he says.

▶ Avoid stick margarine; it tends to be highly hydrogenated. Opt for soft tub-style margarine instead. "The softer the margarine, the lower its content of trans-fatty acids and saturated fat," says Alice H. Lichtenstein, D.Sc., assistant professor of nutrition at Tufts University in Medford, Massachusetts, and a scientist at the Jean Mayer USDA Human Nutrition Research Center on Aging in Boston.

▶ Select a brand with a highest percentage of polyunsaturated fat, advises Dr. Lichtenstein. You might opt for products made from safflower, sunflower, corn or soybean oil.

▶ If possible, select a liquid or semiliquid spread, particularly for cooking, says Dr. Lichtenstein. When she compared three diets—a baseline diet with 35 percent of calories from fat, a corn oil margarine–enriched diet with 30 percent

Margarine's New Dark Side

Harvard University researchers who followed the health and eating habits of 85,095 women for eight years recently uncovered a disturbing link: The more margarine—as well as cookies, cakes and biscuits—that the women ate, the higher their risk of heart disease.

The researchers, working on the ongoing Nurses' Health Study, found that women who ate four or more teaspoons of margarine a day had a 66 percent greater risk for heart disease than women who ate less than one teaspoon a month.

The culprit? Trans-fatty acids—vegetable oils converted into solid fats.

"These fats are solid at room temperature, like animal fats," explains researcher Walter C. Willett, M.D., Dr.P.H., professor of epidemiology and nutrition at the Harvard University School of Public Health. Dr. Willett and some other experts believe that in your body they may be significantly worse than animal fats—even though for years margarine was considered the healthy alternative to butter and other animal fats.

"If you're really concerned about your health, you want to stay away from trans-fats as much as possible," Dr. Willett says.

Avoid them completely by spreading olive oil, sesame oil or even peanut butter on your bread instead of margarine. And try baking with canola oil instead of margarine. "Olive oil on bread tastes good, even at breakfast," he notes. "And a small amount of butter once in a while is all right."

HEALTH FLASH

of calories from fat and a liquid corn oil–enriched diet with 30 percent of calories from fat—the liquid corn oil was found to cut LDL cholesterol by 17 percent compared with the baseline diet. The corn oil margarine cut LDL by 10 percent compared with baseline.

▶ Spare the spread altogether. "We've been raised to think that we should smear something on our toast," says Dr. Lichtenstein. "But if we eat tasty bread, we may not need to." Another option: Top your toast with a small amount of jelly or jam, which contains no saturated fat.

▶ Avoid products that contain partially hydrogenated vegetable oil, another term for trans-fatty acids. "In particular, watch out for fried foods, cakes and cookies," says Dr. Lichtenstein.

▶ Consume all fat in moderation, says Dr. Lichtenstein. "If you're concerned about obesity, heart disease and cancer, the point is to cut as much fat as possible out of your diet."

Olestra: Olé or Oh No?

The hope that fat substitutes would transform our favorite foods into guilt-free pleasures has yet to be fulfilled. Olestra, the new fat substitute that hit selected supermarkets late last year, remains controversial, thanks to potential negative health effects.

Meanwhile, the benefits of the thousands of fat-free and low-fat foods that have come onto the market in the past few years remain murkier. Why? These foods provide new options, and they sound healthier than the products they replace. But they may not have the benefits that we had wished for. One thing is for certain: Despite the ever-widening availability of these foods, Americans aren't getting any thinner.

Fake-Fat Furor

A chemical synthesis of sugar and vegetable oil, Olestra sounds like the dieter's dream. It functions like fat in frying but supplies no calories, passing through the body undigested. Potato chips made with olestra are fried but fat-free and have less than half the calories of regular chips.

But there's a downside: Olestra can cause diarrhea-like symptoms and intestinal gas in some users. (Foods made with olestra carry a warning about those side effects.)

Olestra also impedes the absorption of some essential nutrients. To correct that, it would have to be fortified with vitamins A, D, E and K. But beyond that, olestra also interferes with the absorption of carotenoids. These are among the substances in fruits and vegetables that some scientists believe protect cells from damage and help ward off cancer and other chronic illnesses.

The benefits of carotenoids are as yet unproved. But since daily consumption of as little as eight grams of olestra (less than the amount in a one-ounce packet of potato chips) can reduce carotenoid levels substantially, scientists who oppose olestra fear that decades from now, olestra users could suffer higher rates of cancer, heart disease and other debilitating illnesses.

Other substitutes are currently in development and may come to the market in the near future. It's unlikely that any of them will turn out to be a diet miracle, and some may prove to have unanticipated negative health effects, experts say.

A Case of False Hope

Even the most widely used fat replacements are carbohydrate- and protein-based compounds. While they have no negative effects on health, there is one key drawback: Many of the foods they're used in become lower in fat but not significantly lower in calories.

"Don't bank on fat-free foods to make you slimmer. The desire for these products is enormous, but to a certain degree, it's a case of false hope," says Fred Caporaso, Ph.D., chairman of the Department of Food Science and

The Lowdown on Olestra

If you're a snack-food fan looking to cut calories without sacrificing taste or even quantity, the new fake fat called olestra is worth a try, says obesity expert G. Ken Goodrick, Ph.D., assistant professor of medicine at Baylor College of Medicine in Houston.

"If a person just has to eat chips, they may as well be chips made with olestra," Dr. Goodrick says. "I don't think anyone's going to lose much weight by eating them, but in moderate amounts, they probably won't cause big problems."

With zero calories, zero fat and a formula that can be fried into potato chips, fake fat certainly sounds tempting. But will olestra let you eat like Roseanne while keeping a Cindy Crawford figure? Doubtful, says Dr. Goodrick, unless you can stop after a nibble instead of downing a bowlful of these greasy taste-treats.

After all, even a bowlful of low-cal chips can add up to a lot of calories—and Americans tend to eat salty snacks such as potato chips in large quantities.

"My best advice is, eat foods closer to nature—fruit, vegetables, whole grains. They're low in fat and full of the nutrients we need," Dr. Goodrick says.

By the way—chances are that you won't find the name olestra on the front of packages for fat-free foods at the supermarket. Instead, look for the brand name Olean. Olestra is this fake fat's chemical name and will appear in the ingredients list on the back of the package.

HEALTH FLASH

Low Fat = Low Calorie? Not Always

Doctors are noticing that a lot of people are scrupulous about buying only fat-free products yet still can't lose weight. Some even gain weight.

What's going on?

Reading nutrition labels provides one important clue. Take that luscious-looking chocolate frozen yogurt, for example, that boasts a mere four grams of fat per half-cup serving. Before you fill 'er up, take a second look at the label. As it turns out, one serving of this treat also contains 140 calories—about as much as in the same amount of regular ice cream.

Further detective work reveals that other fat-free or low-fat products may also be quite high in calories. Sure, they may not have much fat. But something makes them taste good, and in some cases, that "something" adds calories. According to James J. Kenney, R.D., Ph.D., nutrition research specialist at the Pritikin Longevity Center in Santa Monica, California, fat-free products don't automatically cut calories or lead to weight loss, because the fat in the products has been replaced with sugar and white flour, actually increasing the calorie density.

"Products are formulated to achieve a fatlike taste, appearance and texture, and each manufacturer blends a variety of ingredients to do that," explains Angela Miraglio, R.D., head of AMM Nutrition Services in Chicago. "Some products end up with fewer calories, and some do not."

Here's the math: If you have a cookie that contains four grams of fat, at 9 calories per gram (the number of calories in one gram of fat), the total calories from fat are 36, says Miraglio. If the manufacturer makes a fat-free version of the cookie, you "save" four grams of fat and 36 calories.

But to maintain a flavorful cookie, the cookie makers may put in, say, a bit of emulsifier, an additive that may contain nine calories per gram (the same as fat). Or they may add extra sugar (which contains no fat), accounting for a fair number of calories. Add it all up, and a fat-free cookie may have fewer calories than a regular cookie—but don't count on it.

Nutrition at Chapman University in Orange, California.

Fat substitutes can duplicate some of the sensory pleasures of fat, but they don't provide the same sense of satisfaction, says Dr. Caporaso. As a result, people eat more of other foods, which compensates for the calories they saved by eating fat-free products. So if you're using lower-fat products in the hope that you'll shed pounds, you may be disappointed unless you're making an overall effort to cut calories or to burn more calories than you take in with a stepped-up exercise regimen.

Using lots of no- and low-fat foods isn't an automatic nutrition improvement, either.

"We've oversimplified nutrition by saying that low fat equals healthy," says Alicia Moag-Stahlberg, R.D., a dietitian in Chicago and a spokesperson for the American Dietetic Association. "But overfocusing on avoiding fat can result in other nutrients becoming unbalanced. If you're eating a lot of fat-free foods and omitting fat-containing foods (even lean meat and low-fat dairy and whole grains), the percentage of fat in your diet may be low, but you may also be low in a range of other key nutrients: iron, zinc, beta-carotene, selenium, calcium, folate and vitamins A, C, D and E."

Fat substitutes can make you feel a lot less guilty about eating foods such as chips, ice cream and cookies, so you're likely to eat more of them no matter how low in fat they may be. Therefore, you still need to make the diet changes that improve health, such as eating more of the original fat-free and low-fat foods: fruits, vegetables and whole grains.

"You can't eat in ways you shouldn't and then count on fat substitutes to save the day for you," says Dr. Caporaso. "If you want to be healthy, the number one thing is to have an exercise program that burns calories."

Brave New Breakfast

W hen you were a kid, cereal makers wooed you with sugary, fruit-flavored breakfast flakes—packed with prizes like decoder rings, snap-together plastic toys, even send-away coupons for T-shirts and monogrammed pencils.

Fast-forward to 1997: Cereal manufacturers are *still* conspiring to woo you, this time with a different sort of prize—health benefits. Commercials tout a ton of them: high fiber, low sugar, piles of vitamins and minerals. And these benefits actually live up to the promises. (What toy was ever as terrific as the hype on the back of the cereal box?)

"You can't find another food to nutritionally match any fortified cereal," says Liz Applegate, Ph.D., sports nutritionist at the University of California, Davis, and author of *Power Foods*. In fact, according to Dr. Applegate, you really can't go wrong with any cereal (the kiddie kind included).

How? By optimizing every snap, crackle and pop, thanks to brands that please your palate as well as your diet. This is especially good news for busy women who'd like to eat breakfast—if it took less than 30 seconds to prepare. What's faster than pouring flakes and milk into a bowl?

So grab a spoon. We'll revisit Toucan Sam, Cap'n Crunch, the Lucky Charms elf and all the rest.

Box Dynamics

While less intriguing than the back-of-the-box offers for prize toys, the nutrition information on the side is, well, at least a bit more specific than it used to be. Thanks to new government regulations, cereal manufacturers are required to divulge more nutritional data (including the sugar content, which many companies used to mask under total carbohydrates) than they once did.

The result: a label that's a little more accurate and a lot more extensive.

How can you use it? Happily, you don't have to analyze every entry, just a few key categories. From the label's top to bottom, here's our guide to understanding—and using—the new label to your own advantage.

Consider the Real Serving Size

A sticky issue. Until fairly recently, all side-of-the-box nutritional data was based on a serving size of one ounce by weight. But an ounce of a light-weight cereal such as Cheerios amounts to a stomach-satisfying cup of O's (400 of them, to be exact), whereas an ounce of a heavier cereal, such as Grape-Nuts, barely coats the bottom of your bowl.

Of course, Grape-Nuts lovers weren't deterred by their tiny allowance (who knows how much an ounce equals, anyway?) and routinely filled their bowls with the stuff, consuming many more calories than they bargained for in the process.

Enter the U.S. Food and Drug Administration—the FDA. Last year, the FDA began requiring manufacturers to increase the serving size of dense cereals to a more realistic two ounces by weight (usually ½ to 1¼ cups). And as a result, the calories and fat listed on the label nearly doubled. For instance, one serving of Grape-Nuts now sets you back 200 calories, whereas one serving of Cheerios (still about one ounce by weight) packs only 110 calories.

Logical, yes. Simple, no. "The new serving sizes do more accurately reflect how much you're likely to eat," says Patricia Harper, R.D., a nutrition consultant in Pittsburgh and a spokesperson for the American Dietetic Association. "But don't be misled into thinking that some cereals are more fattening than others, because you might actually be comparing one ounce of one cereal to two ounces of another. Actually, ounce-for-ounce, most cereals are just about equal in calories."

Reap the Low-Cal Bonus

The calorie count in breakfast cereals is a real steal. The vast majority of cereals contain just 100 to 210 calories per serving, and some, such as Fiber One and All-Bran, pack 80 or less.

So if you curb your enthusiasm and eat no more than the recommended portion size (an admittedly tough assignment), you should be okay. But read labels regardless—and deep-six the handful of cereals such as Post Hearty Granola that actually exceed 210 calories per serving.

Check the Fat

The fat content of flakes can be tricky. True, most cereals (even the kiddie kind) contain little fat. In fact, three grams of fat or less per 110- to 200-calorie serving is about average. No problem there. The tricky part: Some seemingly healthful cereals such as Post Hearty Granola and Cracklin' Oat Bran contain eight or nine grams of fat per serving.

Granted, given their overall calorie counts, the percentage of calories that come from fat falls right around 33 percent in both cereals (34 percent in Post Hearty Granola, 32 percent in Cracklin' Oat Bran). So neither is necessarily high in fat; they're just not low-fat. Which begs the question: Do you really want to use up all of your daily fat allowance on—of all things—*cereal*? Of course not!

So dyed-in-the-wool granola-lovers can try the low-fat versions made by Kellogg's and General Mills, both of which contain just 2½ to 3 grams of fat per serving. Or you can sprinkle the original over a more healthful (nonfat) alternative, such as Cheerios or Kellogg's Corn Flakes, for a twice-the-flavor, half-the-fat combination.

Spoon Up the Salt Bargain

The sodium, or salt, content in most cereals is negligible—so low, it's small potatoes. Most cereals contain only a sprinkling of sodium, usually no more than 300 milligrams.

So don't worry about scanning the label for salt content as well as fat, fiber and calories—unless, of course, you're on a low-sodium diet prescribed by your doctor. In that case, you should stick with cereals that contain less than

New Study: Breakfast-Eaters Get Nutrition Edge

H E A L T H F L A S H

You knew breakfast was important—but now there's brand-new evidence reinforcing just how vital that morning meal is.

In an analysis of the dietary habits of over 11,000 women and men, researchers found that those who woke up to everyday breakfast foods like cereal, milk, orange juice, yogurt and fresh fruit got a huge nutritional head start. Many met one-third to one-half of their daily needs for some key nutrients.

Meanwhile, breakfast skippers never caught up nutritionally—though ironically, missing breakfast did not mean they ate less calories over the course of the day.

"Our analysis indicates women can benefit especially from eating breakfast," says Beth Olson, Ph.D., senior nutrition scientist for Kellogg Company, in Battle Creek, Michigan. Morning meals are rich in nutrients like folate, which reduces the risk of birth defects and heart disease; vitamin C, which may provide protection against cervical and breast cancers; iron, a preventive of anemia; and calcium, which can ward off osteoporosis.

What if traditional breakfast foods don't appeal to you? Try cereal bars or low-fat granola bars, precut veggies or low-fat cottage cheese. "If you eat these instead of going without breakfast, you'll be ahead of the game nutritionally," she says. "But I think they'd make great breakfast foods."

Mix and Match the Flakes

Television comedian Jerry Seinfeld does it. We assume Shoshanna Lonstein (a.k.a. "the girlfriend") does it, too. And why not? We're talking mixing 'n' matching your cereal.

"I encourage my clients to combine cereal brands for optimal taste and nutrient content," says Pittsburgh-based nutrition consultant Patricia Harper, R.D., who regularly satisfies her own sweet tooth (and her conscience) by liberally flavoring her original Cheerios with their more flamboyant sibling—Honey Nut Cheerios.

To engineer the perfect personalized blend, breeze through the following suggestions.

▶ Corn Chex, a nonfat, low-sugar, low-calorie choice, with Raisin Bran, a sweet treat that packs seven grams of fiber per serving but is moderately high in calories.
▶ Kellogg's Corn Flakes, an old standby that contains no fat and only two grams of sugar per serving, with Frosted Mini-Wheats, a moderately sweet choice with six grams of fiber per serving.
▶ Fiber One, a fiber powerhouse with 13 grams per serving, with Rice Krispies, a welcome dose of sweetness and a satisfying crunch.
▶ Nut & Honey Crunch, a deliciously sweet pick that is low in fiber and moderately high in calories, with Cheerios, a less sweet staple that is lower in calories and a bit higher in fiber.

140 milligrams per serving such as Shredded Wheat and Healthy Choice Multi-Grain Squares (both sodium-free) or Kellogg's Blueberry or Strawberry Squares (less than 20 milligrams per serving).

Customize That Fiber Crunch

The facts behind the hype: Bran cereals provide a lot of insoluble fiber, which ushers food through your digestive system, prevents constipation and reduces your risk of colon cancer. They may also contain soluble fiber, which may help lower your cholesterol level.

In tandem, the two types are dubbed dietary fiber, and the National Cancer Institute recommends women get 20 to 30 grams of it daily through fruits, green leafy vegetables, legumes and whole grains such as those found in cereal.

Most cereals contain at least 1 gram of dietary fiber per serving—and some, such as Fiber One or All-Bran, boast as many as 13 grams per serving. Opt for the brand that best complements your diet.

For instance, if you consistently eat plenty of high-fiber foods like salads, beans and bread, choose a cereal that provides two to five grams per serving.

If, on the other hand, you want to boost your fiber quotient, try eating a fiber-rich cereal such as All-Bran every other day, or you can go the tastier route and add some to your Froot Loops every morning.

A word of warning: Cereals that contain more than ten grams of fiber per serving can trigger severe bloating or diarrhea if your system isn't accustomed to the added bulk. So introduce fiber to your diet gradually. Give your body time to adjust.

Avoid Sweet Nothings

How much sugar do you want in the morning. It's up to you. After all, sugar hasn't been proven to hamper overall good health—except by causing an occasional cavity or two (and now starches such as bread and pasta are thought to be bigger offenders on that score than sugar).

Even people with diabetes can eat sugary cereal—provided the total amount of carbohydrates they eat during a meal doesn't exceed the amount physicians recommend.

So why does sugar have such a bad reputation? It's a question of space. Seems that by adding lots of sugar to their cereals, manufacturers are left with little room to include more important nutrients such as fiber. Consider Cheerios, for instance. The ordinary O's contain 1 gram of sugar and 3 grams of fiber per serving. Add some apple-cinnamon coating, however, and you gain 11 grams of sugar per serving (almost a tablespoon) and lose 2 grams of fiber.

Some exceptions: Total Raisin Bran and Bran'nola both contain more sugar per serving than either Lucky Charms or Cocoa Krispies, yet they pack a decent amount of fiber, too. Read labels and get some fiber whenever possible.

Reconsider Those Extra Vitamins

The more vitamins and minerals, the merrier, right? Not necessarily. Why pay for more vitamins than your body can use?

The fact is, most cereals are fortified with 25 percent of your Daily Value (the new term for "Recommended Daily Allowance") for vitamin C, iron, thiamin, riboflavin, niacin, vitamin B_6 and folic acid. (Folic acid, the supplemental form of folate, is an especially important nutrient for women because it greatly lowers the risk of giving birth to a baby with severe spinal-cord damage such as spina bifida.)

A half-cup of skim milk provides 15 percent of your daily needs for calcium. Put the two together (by grabbing a bowl of Froot Loops or Frosted Flakes topped with milk) and

More Reasons Not to Miss Breakfast

If your biggest meal of the day is dinner or an all-evening snack-a-thon, you have lots of good company. A new study shows that the average American woman eats almost half of her daily calories (46 percent, to be exact) after 5 P.M.

What's even more surprising is that women who eat more at night don't seem to be heavier than women who eat more at breakfast or lunch. That contradicts recent studies suggesting that calories eaten late in the day lead to weight gain—so this story isn't over. But look what else turned up. Women eating the most after 5 P.M. consumed more fat and alcohol, and less vitamin C, vitamin B_6 and folate. (Who eats asparagus in front of the TV?) The bottom line: If you're a big evening eater, don't let good nutrition go down with the sun. Grab an orange. Savor lentil soup-in-a-cup.

And try increasing your intake at breakfast and lunch—you may eat less in the evening if you're not feeling hungry and deprived. Plus, you will likely be getting more of the nutrition women need most.

you're as good as gold. No kidding.

Despite popular belief, most reasonably healthy people who eat fairly well don't need to buy the higher-priced cereals such as Total or Product 19 that offer 100 percent of your daily needs for many vitamins and minerals. Of course, if you have iron-deficiency anemia (as diagnosed by your doctor) or eat very little red meat, you may want to choose a cereal that contains more iron than most, such as Blueberry Squares (which provides 90 percent of your daily needs), Corn Chex (50 percent of daily needs) or Life (45 percent of the daily needs—oh, and remember that Mikey, the little kid in the commercial, liked it). Otherwise, stick with your favorite. It provides you with plenty.

And finally, if you absolutely, positively can't work cereal into your morning routine, consider this: Cereal makes a great snack, either right out of the box or topped with cold milk.

NATURAL HEALING

Part 3

Alternative remedies are a much better use of my time, money and energy.

—Pam, a Seattle nurse

Female Advantage

Women lead the way when it comes to experimenting with alternative medicine—from herbal remedies to yoga, homeopathy to acupuncture, massage to food therapy.

"About 75 percent of all doctor's office visits are made by women. And based on what we see in our naturopathic practice, that number is often even higher for alternative medicine," notes Tori Hudson, a doctor of naturopathy, professor at the National College of Naturopathic Medicine and director of A Woman's Time, a women's menopause and natural health clinic specializing in natural treatments, both in Portland, Oregon.

Why are nature's cures so attractive for women? "Women biologically tend to be more nurturing creatures than men are," says Thomas A. Kruzel, a doctor of naturopathy and president of the American Association of Naturopathic Physicians, based in Seattle. "So it makes sense that they will gravitate toward safer, more natural therapies when it comes to caring for themselves and their families."

This willingness to explore new health care options can pay off in many ways. Here are just a few.

▶ Kinder, gentler medicine. Most herbal, nutritional and natural homeopathic remedies are gentler and have fewer side effects than pharmaceutical drugs, says Dr. Hudson.

▶ Better overall health. "We stress prevention," Dr. Kruzel says. "We'll counsel families on how to stay well."

▶ Less costly options. Natural remedies are often less expensive than prescription drugs. And if preventive treatments keep you out of the doctor's office, you save the cost of medical bills—a big plus for women, who often make less money than men.

▶ Less surgery. Alternative medicine seeks to avoid harsh drugs and surgery. "For women, that philosophy translates into fewer unnecessary surgeries to remove breasts, uteruses and ovaries," says Dr. Hudson. (Surgery and drug treatment may still be necessary, however, in the case of advanced disease.)

▶ A chance to be heard. Alternative practitioners say they listen carefully to women who come to them. "It's a great benefit for a woman to be able to talk about what is going on with her body and to be heard," says Dr. Hudson. "She has a better chance of getting well faster."

Alternative Healing: New Options for Women

Here's a scene you could have dubbed fiction back in the 1980s: A 39-year-old woman who has just had surgery to remove a cancerous breast tumor meets with radiation oncologist Jerold Green, M.D., at California Pacific Medical Center's gleaming, high-tech radiation oncology unit in San Francisco.

Dr. Green explains how he plans to treat her breast with x-rays to kill any cancer cells that the surgery missed. He also explains that, unless she takes precautions, the treatments would cause a radiation burn on her breast resembling a bad sunburn. His recommendation: Aloe vera gel, from an herb that has been used to treat burns for more than 3,000 years. "Buy it at our pharmacy or at any health food store," Dr. Green says. "Just rub it on your breast before and after each treatment."

A decade ago, most physicians scoffed at medicinal herbs. Some still do. But today, medical journals are publishing more herb research than ever. Consumers, who are fascinated by herbal medicine, continually ask their doctors about it. And the threat of plant extinctions has spurred new scientific interest in the healing power of botanicals. As a result, many mainstream doctors are now incorporating herbs into their practices.

Ancient, Yet Thoroughly Modern

The botanical roots of modern medicine are everywhere—if you know where to look. Ancient India's traditional Ayurvedic medicine dates back 4,500 years to the ancient Hindu text, the *Rig Veda*, which mentions 67 medicinal herbs, including senna to treat constipation and cinnamon for stomach upsets. These herbs are still used medicinally.

"Senna contains anthraquinone glycosides, chemicals that have powerful laxative action," says James Duke, Ph.D., a botanist with the U.S. Department of Agriculture's Research Station in Beltsville, Maryland, and author of many herb guides, including *The Handbook of Medicinal Herbs*. Senna is an ingredient in many commercial laxatives, including Gentlax, Senokot, Fletcher's Castoria and Innerclean Herbal Laxative.

"Cinnamon helps relieve stomach distress because its oil has antimicrobial properties," says Daniel Mowrey, Ph.D., director of the American Phytotherapy (plant medicine) Research Laboratory in Salt Lake City and author of *The Scientific Validation of Herbal Medicine*. Today, we have better treatments for intestinal infections, but cinnamon has been incorporated into several toothpastes, in part because it tastes good but also because its antibiotic action helps kill the bacteria that cause tooth decay and gum disease.

Untold numbers of herbs used in healing during ancient times are still in use today, many of them incorporated into common over-the-counter and prescription medications. And researchers are continually finding new uses for medicinal plants.

These days, ever-increasing numbers of people are returning to herbs—or learning about them for the first time. Herbal beverage teas line supermarket shelves, and most health food stores do a brisk business in medicinal herb tinctures (the liquid form of the herb plus alcohol) and teas.

Concerns about Safety

If herbs really have medicinal value, are they safe to use?

While the vast majority of herbal medicines present no danger to the public health, using them does require knowledge and proper caution. Too much of any good thing can cause harm, and recent studies show that a few herbs that were once considered safe for internal use are, in fact, hazardous. In large doses, comfrey—a traditional digestive remedy—can cause liver damage. So can coltsfoot, an herb long used to treat cough. In addition, just about any herb may cause an allergic reaction.

For healthy individuals who are not pregnant, the herbs in this book are all considered safe in recommended amounts. Pregnant women, however, should consult their physicians before using any medicinal herbs (or pharmaceuticals). Most herbal medicines should not be given to children under age 2. Children under 16 and anyone over 65 should dilute herbal preparations to reduce the dose. And those with chronic medical conditions should consult their physicians before supplementing medical therapies with herbs.

Best Herbs for Women

Once you decide that you want to use herbs, you're still left with some key questions. Which herbs? And how do you use them? Here is a list of common, safe and effective herbs to choose from, along with information about the conditions that they treat and directions for their use.

Aloe Vera

In ancient Egypt (1500 B.C.), the *Ebers Papyrus* recommended aloe vera for skin problems, and the world has been using this herb ever since. Chinese, Greek, Roman and Arab herbalists recommended it for wounds, burns, rashes and hemorrhoids. During the 1930s, radiologists discovered aloe vera's effec-

The New

Feel-

Good

Herb

New research shows that the extract from an early summer flower can help women relieve the blues and blahs of mild depression.

In carefully controlled European studies, roughly two out of three women and men who felt fatigued, had trouble sleeping and showed other signs of mild depression were helped by an extract of St.-John's-wort, a flower also known by its Latin name *Hypericum perforatum*.

Another study from Europe (where herbs are much more commonly used than in the United States) compared the herb with imipramine (Tofranil), a drug often used to treat depression. This research was carried out at 20 different health centers, with 135 depressive patients. After six weeks of treatment, the St.-John's-wort extract proved just as effective as the drug, but with fewer side effects.

But use caution with St.-John's-wort. Because of this herb's generally stimulating effect, it shouldn't be taken at bedtime, advises Varro E. Tyler, Ph.D., professor of pharmacognosy at the Purdue University School of Pharmacy in West Lafayette, Indiana, and author of *The New Honest Herbal*. Dr. Tyler adds that cases of severe depression probably won't be helped by the herb; seek medical attention without delay.

His advice? Don't take huge doses (no more than 300 milligrams at one time and a maximum of 900 milligrams a day) and don't sunbathe after taking it. St.-John's-wort is photoreactive and can make your skin super-sensitive to the sun's rays.

HEALTH FLASH

tiveness in treating radiation burns. The latest scientific studies show that the herb has clear value in treating minor cuts, scrapes and burns.

How to use: "Keep a potted aloe plant in your kitchen, where most household burns occur," says Dr. Mowrey. "That way, it's handy when you need it." Snip off a leaf, slit it open, scoop out the jellylike material and apply it to the affected area. Aloe vera gel may also be purchased commercially, but fresh gel works best. (Snipping an occasional leaf doesn't harm the plant.)

Chamomile

When Peter Rabbit ate himself sick in Mr. McGregor's garden and got chased out with the wrong end of a hoe, his mother gave him chamomile tea, a traditional remedy for indigestion, anxiety and wounds. German herbalists once used chamomile so extensively, they called it *alles zutraut*, "capable of anything."

Recent studies show that this popular beverage herb does indeed calm jangled nerves, relieve stomach distress, prevent ulcers and speed their healing and help fight infection by stimulating the immune system.

How to use: For an infusion—a type of tea in which the herb is extracted by letting it steep in very hot water—use two to three heaping teaspoons of dried or fresh flowers per cup of water that has come to the boiling point. Steep for 10 to 20 minutes. Reheat, if desired. Drink up to three cups a day.

In a tincture—a concentrated extract—use one-half to one teaspoon up to three times a day.

When using commercial preparations, follow package directions.

For a relaxing herbal bath, fill a cloth bag with a few handfuls of dried or fresh flowers and let the water run over it.

Feverfew

The name *feverfew* is actually a corruption of the Old English *featherfew*, a reference to the plant's feathery leaf borders. The ancient Greeks and Romans prescribed it for gynecological problems, and British herbalists recognized its abilities to ease headache pain in the seventeenth and eighteenth centuries. But their recommendations were largely forgotten.

Then about ten years ago, a happy accident occurred. The wife of a doctor with the British National Coal Board had migraines. A coal miner confided that he had been cursed with the horrible headaches until he began chewing two feverfew leaves a day. The woman tried the herb and noticed immediate improvement—fewer and less severe migraines. Intrigued, her husband urged a London migraine specialist to test feverfew. Now several studies have shown it to be effective. Feverfew also calms the digestive tract and may help reduce blood pressure.

How to use: For migraine control, chew two fresh (or frozen) leaves a day or take a pill or capsule containing 85 milligrams of leaf material. Most people prefer pills or capsules to leaves, since feverfew is quite bitter.

For an infusion, use one-half to one teaspoon per cup of boiling water. Steep for five to ten minutes. Reheat, if desired. Drink up to two cups a day.

In a tincture, take up to one teaspoon a day.

When using commercial preparations, follow package directions. Don't give feverfew to children under the age of 2. For older children or people over 65, start with low-strength preparations and increase strength, if necessary.

Garlic

Garlic is considered the world's second oldest medicine (along with its close botanical relatives onions, scallions, leeks, chives and shallots).

"Garlic is a very useful herb," says Dr. Duke. "Studies show that it helps protect against stomach cancer and reduces risk of heart disease by lowering blood pressure, reducing cholesterol and decreasing the likelihood of blood clots that can trigger heart attack."

How to use: In food, use as a seasoning to taste. The cloves' papery skins peel easily if you smash them with the flat side of a cleaver.

For an infusion, use six chopped cloves per cup of cool water and steep for six hours.

In a tincture, take up to three tablespoons a day.

Ginger

Scientific research has shown that ginger fights nausea better than the over-the-counter anti-nausea drug Dramamine. This root herb does more than simply soothe the stomach, however. An ancient Indian proverb says, "Every good quality is contained in ginger." Well, not quite, but studies show that it also boosts the immune system's ability to fight infection. And like garlic, it lowers blood pressure and cholesterol and helps prevent the blood clots that trigger heart attack.

How to use: For motion sickness, take 1,500 milligrams 30 minutes before departure. Ginger capsules are usually most convenient, but a 12-ounce glass of ginger ale also provides the recommended amount—if it's made with real ginger, not artificial flavor.

For an infusion, use two teaspoons of powdered or grated gingerroot per cup of boiling water. Steep for ten minutes. Drink up to three cups a day. If you buy whole root, refrigerate it.

Ginkgo

A relic of the dinosaur age, ginkgo is the oldest surviving tree on Earth. Poetically, it helps the oldest people. China's first historically recognized herbalist, Shen Nung (circa 3000 B.C.), called ginkgo "good for the heart and lungs." And traditional Chinese physicians have used it for thousands of years to treat asthma.

Studies show that ginkgo helps prevent asthma attacks. But its effectiveness against many infirmities of old age is astonishing.

When cholesterol deposits narrow the arteries in the legs, the result is a painful condition called intermittent claudication. In one study ginkgo produced "significantly greater pain relief than standard therapy." Finally, studies show ginkgo to be effective in the treatment of chronic ringing in the ears (tinnitus), one form of hearing loss (cochlear deafness) and age-related vision loss (macular degeneration).

How to use: Bulk ginkgo cannot be used because it takes a huge number of leaves to make a small amount of medicinal preparation. Many herb companies market ginkgo products. Follow package directions.

Ginseng

Prized above gold for thousands of years, ginseng root has been Asia's most revered tonic.

Until recently, Western scientists scoffed at ginseng claims. But research evidence is mounting that the herb helps the body resist illness and damage from stress. Studies show that ginseng stimulates the immune system, helps reduce cholesterol, protects the liver from toxic substances and increases stamina and nutrient absorption from the intestines. Asian Olympic athletes take it regularly to boost their performance.

How to use: Herb companies market ginseng teas, capsules, tablets and tinctures. Follow package directions.

For a decoction—a type of tea in which the herb is extracted by a long immersion in boiling water—add one-half teaspoon of powdered ginseng root per cup of boiling water. Simmer for about ten minutes. Drink up to two cups a day.

Goldenseal

A favorite Native American infection fighter, goldenseal was widely used to treat battle wounds during the Civil War and has been a popular folk antibiotic ever since. A survey of folk healing in Indiana showed that goldenseal is still used extensively to treat wounds and infections. No wonder: "Many studies show that it's a powerful antibiotic," Dr. Mowrey says. "It also has immune stimulant properties."

How to use: For an infusion, use one-half to one teaspoon of powdered goldenseal root per cup of boiling water. Steep for ten minutes. Drink up to two cups a day.

In a tincture, take one-half to one teaspoon up to twice a day.

When using commercial preparations, follow package directions.

Mint

The ancient Egyptians relied on peppermint and spearmint to relax the digestive tract. Chinese and traditional Indian Ayurvedic physicians used them to treat colds, coughs and fever. Native Americans employed mint for all these uses, as did European herbalists.

"Mints continue to be widely used as stomach soothers," says Varro E. Tyler, Ph.D., professor of pharmacognosy at the Purdue University School of Pharmacy in West Lafayette, Indiana, and author of *The New Honest Herbal*. Try a cup of mint tea after eating. In addition, mint oil (menthol) is an ingredient in several over-the-counter indigestion remedies, including milk of magnesia. Menthol is also a Food and Drug Administration–approved decongestant used in such cold formulas as Vicks VapoRub. Finally, menthol has anesthetic properties. It's an ingredient in several pain-relieving skin creams, including Solarcaine.

How to use: For an infusion, use one teaspoon of fresh herb or two teaspoons of dried leaves per cup of boiling water. Steep for ten minutes. Reheat, if desired. Drink up to three cups a day. Peppermint has a sharper taste than spearmint, and it feels cooler in the mouth.

In a tincture, take one-quarter to one teaspoon up to three times a day.

When using commercial preparations, follow package directions.

For a relaxing herbal bath, fill a cloth bag with a few handfuls of dried or fresh leaves and let the water run over it.

Slippery Elm Bark

The colonists found Native Americans using the inner portion of slippery elm bark as a food and as treatment for wounds, sore throat, cough— anything that needed soothing. As the young nation grew, slippery elm sore-throat lozenges became a fixture in home medicine chests.

Today, tragically, Dutch elm disease has decimated our elm forests, and our landscape and herbalism are poorer as a result. But the beneficial bark is still available in bulk and in herbal cough drops and sore-throat lozenges.

How to use: For a poultice, mix the powdered bark with water to make a paste. Apply the paste to the affected area, then cover it with a bandage. Change the bandage and slippery elm preparation daily.

For a soothing decoction, use one to three teaspoons of powdered bark per cup of water. Blend a little water in first to prevent lumpiness. Bring to a boil and simmer for 15 minutes. Drink up to three cups a day.

Valerian

Studies show that valerian, which contains hypnotic chemicals similar to catnip, has tranquilizing and sedative properties similar to Valium's, but it's nonaddictive. In Europe, dozens of valerian-based sleep aids are sold over the counter. "It works," says Dr. Mowrey, "and it's safer than most pharmaceutical sleeping pills."

How to use: Valerian is quite bitter. Commercial preparations and tinctures are usually more palatable than the infusion. Follow package directions.

If you would like to try the infusion, use two teaspoons of powdered valerian root per cup of boiling water. Steep for 10 to 15 minutes. Add sugar, honey or lemon or mix it with a beverage tea. Drink one cup before bed.

The Mind-Body Connection: Stronger Than Ever

There's strong new evidence that mind-body medicine alleviates the suffering of infertility. It calms the flaring symptoms of premenstrual syndrome (PMS). It ameliorates the discomforts of menopause. It promotes the well-being of breast cancer patients and may even extend their lives.

It reduces chronic pain in women with endometriosis and other pelvic conditions. It helps women beset by eating disorders. It liberates women from the disabling emotional and physical consequences of chronic anxiety.

Harvard University psychologist Alice Domar, Ph.D., co-author of Healing Mind, Healthy Woman, and other researchers have discovered that mind-body approaches can ease suffering among women with almost any medical condition.

What explains the vast potential of a mental approach to physical ills? One reason is clear. The stress in our lives, and the internal distress it causes, can wreak havoc on our bodies. Our hearts get overstimulated, our hormonal output becomes imbalanced and our immune systems—those inner networks of healing and defense—are weakened. There's even proof that women's reproductive systems can be affected by stress and ongoing emotional upset.

The Short Path to Better Health

When we learn to manage stress and free ourselves from chronic unhappiness, we alter our physiology in favor of health. Mind-body methods can remove the albatross of stress from all our biological systems, including our reproductive systems. For women, this may mean fewer and less severe symptoms of the disorders that commonly afflict us.

One way to manage stress is through exercises in deep breathing called mini-relaxations.

Women have special difficulty with deep breathing. It has nothing to do with genetic differences between men and women, or the fact that men have wider chest cavities. Our difficulty is strictly societal: We've been taught to hold in our stomachs because the hallmark of beauty is thinness.

To understand the effects of chest breathing, try this exercise. Sit or lie down and contract your abdominal muscles with all your might. As you do, take note of your breathing. Only your chest will rise as you inhale. Notice that your diaphragm is stuck in place and that air fills only the uppermost portions of your lungs. Now relax your stomach muscles and breathe into your abdomen. Notice how your diaphragm moves downward and the lower portions of your lungs fill up. While you're at it, take note of differences in how you feel, in mind and body, as you engage in chest versus abdominal breathing.

After doing this exercise, you may recognize that how you breathed when you held in your stomach is a mere exaggeration of how you normally breathe. And sensations associated with shallow breathing—constriction, lightheadedness, mild anxiety—may be modest exaggerations of how you often feel, especially when stressed out. That's what happens when we chronically hold in our stomachs. We may be robbed of the rich oxygenation that we need to run every cell in our bodies.

After years of holding in our bellies, the process becomes unconscious, automatic. Often, we don't know that we're tensing our abdomens, and the muscular tensions become chronic. We therefore must make a conscious effort to relax those tensions, to restore normal function to our diaphragms and to once again take deep, natural abdominal breaths. That's where mini-relaxations come in. Practiced regularly, these exercises—called minis for short—can change our bad breathing habits. By doing so, minis can instantaneously help to break the vicious circle of tension and anxiety.

By shifting our breathing patterns, minis perform a similar function to longer exercises in relaxation. But they don't last long enough to elicit our inborn physiologic "relaxation response" and therefore do not carry the same short- and long-term benefits. But minis do bring about beneficial psychological and physiological changes within minutes or even seconds. Thus, you can do a mini in the midst of almost any event that taxes your patience, energy or capacity to cope.

Practice minis as well as longer relaxation exercises for about 20 minutes at a stretch. The minis can pull you through tight situations, while longer exercises can, over the long haul, bring about a deeper enhancement of mind-body health.

Instant Relaxation

You can practice mini-relaxations anywhere, anytime. You can do them with your eyes open or closed. You can do a mini whenever you are feeling anxious, or even when you anticipate feeling anxious. You can do them in the presence of others, and more often than not, they won't even know you are practicing a mind-body technique.

In their book *Healing Mind, Healthy Woman*, Dr. Domar and co-author Henry Dreher recommend four methods of mini-relaxation. The first helps you to learn the basic approach for switching from chest to abdominal

Stress: A Growing Health Hazard for Women

Harvard psychologist Alice Domar, Ph.D., co-author of the new best-seller *Healing Mind, Healthy Woman*, says stress affects women more than most of us realize—leading to infertility, eating disorders, digestive disease, autoimmune problems and possibly even some forms of cancer.

"Our lifestyles now are so stressful that we have to take care of ourselves . . . guilt-free," says Dr. Domar, who is also assistant professor of medicine at Harvard Medical School and director of women's health programs in the Division of Behavioral Medicine at New England Deaconess Hospital, both in Boston.

Stress relief, she says, is a health priority—not a luxury. But instead of taking time out for a stroll, a good workout or an hour spent reading a novel in the backyard, we race through life trying to be the perfect employee, perfect mother, perfect wife, perfect community volunteer, perfect cook . . . it goes on and on.

Relieving stress can have far-reaching health benefits and can prevent future health problems. "Recognizing how stress affects you is half the battle," says Dr. Domar.

The next step is examining your life for ways that you can tailor a prescription for stress reduction to your specific pressure points. If you get a headache every day after lunch, perhaps a peaceful walk during your lunch hour will help, says Dr. Domar. Are you combating fatigue with too much coffee? Cut back gradually as you integrate 20 minutes of yoga or relaxation exercises into your day, she suggests.

HEALTH FLASH

breathing. It can be practiced in any position, but it is useful initially to lie down, a position that makes you more aware of your breathing patterns. Otherwise, you can practice minis sitting, standing, hanging by your feet from a chandelier—any position you find yourself in when you're stressed out.

Mini Number One

Sit down or, preferably, lie down in a comfortable position. Take a deep, slow breath. Notice any movement in your chest and any movement of your abdomen. Place a hand on your abdomen, just on top of your belly button. Allow your abdomen to rise about an inch as you inhale. As you exhale, notice that your abdomen will fall about an inch. Also notice that your chest will rise slightly at the same time that your abdomen rises. Abdominal breathing does not mean that you don't take air into your upper chest; you do. But now, you are also bringing air down into the lower portion of your lungs by using your diaphragm to expand the entire chest cavity.

Become aware of your diaphragm moving down as you inhale, back up as you exhale. Remember that it is impossible to breathe abdominally if your diaphragm does not move down. And it is impossible to let your diaphragm move down if your stomach muscles are tight. So, relax your stomach muscles. If you are having trouble, try breathing in through your nose and out your mouth. Enjoy the sensations of abdominal breathing for several breaths or for as long as you desire.

Mini Number Two

Make the shift from chest breathing to deep abdominal breathing. With each complete breath—one inhalation, one exhalation—count down from ten to zero. Thus, with your first abdominal breath, you say "ten" to yourself, with the next breath you say "nine," and so on. If you start to feel light-headed or dizzy, slow down your counting. When you get to zero, see how you are feeling. If you are feeling better, great. If not, try doing it again.

Mini Number Three

Make the shift from chest breathing to deep abdominal breathing. As you inhale, count very slowly from one to four. As you exhale, count slowly back down, from four to one. Thus, as you inhale, you say silently to yourself, "one, two, three, four." As you exhale, you say silently to yourself, "four, three, two, one." Do this for several breaths, or for as long as you wish.

Mini Number Four

Make the shift from chest breathing to deep abdominal breathing. Use any of the other three methods as you breathe: Simply breathe as you feel your stomach rise, adding a one-to-ten count with each breath; or adding a four-to-one, one-to-four count as you inhale and exhale. But this time, regardless of what method you use, pause for a few seconds after each in-breath. Pause again for a few seconds after each out-breath. Do this for several breaths, or for as long as you wish.

Minis in Your Daily Life

What do rosary beads, Valium pills, amulets, teddy bears and talismans have in common? They are things that people carry around to ease their anxieties in circumstances that threaten to overwhelm. Yet they have something else in common. They are things people can forget to take with them.

But we can't forget our lungs, no matter where we go. And our lungs can be an immediate source of relaxation, comfort and control—if we use them properly. When we practice minis, we use our lungs to restore balance to our breathing and balance to our perspective about events swirling around us.

You can use minis while driving in heavy traffic. You can use them during a family argument. You can use them in any high-pressure job situation. You can use them during a bout of acute or chronic pain. You can use them as you anticipate or undergo stressful medical procedures. You can use minis anytime you are upset, anxious, fearful or in pain. Here are a few everyday instances that would call out for a mini.

> You are already running late for an important meeting or appointment, and traffic is bumper-to-bumper.
> You are the mother of several young children, with a husband at work. You're trying to cook dinner while keeping watch over the kids, who roam about the house making noises that suggest breakage of household items.
> You feel awkward as you attend a party with many interesting, attractive people, none of whom you know.
> Your husband has a group of friends over to watch a sporting event, and they don't clean up their own mess, expecting you to do it.
> Your teenage daughter is two hours late coming home from a Saturday-night date.
> A friend who is going through a period of depression calls for the umpteenth time, and you don't know if you can listen anymore.
> After a shopping spree, the credit card bills arrive. You know that you have to sit down with your partner that evening to figure out how you are going to pay these bills.

Minis not only improve oxygen exchange and lower heart rate and blood pressure. The psychological effects are also pronounced. Why? First, minis are a distraction. They momentarily take your mind off fear or pain, especially during stressful or unpleasant medical procedures. Second, minis enhance your perception of control. When you know you can count on minis to make you feel physically and emotionally better, you regain that sense of control. Third, minis can be psychological touchstones—mini-reminders that you can find your center, even when events or other people seem utterly out of control.

Minis, Medicine and You

Minis can also help people get through some of the big stuff. Women dealing with medical conditions can use minis to calm their fears, and in some cases, quell their symptoms. Minis are particularly useful and effective for women who suffer with PMS or menopausal hot flashes.

Minis can also be anxiety blockers for women with breast or gynecologic cancers, who frequently feel overwhelmed by their medical treatments, side effects and the sheer emotional impact of their diagnoses. The same holds true for women with infertility or multiple miscarriages who are faced daily with painful reminders of their plight: friends or relatives with babies, friends or relatives who are pregnant, friends or relatives who make unknowingly insensitive comments, spanning the spectrum from, "Oh, of course you'll come to term," to "Maybe it's time for you to let go." These quick relaxation routines can also relieve tension during pelvic exams.

In addition, consider doing mini-relaxations:

▶ Prior to and during any blood test
▶ Prior to and during any injection
▶ Before and during insertion of an intravenous needle prior to surgery
▶ During any stressful phase of preparation for surgery
▶ During a mammogram
▶ Before and during every phase of chemotherapy for cancer: As you anticipate treatment, during insertion of intravenous needles, immediately afterward and later, when nausea may occur
▶ Before and during radiation therapy for cancer
▶ During any ultrasound test, including those used at various phases of treatment for infertility and those used during pregnancy
▶ Before calling the doctor's office for test results
▶ When you are awaiting a call from your doctor
▶ When you are put on hold by your doctor's office

Uncommon Relief from the Common Cold

For about six months every year, Pam, a 47-year-old registered nurse in Seattle, was forced to take antibiotics and antihistamines. She didn't like the medication or its side effects.

"I had mostly head colds—lots of sinus congestion, headaches and eye pain," she laments. "Eventually, I started getting tired of depending on medications. Every time I'd be on antibiotics, I'd get a yeast infection."

But about five years ago, colleagues introduced Pam to acupuncture (inserting tiny needles into specific areas of the skin to remedy various ills). When she felt a cold coming on, she would head to the acupuncturist once or twice a week. She also began to take specially prescribed Chinese herbs.

"I'm much healthier now than I've ever been," she says. "As someone who practices conventional medicine, I believe Western treatments have their place in treating serious infections. But alternative remedies for colds and flu are a much better use of my time, money and energy."

Stifle Sniffles, Calm a Cough

Pam is not alone. One-third of Americans polled in a recent study now use alternative treatments, including herbs, acupuncture and simple home remedies, to fight illnesses that range from the sniffles to cancer. Sales of

herbs will climb to more than $1.5 billion in the United States this year—
and they're growing by 25 percent annually, says Varro E. Tyler, Ph.D., professor of pharmacognosy at the Purdue University School of Pharmacy in
West Lafayette, Indiana, and author of *The New Honest Herbal*.

Acupuncture is equally popular. According to a recent Food and Drug Administration (FDA) report, there are between 9 million and 12 million visits
to acupuncturists every year.

It's easy to understand why: Not only do alternative remedies often cost
half as much as synthetic drugs, but some seem to attack the viruses that
cause colds and flu, whereas Western medicine only alleviates symptoms.
Better still, many natural therapies may actually prevent illness.

As more patients use these remedies, doctors are becoming increasingly
aware—and accepting—of them. "We should be using more of these methods,"
says internist and certified acupuncturist Margaret Mullins, M.D., of Annapolis,
Maryland. "We've overused antibiotics, making many less effective."

The fact that these remedies are cheaper than synthetic drugs even has in
surance companies sitting up and taking notice. Many—including Pruden-
tial and Mutual of Omaha—are starting to pay for nontraditional remedies,
including acupuncture. Still, according to Richard Coorsh, spokesperson for
the Washington, D.C.–based Health Insurance Association of America,
"most of us are still waiting for the science to show safety and effectiveness."

That's the catch. Although many natural remedies have been studied and
are widely accepted as medicines in other countries, research is still in its infancy in the United States. This may soon change; between 1993 and 1995,
for example, Congress more than doubled the budget of the recently established Office of Alternative Medicine at the National Institutes of Health,
raising it from $2 million to $5 million.

But until science catches up, alternative remedies must be used carefully.
Just like any Western medicine, they can have side effects, especially if you're
pregnant or nursing. So if you decide to try one of these therapies, look for a
certified practitioner and use herbal products without any added ingredients.
Always follow the directions on the package, and tell your physician what
you're using.

Natural Soothers

As inexpensive and promising as natural remedies may be, always add a
dose of common sense. Don't rely on natural methods to push you through
an illness in the midst of a hectic schedule.

"These methods are an aid to healing; they are not a substitute for rest,
which is absolutely necessary when you're ill," Dr. Mullins says. If your
symptoms don't improve in a few days, stop using alternative therapy. You
may have a more serious condition. See your doctor immediately.

The key is to keep an open but cautious mind. As Pam, the acupuncture advocate, says, "I'll always start with an alternative method, but if it's not effective, I'll use a prescription medicine."

In that spirit, consider these popular, natural ways to beat the woes of a cold or flu.

Preventing Colds and Flu

Echinacea

Also known as the purple coneflower, this herb is taken to stave off a cold or the flu and to ease symptoms. "Studies in Europe have shown that it shortens a viral infection by about three or four days," says Dr. Tyler. (A cold

Women: Magnets for the Common Cold

Now, the National Center for Health Statistics has confirmed something that you may have been noticing for years: Women catch more colds than men—often for surprising reasons.

Overall, we cough and sniffle about 8 percent more than men. Among 18- to 44-year-olds, women catch colds 12 percent more often than the guys do.

Cold germs can invade your body through any orifice, says Katherine Sherif, M.D., instructor of medicine at the Institute for Women's Health of the Medical College of Pennsylvania and Hahnemann University in Philadelphia.

Unwrapping a tampon or sanitary napkin can transfer germs to its surface if you don't wash your hands first. Inserting the tampon or wearing the napkin could introduce cold germs into your system, setting up the whole sneezing, coughing, runny nose cycle, she says.

And where do we get those germs? Often, from the people we take care of. "Women are the primary caregivers; they tend to take care of sick family members and that increases risk," Dr. Sherif says. Women—whether mothers, day care workers, aunts or grandmothers—also tend to spend more time than dads around children. And kids can be little cold-germ factories, averaging eight colds a year. "On top of all this," Dr. Sherif adds, "today's women are overwhelmed with home and job responsibilities, and the cumulative stress can weaken the body's immunity."

But before you load up on aspirin and chicken soup, stock up on some free advice from Dr. Sherif. Keep your hands away from your face, she suggests. Also, wash your hands after contact with someone who has a cold, and both before and after you use the bathroom.

HEALTH FLASH

usually lasts a week to ten days.) Research indicates that echinacea works by stimulating the immune system's fighter cells, which destroy infection.

Dr. Tyler recommends taking one capsule of echinacea every four hours at the first signs of a cold, then three capsules a day after that. But don't take it long-term. "There's evidence that after eight weeks of continuous use, it may no longer work because your body gets used to it," says Dr. Tyler.

Vitamin C

Research on vitamin C's power over the common cold remains controversial. Experts who swear by it say that taking 250 to 500 milligrams daily prevents colds and other viral infections from developing. Taking even higher doses—1,000 to 2,000 milligrams—may cut a cold short, according to Tom Wilson, a pharmacist and owner of Cape Drugs, specializing in natural and homeopathic medicines, in Annapolis, Maryland.

While some experts believe that high doses of vitamin C pose no harm because the body eliminates what it can't use, others caution that more than 1,000 milligrams a day may cause kidney stones.

Acupuncture

The theory behind this procedure, which Pam, the Seattle nurse, relies on to prevent colds and the flu and to treat symptoms when they occur, is that illness results from imbalances in the body's energy, or "chi." An imbalance may be caused by weather changes, stress, lack of sleep or poor diet. Anecdotal evidence indicates that if your body is "restored" regularly with acupuncture, you may be less likely to come down with a viral infection.

In general, acupuncture is safe and effective if it's performed by a qualified practitioner. The needles used to treat imbalances are so fine that most patients hardly notice them or may experience only minor pain, says Dr. Mullins. If acupuncture is not performed properly, however, needles can break off (in rare instances) and bleeding or bruising may occur. In addition, needles should be sterilized or disposed of after use.

Look for practitioners certified by the National Commission for the Certification of Acupuncturists; in some states, they need to be licensed. Check with your state health department.

Curb Congestion

Capsaicin

Found in cayenne peppers as well as in capsules, capsaicin relieves nasal stuffiness because it increases secretions in the nose and throat, allowing them to pass out of the body through coughing or a runny nose. You can eat either red or cayenne peppers (not to be confused with red bell peppers) in a salad, pasta or salsa, for instance, or take a capsule up to four times a day, as needed.

Steam

To temporarily clear your sinuses, add a drop or two of peppermint, eucalyptus or thyme oil to boiling water and put it in the sink. Place your face 18 inches over the water (not so close that the steam will burn your face) and cover your head and the sink with a towel. Inhale for several minutes.

Fluids

Grandma was right about drinking six to eight eight-ounce glasses of water, juice or tea a day to keep your nose and throat lubricated. Like capsaicin, moisture helps thin respiratory-tract secretions so that they drain more readily. Avoid alcohol, which will dry out the nose and throat, and mucus-producing drinks like milk.

Calm a Cough

Licorice

This herb, which comes in the form of lozenges and a coarsely ground powder that can be made into a tea, eases coughs because it's a good expectorant, says Dr. Tyler. "It also stimulates saliva production, which suppresses the cough reflex," he adds. Licorice works especially well when you have a cough accompanied by a lot of phlegm.

To make the tea, which tastes sweet like the candy, add a teaspoon of licorice powder to a cup of hot water. Sip it throughout the day. But don't use more than a half-ounce (equivalent to three teaspoons) of the powder daily over several weeks. Larger doses can cause headaches, lethargy, salt and water retention, and excess excretion of potassium, which can lead to high blood pressure and heart problems. And forget about eating candy licorice to stave off a cough; it may not even contain the medicinal herb.

Horehound

This flower, which has been used as a cough remedy in the United States and western Europe for about 400 years, works by thinning secretions of bronchial mucus.

Lozenges are available in most health food stores, or you can brew a tea with one to two teaspoons of the herb and a cup of hot water. Both are equally effective. If you prefer tea, drink three to five cups daily.

Slippery Elm Bark

Derived from the inner bark of the elm tree, this herblike remedy has been reviewed by the FDA as safe and effective for treating sore throats. It also can be used for coughs because it coats the throat with a gel, stopping the coughing reflex.

Slippery elm lozenges and powder are available. Teas can be made by adding one teaspoon of slippery elm powder to a cup of hot water or by using the ready-made tea mix available in health food stores. To sweeten, add honey or sugar.

Ease Other Cold Symptoms

Saltwater
Pamper an irritated throat by gargling with warm saltwater. "The salt inhibits the growth of bacteria, like that which are present in strep throat," says Wilson. Mix one tablespoon of table salt with an eight-ounce glass of warm water. Don't swallow the solution, however—besides tasting terrible, too much salt can lead to dehydration.

Feverfew
Part of the chrysanthemum family, this herb is used to reduce migraine pain and headache. It works by preventing blood vessels from dilating. Feverfew comes in capsules. Take one capsule containing 85 milligrams of leaf material daily.

Vitamin E Cream
To relieve skin rubbed raw by blowing and wiping, dab on some vitamin E cream. Better yet, start creaming your nose as soon as you feel a cold coming on.

New Thinking That Outsmarts the Blues

A re you depressed? Are you anxious or troubled by guilt, frustration, anger or other negative emotions?

If you're a woman, you're more likely to answer yes. Though the gender gap is narrowing when it comes to such negative emotions, this year women will still be nearly twice as likely as men to experience depression. New research shows that this isn't just an American phenomenon—women in cultures around the globe have similar experiences.

While you should never try to handle major depression on your own, the new self-talk therapy could help ease milder negative emotions, freeing you from the self-criticism, self-blame and low self-esteem that can hold you back in relationships and on the job. This approach can be a viable alternative to antidepressants and even to psychotherapy, and is certainly a better alternative to feeling bad and then blaming yourself for the way you feel.

A Fresh Look at an Old Problem

The true cause of negative emotions is a matter of opinion. To Freudian psychoanalysts, they are the result of repressed feelings that typically date back to childhood relationships with one's parents. To biological psychiatrists, they stem from chemical imbalances in the brain.

But to cognitive therapists, they represent distorted thinking. The word *cognitive* refers to thought processes. Cognitive therapy is a deceptively simple, powerful self-help technique for dealing with emotional negativity by consciously changing the way we think.

This view may be comparatively new to the mental health profession, but it was first espoused nearly 2,000 years ago by the Greek philosopher Epictetus, who said, "People are not disturbed by events themselves, but rather by the views they take of them."

Some emotional turmoil is clearly the result of problems early in life—for example, childhood abuse—and Freudian-style talk therapies can help. "But most people don't have to spend a great deal of time understanding the past to improve how they react to potentially upsetting situations in the present," says psychologist Mark Sisti, Ph.D., associate director of the Center for Cognitive Therapy in New York City.

Some mental health problems are caused by chemical imbalances in the brain, and in recent years new antidepressants have been hailed by some biological psychiatrists as the answer to all mood problems. "Antidepressants can help people with severe depression," Dr. Sisti says, "but in mild to moderate depression, cognitive therapy works as well or better. In addition, it costs less and has no side effects. For other mood problems—anxiety, stress, guilt or phobias—cognitive therapy is more helpful than medication."

Scientific research supports Dr. Sisti. In a study, researchers at the University of British Columbia in Vancouver analyzed 28 separate studies comparing how people fared after different types of mental health therapy. Those using cognitive therapy did better than 98 percent of those who had no other therapy, better than 70 percent of those who took antidepressant drugs, better than 70 percent of those who tried the various forms of talk psychotherapy and better than 67 percent of those who tried behavior therapy (such as changing routines to break bad habits).

Ten Forms of Distorted Thinking

Could cognitive therapy help you deal with negative emotions? Perhaps.

There are many types of distorted thinking that lead to problems with negative emotions, according to David D. Burns, M.D., professor of psychiatry and research clinical psychiatrist at the University of Pennsylvania Medical Center in Philadelphia and author of *Feeling Good: The New Mood Therapy* and *The Feeling Good Handbook*. Dr. Burns has documented ten types of distorted thinking. How many of these emotional traps have you fallen into?

All-or-nothing thinking. You see things as black or white. If you're not perfect, you think of yourself as a total failure. You make one mistake at work and decide you're going to be fired. You get a B on a test, and it's the end of the world. Your husband reprimands you for not checking the oil when you got gas, and you decide he doesn't love you.

Labeling. This practice is an extension of all-or-nothing thinking. You make a mistake, but instead of thinking, "I made a mistake," you label yourself: "I'm a jerk." Your girlfriend breaks up with you, but instead of thinking, "She doesn't love me," you decide, "I'm unlovable."

Overgeneralizing. The tip-offs to this kind of distorted thinking are the use of the words "always" or "never." You drop something and think, "I'm always so clumsy." You make a mistake and think, "I'll never get it right."

Mental filtering. In complicated situations that involve both positive and negative elements, you dwell on the negative. Your mother clearly enjoys the dinner party you throw in her honor but comments that the cake was a bit dry. You filter out all her positive comments and whip yourself for being such a lousy baker.

Discounting the positive. The tip-offs to this kind of distorted thinking are the phrases "That doesn't count," "That wasn't good enough" or "Anyone

---

Early Bedtime Brightens Mood

Recent research suggests that going to sleep a little earlier than usual may be all that it takes to ensure that you'll rise in a good mood tomorrow.

Researchers had 30 women and men take stock of their moods and sleep habits for two weeks. They found that when folks fell asleep a little earlier than usual, they rated themselves as more cheerful the following day—even if they slept the same number of hours as they normally did.

What's at work here may be the same thing that happens when you turn the clock ahead one hour in the spring. You rise and wake according to the change (without altering your total sleep time) and end up feeling extra refreshed and chipper in the morning.

According to researcher Peter Totterdell, a psychologist at the University of Sheffield in England, this may be because you have made a change not only to your sleep cycle but to your "cheerfulness cycle" as well. Totterdell and co-workers have found evidence supporting the notion of such a cycle—one that's intimately tied to the sleep cycle. Because of this, a little change in your sleep habits may be just enough to give you an extra dose of cheer.

Without waiting for next April, you can "spring" out of bed with a smile simply by going to sleep a little earlier. But be aware: This will only work once in a while. If your usual bedtime becomes the new, early bedtime, then your body's going to adapt quickly. So save the trick for the night before you're going to tackle your taxes—or any other time when your mood's sure to need a next-day boost.

could have done it." You do well on a test and think, "It doesn't count." Your colleagues praise a presentation and you think, "It wasn't good enough." You win a commendation and think, "Anyone could have done it."

Jumping to conclusions. You assume the worst based on no evidence. There are two subcategories here—mind reading and fortune-telling. In mind reading, you decide that another person is reacting negatively to you. Two of your co-workers are chatting at the coffee machine at work, but as you approach, they fall silent. Chances are, they had simply finished their conversation, but you assume they have been criticizing you behind your back.

In fortune-telling, you predict the worst possible outcome. A test is difficult, so you decide you'll fail. The sky is cloudy before your lawn party, so you decide a thunderstorm must be imminent.

Magnifying. In this kind of distorted thinking, you exaggerate the importance of problems, shortcomings and minor annoyances. Your toilet backs up and you believe that you need your entire plumbing system replaced. You forget to close a window before it rains and imagine that you'll return to a flooded home. A neighbor's dog tramples a few flowers and you decide that your garden is ruined.

Emotional reasoning. When you fall into emotional reasoning, you mistake your emotions for reality. "I feel nervous about flying, therefore it must be dangerous." "I feel guilty about forgetting my brother's birthday, therefore I'm a bad person." "I feel lonely, therefore I must not be good company."

Blaming yourself with "should" and "shouldn't" statements. This kind of thinking involves blaming yourself. You play well in the company volleyball tournament but miss one shot and berate yourself: "I should have made that shot. I shouldn't have missed." You eat a doughnut and think, "I shouldn't have done that. I should lose ten pounds." Other self-denigrating tip-offs include "must," "ought to" and "have to."

Personalizing the blame. Here you hold yourself personally responsible for things beyond your control. Your child misbehaves at school and you think, "I'm a bad mother."

Seven Ways to Untwist Your Thinking

"When you feel bad," Dr. Burns explains, "your thinking becomes negative. This is the A B C of emotion: A stands for the actual event, B for your beliefs about it and C for the consequences you experience because of your beliefs." If you can somehow prevent erroneous negative beliefs from forming around an actual event, you have gone a long way toward protecting yourself from the unnecessary negative emotions that are sure to follow from such distorted thinking.

Dr. Burns recommends seven special techniques to protect yourself from negative, distorted thinking. These techniques work for any number of un-

Tunes That Battle the Blues

So you find the stuff under the New Age/Relaxation section of the record store about as relaxing as water torture? Just because your taste runs more to Sousa than to soothing doesn't mean you can't reap all these relaxation benefits that music is supposed to have.

"If you're in a very anxious state, you can't expect to be able to relax immediately upon listening to some very slow, New Age kind of music," says Suzanne Hanser, Ed.D., chair of the music therapy department at Berklee College of Music in Boston. Match the music to your mood, and then slowly change the music, she says. For a lot of anxiety, you might put on music that's very rhythmic and fast. "Gradually make the music flow or the melodies flow more," she says.

This is one of the strategies she taught 20 older people in a study she did at Stanford University with Larry Thompson, Ph.D., co-director of the center for the study of psychotherapy and aging at the VA Medical Center in Palo Alto, California. As part of the study, she made weekly phone calls to 10 of the people; the other 10 she visited every week, supplementing this idea with other relax-to-music strategies. Eight weeks later, these previously down-in-the-dumps seniors were significantly closer to their usual spirits than were the 10 people who received neither music training nor personal attention.

It could have been the phone call or visit that lifted their spirits, says Dr. Thompson. But it's possible that the music played a part, too. "In people who are depressed, the ratio of pleasant to unpleasant events gets out of balance," he says. It's likely that both the music and the human contact increased the number of pleasant events for the people involved. "With music, it's not just that these pleasant events are happening to you. You are in some way taking control and making these pleasant events happen," he says.

If anxiety is involved in depression, as it often is, the right kind of music may help someone de-stress. This doesn't necessarily mean your kids can blast Pearl Jam and call it therapy, or that you can write off your CD collection as a medical expense. But it might reinforce your idea that Glenn Miller means more than ocean sounds to your mental state.

pleasant experiences, but let's use as an example a particularly unpleasant divorce.

In the throes of a nasty divorce, you may be tempted to believe many of the charges that your ex levels against you: You're selfish, uncaring and vindictive, and not only that, you're lousy in bed. If you buy into this picture of yourself, the consequences may well be low self-esteem and guilt, not to mention severe depression. Cognitive therapy tries to change the Bs—your beliefs—so you don't experience the Cs—negative consequences. Here's how to cope.

Talk to yourself as you would to a best friend. Suppose a friend were getting divorced and felt like a selfish, uncaring, vindictive failure, Dr. Burns says. What would you say? Probably something like: "You're not a failure simply because your relationship ended. Many marriages end in divorce, and many winning teams lose a game now and then. It's rough to endure a divorce, and breakups never bring out the best in people, but I've known you for years, and you're a warm, kind, caring person."

Examine the evidence. Take in the big picture. Write it down if you have to. Your ex says that you're lousy in bed, but are you really? Until you learned of your ex's unfaithfulness, the two of you had a great sexual relationship. Of course, after your heart was broken, you didn't have any energy for sex, especially with the person who had rejected you. That's not being lousy in bed. That's a normal reaction to betrayal.

Experiment. See how this negative thinking about yourself in this one area stacks up against your behavior in other areas. Your ex called you selfish for wanting to keep the house, but are you really? If you were truly selfish, you wouldn't give to charity, wouldn't help friends in need and wouldn't share credit for your group's accomplishments at work. Test your reactions the next time a charitable solicitation arrives or a friend calls with a problem or your group's efforts are recognized. If you write a check, offer to lend a hand or praise a co-worker, you're not entirely selfish. You may not be as magnanimous as you would like to be, but you're not the ogre your ex says you are.

Look for partial successes. Instead of thinking that your marriage was a complete failure, consider the many ways that it was successful: You took turns putting each other through school, and now you both have much more fulfilling careers than you had when you met. You have two great kids, and the problems that led to your breakup have given you valuable new insights into the kind of person you'll look for in your next relationship.

Take a survey. Your ex insists that your refusal to take the kids for an extra day after a holiday weekend proves that you're vindictive. You maintain that you're open to rescheduling time with the children but not when the real reason is to allow your ex to jet off to a luxurious resort with a new lover. You feel justified, but after a screaming argument on the phone, your confidence is shaken. Perhaps you are a vindictive creep. Now's the time to call a few friends and solicit their views. Chances are, they'll say you're justified.

Define your terms. You had no idea that your ex was having affairs. You were blind. Define *blind*. The dictionary says "completely without sight." That wasn't you. You saw that your ex was withdrawn from you and was spending an enormous amount of time "working late." You weren't blind, just too trusting of someone you had every reason to believe was trustworthy.

Solve the problem. You blew up when you came home early and found your ex, who moved out months ago, unexpectedly in your house. Since that ugly scene, you have been thinking that your "terrible temper" has turned you into a monster. Possibly, but the problem in this case is not your temper. The real problem is that your ex still has keys to your house. Maybe it's time to change the locks.

Feeling Better

What if negative thinking does creep in and you find yourself mired in unpleasant emotions?

Cognitive therapy calls for tackling the problem in seven easy steps. Seven steps may not sound like many, but "simplicity is one of cognitive therapy's major strengths," Dr. Sisti explains. "It's quick and easy, and once people understand the basic concepts, almost anyone can practice it."

Sometimes, though, cognitive therapy's very simplicity puts people off. They say, "It's so simple, it can't work." When that happens, Dr. Sisti points out that they're jumping to a conclusion—the fortune-telling kind—and urges them to try the steps anyway. Give it a try for any given problem and see what happens.

Step 1: Write everything down. "The act of writing automatically puts some distance between you and your negative thought," Dr. Sisti says. "Jotting things down provides perspective and helps people detect distorted thinking more easily." If you are in a situation where you just can't put pen to paper, Dr. Sisti recommends saying things out loud.

Step 2: Identify the upsetting event. What's really bothering you? Is it simply the fact that you got a flat tire? Or is it that you soiled your outfit while changing the tire? Or that you knew you needed a new tire but didn't replace it? Or that the flat made you late for your daughter's soccer game?

Step 3: Identify your negative emotions. You may feel annoyed about the flat, frustrated that replacing it soiled your outfit, angry at yourself for not replacing it in time and guilty for being late for the soccer game.

Step 4: Identify the negative thoughts that accompany your negative emotions. About failing to replace the tire: "I always procrastinate. I never take care of things in time." About soiling the outfit: "I'm a slob. I can't go anywhere and look okay." About being late for the game: "My daughter will make a scene. She'll think I don't love her. And the other adults there will think I'm a bad parent."

Step 5: Identify distortions and substitute rational responses. About the tire: "I don't always procrastinate. I juggle my job and family and accomplish just about everything that has to get done. I would have replaced that tire in time, but I had to deal with an emergency at work, and the tire just got by me."

About the stained outfit: "I'm not a slob. I'm usually very careful about my appearance, more so than most people, which is why things like this upset me."

About the tardiness: "My daughter knows I love her. She knows that if I'm late, whatever detained me was beyond my control. She's unlikely to make a scene, but if she does, the other adults there will comfort her. I've done the same for their kids and never thought them to be bad parents. No one will think the worst of me."

Step 6: Reconsider your upset. Are you still heading for an emotional tailspin? Probably not. But you still feel annoyed about getting the flat.

Step 7: Plan corrective action. "As soon as the game is over, we're getting that tire. That will take the time I had planned to spend cooking dinner, so I'll pick up some takeout instead."

Count Your Blessings

"A major task of adulthood is to balance striving to do well and accepting one's limits," Dr. Burns says. "Cognitive therapy has helped me accept my limits without feeling ashamed."

"Cognitive therapy is simply a more organized way to implement traditional psychological self-care advice," says psychotherapist Alan Elkin, Ph.D., director of the Stress Management Counseling Center in New York City. "It boils down to counting your blessings. Most stressful, depressing or anxiety-producing events are not inherently awful. What makes them feel awful is the way that we react to them. Counting your blessings forces you to step back, get some perspective and see challenges in a larger context.

"The problem with 'count your blessings' is that it's vague. Cognitive therapy is a step-by-step program, and when negative thoughts are spinning out of control, an organized program helps," says Dr. Elkin.

OUTSMARTING DISEASE

Part 4

Too often,
doctors
dismiss signs
of heart
disease in
women.

—cardiologist Mary Ann
Malloy, M.D.

Female Advantage

Women often complain about their hormones. When we feel like bursting into tears one day and then feel frisky the next, we blame those pesky chemicals racing around in our bodies.

Yet one hormone that we have in abundance, estrogen, may actually be a woman's best friend. This "female" hormone gives women significant health benefits that men—whose bodies are rich in testosterone—miss out on.

What's estrogen? A substance essential for a healthy reproductive system—and more. While men's and women's bodies both produce estrogen, we make more. And researchers are discovering that this extra estrogen has definite advantages.

(Small wonder, then, that hormone replacement therapy is often prescribed for women at menopause, when levels of natural estrogen fall and the positive effects of this hormone would otherwise be lost.)

Among the health-promoting roles of our female hormone are these.

▶ Bone builder. Bone tissue constantly breaks down and rebuilds itself— and estrogen is thought to aid this process. That's one of the reasons why estrogen helps prevent brittle-bone disease.

▶ Heart protector. Estrogen lowers dangerous blood cholesterol levels, decreasing the risk of heart disease—giving women an estrogen-rich advantage over men.

▶ Arthritis stopper. Among postmenopausal women in one study, those taking estrogen had a 30 percent lower chance of getting arthritis than women who didn't take this hormone.

▶ Tooth maintainer. Lower rates of tooth loss and gum disease were reported among postmenopausal women taking estrogen, when compared with women who were not taking estrogen, according to one study from the State University of New York at Buffalo.

▶ Memory enhancer. Recent research suggests that estrogen can positively affect memory. In one study, 28 women taking estrogen did significantly better on four tests of verbal memory than 43 who weren't taking it.

Unfortunately, estrogen doesn't score high marks in all health categories. There is still a question as to whether or not the hormone promotes certain forms of cancer, particularly ovarian and breast cancer.

Build Stronger Bones at Any Age

Ｔhe enemy is osteoporosis—and a formidable foe it is. Experts estimate that this year, as many as 20 million American women will have this bone-withering disease or be at risk for it.

The fact is, the chances of this happening to you are greater than you think: By age 50, your lifetime odds are almost one in two of breaking a bone due to osteoporosis. Characterized by thin and brittle bones that can crack like weather-beaten concrete, the condition is now a major cause of disability among American women.

But you don't have to wait—make that, you should not wait—for that first wrist or hip fracture to find out that you have brittle bones. Bone experts say that a new bone-density test could serve as a critical wake-up call for millions of women.

The test is simple, comfortable and quick. Yet few doctors suggest this safe, reliable and potentially lifesaving checkup to their women patients.

"Bone densitometry equipment in this country sits idle much of the time when it could be saving lives," says John Bilezikian, M.D., professor of medicine at Columbia University College of Physicians and Surgeons in New York City and director of the metabolic bone diseases program at Columbia-Presbyterian Medical Center. "Doctors don't appreciate its value."

The Slow Road to Bone Trouble

Of course, osteoporosis doesn't develop overnight. The deterioration of bone happens slowly and quietly, without your knowing it. Over time, microfractures of the spinal vertebrae can steal inches from a woman's height and collapse her posture.

Eventually, this damage manifests as the deformity known as dowager's hump. And woe be to the woman who stumbles and falls. At age 45, a woman with low bone density may break a wrist and recover; at 75, she may not get off so easily.

"Today's wrist fracture is tomorrow's hip fracture," says Robert Lindsay, M.D., Ph.D., president of the National Osteoporosis Foundation. And hip fractures are by far the most devastating consequence of osteoporosis. They require hospitalization, surgery and months or years of recuperation. That's if you're lucky. As many as one-quarter of those who sustain a hip fracture over age 50 die within the year.

In the vast majority of cases, osteoporosis is not diagnosed until someone suffers her first fracture. By then, the damage is done.

When to Test

There are no official screening guidelines for early detection of osteoporosis as there are for, say, the early detection of breast cancer.

Today only about half of all private insurance policies cover at least part of the cost of bone-density tests, according to the National Osteoporosis Foundation. So, if it's preventive health care you want, you may have to reach into your own pocket.

Is it worth it? Is it worth paying $100 to $200 (or even more) for a bone-density test to save yourself from a debilitating, life-threatening condition that, if you live long enough, will most probably affect you? "If you can possibly afford it, yes, it's definitely worth the cost," says Dr. Bilezikian.

If you agree, here's a bone-saving action plan, developed by *Prevention* magazine after a careful review of all the latest research on osteoporosis prevention and treatment and interviews with the nation's leading osteoporosis experts.

Start with a Good Reading

One problem in being out in front recommending osteoporosis screening is that there are still some kinks in the bone-testing process.

First, though new technology called Dual Energy X-ray Absorptiometry (DEXA for short) is the best test, it isn't universally available. There are only about 800 DEXA machines available to the public in the United States. The good news is that since they are underappreciated, most of them are underused, says Dr. Bilezikian. If there's not a DEXA facility near you, there are other good bone-testing alternatives available.

To be reasonably assured that your test results are interpreted correctly, if at all possible get tested at a major medical center or teaching hospital. Or seek out an endocrinologist, geriatric specialist, rheumatologist or other physician with a special interest in bone. She can refer you to a qualified testing facility and should be knowledgeable enough to recognize whether your test results were properly interpreted.

To be on the safe side, have at least two body sites measured for bone density—preferably the spine and hip—regardless of your age.

In women under 65, it's easier to see changes in the bone of the spine, says Susan L. Greenspan, M.D., director of the osteoporosis prevention and treatment center at Beth Israel Hospital in Boston. As people age, however, calcifications or fractures in the spine can obscure this view. That's why the hip is a critical site in seniors.

The Best Care for Your Bones

Here's the most comprehensive action plan for protecting your precious bones—for women ages 25 to 95—and beyond. First, see which category of bone health describes you. Then, follow the recommended actions, suggested

Women Need D for Healthy Bones

You spent your summer wearing Scarlett O'Hara hats and sunscreen with a sun protection factor of 15. Your skin thanks you—but your bones may have a grudge. Chances are, you soaked up too little sun for your body to make the vitamin D that strong bones require, according to new research from Tufts University in Boston.

Sun avoiders aren't the only ones skimping on vitamin D. "Overworkers who mainly trek from house to car to office probably don't get enough sun either," says researcher Bess Dawson-Hughes, M.D., chief of the calcium and bone metabolism lab at Tufts.

What to do? Make sure that you get the "sunshine vitamin" by mouth—and enough of it. (The Daily Value is 400 international units.) In a new study Dr. Dawson-Hughes found that in two years women getting 200 international units of vitamin D a day (a typical intake) lost over twice as much vulnerable hipbone as women getting 800 international units.

Here's how to get more D: Drink milk (each glass is fortified with 25 percent of the Daily Value for vitamin D) and eat D-fortified breakfast cereals (often 10 percent of the Daily Value per serving). But talk with your doctor before adding a supplement—too much vitamin D can be toxic.

HEALTH FLASH

by the nation's leading osteoporosis experts.

Category I: The Safety Zone

You're in this category if you are at least age 25 and haven't reached menopause, with none of the major risk factors for osteoporosis, and you have an optimal bone-healthy lifestyle.

This means that on three days every week you engage in either one hour of weight-bearing aerobic exercise (such as brisk walking) or at least 30 minutes of resistance exercise (such as weight lifting) or some combination of the two.

In addition, you eat a healthy diet that includes at least 1,000 milligrams calcium and 400 international units of vitamin D per day from food (a great source is vitamin D–fortified skim milk). And embrace a healthy lifestyle—don't smoke or consume excessive amounts of alcohol.

Recommended actions: If Category I describes you, you probably don't need a bone-density measurement at this time. Your goal now is to maintain a strong bone mass so that you face menopause with the highest bone density possible. To do this, it is essential that you continue to follow the bone-healthy lifestyle.

Category II: Bone Loss May Be on Your Horizon

This is your category if you are at least age 25 and haven't reached menopause, but you do not follow the optimal bone-healthy lifestyle described in Category I and/or you have one or more of the major risk factors for osteoporosis.

Major risk factors for osteoporosis include the following:

▷ A personal history of having already broken a bone as an adult from modest trauma, such as breaking your wrist falling from a standing height as opposed to breaking a bone in a car accident
▷ A family history of osteoporosis

- Long-term use of steroid or antiseizure medications or overuse of thyroid medication (a blood test can determine whether you are taking too much now)
- Interrupted menstrual history: any loss of periods for six months or more with the exception of pregnancy
- Hysterectomy prior to menopause with removal of ovaries and without replacement of estrogen. Loss of estrogen is likely to trigger rapid bone loss
- Any period of restricted mobility for six months or longer, especially if it occurred in adolescence

Recommended actions: If Category II describes you, consider having a bone-density test now. And follow the lifestyle suggestions for Category I. They could slow or arrest bone loss (or perhaps even improve density, as some research suggests) so that at menopause you have the highest bone density possible.

Beyond this, Dr. Lindsay suggests that women who discover they have low bone density before menopause step up their calcium intake (from food or supplements or both) to 1,500 milligrams per day, the recommended intake after menopause.

And what about the new Food and Drug Administration–approved treatments? At this point, you may be wise to wait until after menopause or until more is known about the effects of these drugs on younger women (or, in the event of pregnancy, on developing fetuses). "These new drugs are intended and approved for postmenopausal women," says Dr. Bilezikian. "They appear to be safe and well-tolerated by young women, but unfortunately, there's not much research on this yet."

Category III: The Menopause Years

If you suspect that you are in menopause and six months have passed since your last period, or your doctor has confirmed through a blood test that measures FSH (follicle stimulating hormone) that you are in menopause, heed the advice for Category III.

Recommended actions: If Category III describes you, you should have a bone-density measurement now regardless of whether you had a prior test. It is at this time that many women begin to experience the swift and significant bone loss associated with lowered estrogen levels.

If your bone-density measurement is at least +1.0 SD, congratulations. Dr. Lindsay says it's unlikely you'll develop osteoporosis in your lifetime, and you probably don't need another test (about 16 percent of women fall into this category).

Regardless of the results, however, you should maintain a bone-healthy lifestyle. Doctors also advise that, at menopause, women increase their calcium intake (from diet or supplements or both) to 1,500 milligrams per day if they're not on hormone replacement.

If your bone density is low, however, remember that a bone-healthy

Is Sodium Sapping Your Skeleton?

Think of what salt does to the snow on the sidewalks or to a slug in the garden. It turns out that similar stuff is happening in your body, where salt practically shrivels up some of the calcium that you are so conscientiously putting in.

In large quantities, salt acts like a bouncer in the kidneys, rejecting the earnest appeal of the calcium that is trying to get through. Recent research pins down just how serious the effect is. Based on the diets and bone changes over two years in 124 postmenopausal women, scientists recently determined that sodium levels beyond 2,600 milligrams a day may be cheating your body out of as much as 891 milligrams of calcium. That is practically a day's dose of calcium—1,000 milligrams—that the sodium is wiping out.

"Sodium and calcium compete for the same recovery mechanism in the kidney," says osteoporosis expert Robert A. Heaney, M.D., of Creighton University School of Medicine in Omaha, Nebraska. "If you have a high sodium load, then some of that sodium bumps calcium off the conveyor belt."

There are two ways to remedy that: Get more calcium, or get less sodium. Try both—considering that most American women don't get enough calcium and tend to get at least twice the limit of 2,400 milligrams of sodium in a day. A switch from a tablespoon of ketchup (177 milligrams of sodium) on your veggie burger to a slice of tomato (2 milligrams) can start you saving big. Remember that processed foods, not necessarily salt added at the table, are prime sodium offenders. Fortunately, they wear their salt on their sleeves—or at least their labels. So be sure to check before you buy.

lifestyle by itself is not enough to stop the bone drain of menopause. Hormone replacement therapy may be for you. Bone experts agree, taking estrogen is the very best way to prevent and treat osteoporosis after menopause—and to improve other health factors as well.

If you have osteoporosis and you choose not to take estrogen, ask your doctor if you might be a candidate for one of the new FDA-approved drug treatments, such as alendronate (Fosamax) or nasal calcitonin (Miacalcin), or ask whether slow-release sodium fluoride has received final approval from the FDA.

Category IV: Beyond Menopause

You're in this category if you're past menopause and have never had a bone-density measurement.

Recommended actions: If this describes you, you should have a bone-density test now, no matter what your age. Studies show that it is never too late to slow or stop bone loss and perhaps even improve density. But you must take action right away.

By the way, research suggests that there are actually two periods of rapid bone loss in a woman's life. The first is around menopause, but the second is after 65. "We used to think that bone loss stopped or slowed at older ages," says Dennis Black, Ph.D., epidemiologist at the University of California, San Francisco. "But now we know that there's a second wave of bone loss, and if we prevent that, we may be able to prevent many fractures."

Regardless of the outcome of your test, you should follow the optimal bone-healthy lifestyle described in Category I. This will help prevent fractures.

Keep in mind, however, a bone-healthy lifestyle by itself is not enough to stop the bone drain that normally occurs after menopause. So if your bone density is low, and especially if you have osteoporosis, you should consider taking estrogen.

The new FDA-approved drug alendronate is expected to be a great advantage to seniors. Dr. Greenspan, who is conducting studies with alendronate in women over 65, finds that they do very well with it. "Other studies with alendronate have shown that bone mass can be improved even in seniors."

Category V: When Bone Loss Has Happened

If you've had a bone-density test before that yielded a less than optimal score (below +1.0 SD), following the advice for Category V could forestall continued erosion of your skeleton.

Recommended actions: If this describes you, talk to a qualified doctor about tailoring a schedule of follow-up tests for you. Follow-up testing can give you a chance to reassess therapeutic measures and provide additional motivation for maintaining a bone-healthy lifestyle.

Dr. Lindsay suggests the following guidelines as a basis for discussion with your physician: If your bone density is between +1.0 SD and -1.0 SD (as with the majority of women), you probably should have another test again in two to five years. Women with results worse than -1.0 SD should probably be retested every one to two years.

If you are taking bone-saving medication such as estrogen or alendronate, your physician may also want to monitor you with blood and urine tests that measure the rate of bone loss. This permits short-term monitoring of the effectiveness of your particular medication and dosage.

Get
Heart
Smart

At 138 pounds and five feet three inches, Jody admits that she's some-what heavier than she would like to be. Yet she sees the 15 or so pounds that she's put on since finishing law school as a minor cosmetic problem.

"I'm just zaftig," quips Jody, a 34-year-old negligence attorney in New York City. "What's so terrible about that?"

Plenty: The weight she's gained over the last few years may have increased her risk of having a heart attack by 25 percent.

Jody doesn't think she has any reason to be concerned about her heart. On some standard charts her weight is within the normal range for her age and height. She is aware that smoking and having a high blood-cholesterol level are also heart hazards, but she has never smoked and she works to keep her diet low in fat.

What Jody does not know is that heart attack is the number one killer of American women. And researchers have recently uncovered surprising new factors that can contribute to women's risk: While heart disease is most common after menopause, it can occur in younger women as well.

Fortunately, there are steps that you can take to combat both the old and the new risks. The first step is to become informed.

Overlooked for Far Too Long

Too often, doctors dismiss signs of heart disease in women—an oversight that can lead to dangerous delays in diagnosis and treatment, says Mary Ann Malloy, M.D., a cardiologist in Elmhurst, Illinois, who chairs a committee on women and heart disease for the American Heart Association.

"Women are still thought to overreact to or dramatize their symptoms," she says. In addition, some vital heart exams and therapies may be inappropriate for women. For instance:

▶ Women are five times more likely than men to register a false alarm on the standard treadmill stress test, which can detect heart irregularities triggered by exercise.

A better test for women is the thallium treadmill, in which a nuclear marker injected into the blood "lights up" the heart. That way, the heart can be more easily scanned from different angles. The thallium test costs more than the standard test and may not be covered by your health insurance. A less-expensive option for women is exercise echocardiography, which can detect the lack of motion of the heart wall that could signal artery blockage.

▶ Women suffer complications from heart attack treatments more often than men do. One reason is that the drugs used to dissolve clots blocking blood vessels may be given in doses appropriate for males but too high for females, says Dr. Malloy.
▶ Until recently, women were less likely than men to survive coronary angioplasty, a procedure that requires the insertion of flexible tubing called a catheter into blocked arteries. But, thankfully, as women's special needs get more attention, changes have been made.

You can lower your risk for heart disease by knowing your risk factors and taking appropriate actions.

Risk #1: Adult Weight Gain

"Gaining 10 to 15 pounds should be your warning signal to make lifestyle adjustments," stresses JoAnn E. Manson, M.D., associate professor of medicine at Harvard Medical School, co-director of women's health at Brigham and Women's Hospital in Boston and co-investigator for Nurses' Health Study at Harvard Medical School. The 14-year study found that gaining just 11 pounds was enough to produce a small increase in their chances of having a heart attack between the ages of 40 and 70.

Women who had gained 11 to 18 pounds between ages 18 and 40 had a 25 percent higher risk than women who had maintained a steady weight after age 18. In those who had put on 18 to 24 pounds, the risk increased by 65 percent, and for women who had gained more than 24 pounds, the risk rose by more than 100 percent.

"Women who were of average weight or somewhat leaner at age 18 and managed to maintain their weight were the healthiest in the long run," notes study leader Walter C. Willett, M.D., Dr.P.H., professor of epidemiology and nutrition at the Harvard University School of Public Health.

Dr. Willett emphasizes that your healthy-weight goal should not be to become model-slim. Many experts suggest aiming toward the lower end of current height-weight charts. If you're at a reasonably low weight, take steps to avoid even small weight gains. "Once you put on a substantial amount of weight, it's very difficult to lose it," Dr. Willett warns, "and the risk of high blood pressure, diabetes and ultimately heart attack increases greatly."

The researchers caution that the study did not take into account the potential benefits of regular exercise, which would lower heart attack risk even in overweight people. Also, it did not consider the distribution of fat on the body. Having excess weight around the stomach and upper body (the so-called apple-shaped body) puts a woman at higher risk for heart disease than the same number of pounds around the hips.

As your metabolism slows after age 30, you'll need to guard even more closely against overeating and inactivity—especially during the childbearing years. "Try not to gain more than 25 to 30 pounds with each pregnancy, and lose the weight soon after," Dr. Manson advises. "Breastfeeding may also help you shed some pounds."

Risk #2: Childhood Obesity

If you battled a serious weight problem as a child, you may have another strike against you in the fight to protect yourself against coronary artery disease. A study of 217 young people, ages 9 to 22, in Bogalusa, Louisiana, found that those who had gained the most weight over a five-year period developed a thick heart, a dangerous condition that could persist into adulthood.

"Hearts got bigger in the kids who got fatter, especially in the girls," notes Elaine Urbina, M.D., a pediatric cardiologist at Tulane University in New Orleans and a researcher with the ongoing Bogalusa Heart Study, which has followed 14,000 children over its 20 years.

Excess weight during childhood or adulthood appears to stress the heart and cause its left ventricle to grow larger, like the overworked muscles of a bodybuilder. Doctors refer to the condition as left ventricular hypertrophy.

The more developed the heart, the more oxygen it needs; this makes it more vulnerable if arteries become blocked and oxygen-carrying blood can't reach the body's most important muscle.

If you've carried your extra pounds into adulthood, your risk for left ventricular hypertrophy is higher than if you had been thin as a child. If you have since gotten down to a more normal weight, there may be some improvement in your heart, though this has not yet been studied, Dr. Urbina says. You can ask your doctor to check your heart thickness with an echocardiogram, a noninvasive technique that produces pictures of the heart. If you do have this condition, be sure to talk to your doctor about what precautions you should take.

Risk #3: Short Stature

If your height is five feet one inch or shorter, you may face yet another threat to your cardiac health. New data from the Framingham Heart Study in Massachusetts show that short women are more likely than taller ones to suffer a heart attack. For a woman five feet one or shorter, for instance, the risk was 72 percent greater than that of women who were five feet five or taller.

"The reasons aren't clear," says Daniel Levy, M.D., director of the study, "especially when comparing the United States with Asia, where people are shorter yet the heart attack rates are so much lower." It may be that taller people have wider arteries, which are less likely to become blocked than narrower vessels, or that children who are fed more nutritious food grow taller and are less prone to coronary artery disease than others. Or some short Americans may just take in more calories than they need.

"There's nothing you can do about shortness," Dr. Levy notes. "But if knowing it's a risk encourages you to get your blood pressure, cholesterol and glucose levels checked regularly, and to quit smoking and avoid weight gain, then it serves a good purpose."

Women's Hearts Love Lifestyle Changes

HEALTH FLASH

Can women simply choose not to have heart attacks? There's new evidence that with heart-healthy lifestyle choices, women can dramatically reduce the risk of this major health threat.

In a new, five-year study of 20 women and men with serious heart disease, heart specialist Dean Ornish, M.D., assistant clinical professor of medicine at the University of California, San Francisco, School of Medicine and president and director of the Preventive Medicine Research Institute in Sausalito, California, found that the more people adhered to an active, people-oriented, low-stress, low-fat lifestyle, the more improvement there was in crucial blood flow to the heart.

"All your heart cares about is how much blood it's getting," says Dr. Ornish, author of the new book *Everyday Cooking with Dr. Dean Ornish*. "If it's getting more blood, it's getting more oxygen and it's getting better."

The study gave new credence to a heart-healthy program created by Dr. Ornish. It features his brand-name Reversal Diet that gets no more than 10 percent of calories from fat, a stress-reduction plan that calls for an hour a day of meditation and/or yoga, no smoking, moderate exercise three times a week and meaningful connections with other people.

Fizzle Your Anger

Whether it's set off by the traffic jam that made you miss the movie or the teens who spray-painted the sidewalk, anger has for years been in the lineup of heart attack–causing suspects.

Now, new research suggests that aspirin may break the anger–heart attack link.

Mood and heart attack data from 1,623 women and men revealed that an episode of anger more than doubled the risk of heart attack in the two hours after the episode. But there was no added risk for those who took aspirin regularly.

Anger rolls out the red carpet to a heart attack by pushing up levels of the stress hormones adrenaline and noradrenaline. In turn, they increase the heart rate and blood pressure and increase the stickiness of the platelets that form clots, says study leader Murray A. Mittleman, M.D., D.P.H., instructor at Harvard Medical School and physician at New England Deaconess Hospital in Boston.

That is a big problem, since this may lead to disruption of the plaque in the arteries, blocking blood flow to the heart muscle.

"What determines how likely this would be is how clottable the blood is at the moment," says Dr. Mittleman. "Aspirin makes platelets less likely to form clots."

How much should a woman take? A regular-size adult aspirin tablet every other day, or a baby-aspirin size tablet every day is probably enough for benefit, Dr. Mittleman says.

Risk #4: Low Levels of "Good" Cholesterol

In your bloodstream, excess cholesterol can build up inside artery walls. In the arteries leading to your heart or brain, cholesterol buildup can choke off vital blood supplies, causing a heart attack or a stroke, explains Penny Kris-Etherton, R.D., Ph.D., professor of nutrition at Pennsylvania State University in University Park.

But while "bad" low-density lipoprotein (LDL) cholesterol causes the buildup, "good" high-density lipoprotein (HDL) cholesterol helps keep it cleaned up. So it's important, particularly for women, to know how much LDL and HDL they have on board.

According to experts, a desirable total cholesterol level is below 200 milligrams per deciliter, a good HDL level for women is above 50 milligrams per deciliter and a desirable LDL level falls below 130 milligrams per deciliter for people without coronary heart disease and less than 100 for those with heart disease.

A low HDL reading is a tip-off that your body is not repairing the damage caused by LDL deposits and that you need to take action.

Risk #5: A High Triglyceride Level

For years, scientists have debated whether fatty substances in the blood called triglycerides matter a great deal in the development of coronary artery disease. For women, at least, the answer seems to be yes. The Framingham Heart Study found that a high level of triglycerides is associated with a higher risk of heart attack in females.

Like cholesterol, triglycerides can produce abnormal buildups of plaque in the blood vessels that lead to the heart.

In addition, these triglyceride-induced deposits may be even more likely to rupture and cause a heart attack than the lesions that are produced by cholesterol, explains Howard Hodis, M.D., director of the Atherosclerosis Research Unit at the University of Southern California School of Medicine in Los Angeles. High triglyceride levels are also linked to diabetes, a blood-sugar disorder that occurs more frequently in women than in men. Diabetes erases any gender-related protection from heart disease.

Though triglyceride levels below 200 are considered adequate, Dr. Hodis believes that women should aim for below 150. Higher levels are especially alarming when combined with low levels of the protective HDL cholesterol.

An Action Plan That Cuts the Risk

If your triglycerides or blood cholesterol levels are in the danger zone, or if you have any other risk factors for heart disease, these steps can help you cut the risk.

Strive for a healthy weight. To stay trim, Dr. Willett advises not only avoiding high-calorie meals but, more important, committing to regular exercise. "Build it into your daily life," he says, "whether it's going to the gym or just walking to work."

Quit smoking. It's still the number one risk factor. In a recent University of Pittsburgh study that followed 105 women, ages 42 to 50, until five to eight years after their menopause, those who smoked showed greater plaque

Folate Finds

Asparagus. Beans. Brussels sprouts. Mustard greens. Their colors and textures can make dinner look like it was made by Martha Stewart. Best of all, as the eyes enjoy their feast, the heart does, too.

Why? These foods are full of folate, the natural form of folic acid, a B vitamin that has been linked to lowering heart disease risk. In the past year, a blizzard of studies has linked low levels of folate to a high risk of heart disease. Getting enough, researchers say, could lower the rate of artery disease by 6 percent for women.

Studies suggest that folate may lower levels of a factor in the blood called homocysteine. People with high levels of homocysteine also have high levels of artery disease. The link that is still missing is whether lowering homocysteine really prevents deaths from coronary artery disease—no studies have been carried out long enough to tell.

But folate is so easy to get that researchers feel good about recommending 400 micrograms a day for everyone, says Shirley A.A. Beresford, Ph.D., a folate researcher and epidemiologist at the University of Washington in Seattle.

The current Recommended Dietary Allowance is 180 micrograms for women over age 15, and 400 micrograms for women who are pregnant or who are considering pregnancy, to prevent spinal birth defects in their children.

"Increasing fruits and vegetables will increase the amount of folate you're getting," says Dr. Beresford. "But we don't use all of the folate that we get—only 50 percent, on average, can be used by the body. So to get 400 micrograms of folate, you'd have to get roughly 800 micrograms from food. We recommend supplements. You can easily get 400 micrograms a day in most multivitamins."

buildup in the arteries, beginning years before menopause. Among those with no plaque, only 22 percent were smokers; however, 50 percent of those with the highest level of buildup were smokers. To help kick the habit, consider the nicotine patch; its success rate doubles if it's used in tandem with counseling, says Dr. Malloy. (For tips on ways to quit smoking, see "First, Think Smart" on page 138.)

Limit high-fat meat and whole-milk dairy products. "They're high in artery-clogging saturated fats," says Margo A. Denke, M.D., associate professor of internal medicine with the Center for Human Nutrition at the University of Texas Southwestern Medical Center in Dallas and a member of the American Heart Association's Nutrition Committee. If you need a little something on your bread or in the frying pan, switch from butter to monounsaturated fats such as olive or canola oil.

Rev up the produce. A diet rich in fruit, vegetables, grains and low-fat meat and dairy products can lower your cholesterol without drugs, Dr. Denke says. So aim for three to five servings of veggies and two to four servings of fruit a day, particularly those, such as sweet potatoes and cantaloupe, that are loaded with beta-carotene.

Step up the exercise. "It raises HDLs (the 'good' cholesterol), lowers LDLs (the 'bad' cholesterol), triglycerides and blood pressure and helps control obesity," says Dr. Malloy. Try aerobic exercises such as walking, biking or swimming.

Consider taking aspirin, especially after age 50. The Harvard Medical School's Nurses' Health Study found that women who took one to six regular-strength aspirins a week had a 30 percent lower risk of first heart attack. Consult your doctor to see if you're a candidate for aspirin therapy.

Consider estrogen therapy. Hormone replacement after menopause has been shown to decrease heart disease risk factors. Some studies, however, suggest hormone use may increase the risk of breast cancer.

Good, Better, Best Breast Care

Have you started your breast-health action plan yet? Nowadays, you can never assume that you're getting the "whole works" at your annual breast exam. New surveys show that you have to ask for the care you need.

Last year, when 8,000 women in a national survey rated how well their doctors performed in-office breast exams, four out of five said that these important exams were rushed and incomplete. And only one in five said her doctor adequately taught her how to do the monthly breast self-exams crucial for optimal breast health.

Why, you might ask, are top-notch office exams and at-home self-exams so important?

The fact is, one in nine American women will develop breast cancer by age 85. The only way to improve your chances of beating breast cancer is to catch it in its earliest stages. And that is where your doctor can lend a hand.

Would Your Doctor Fail Your Breast Exam?

Breast exams are invaluable tools for detecting tumors that even mammograms sometimes miss.

Rates of breast-cancer detection are consistently higher for women who supplement mammography with regular physical exams from doctors. But to be done correctly and thoroughly, these exams should "take at least five and preferably ten minutes," says Daniel B. Kopans, M.D., director of breast imaging at Massachusetts General Hospital and associate professor of radiology at Harvard Medical School.

Ten minutes? "Most physicians don't take that much time," offers Julie

Abbott, M.D., chairperson of the Division of Preventive and Internal Medicine at the Mayo Clinic in Rochester, Minnesota.

Eight out of ten women in the new survey, commissioned by *Prevention* magazine, said that their doctors took no more than five minutes. And one in five said this crucial step was completed in less than 60 seconds. "My worst experience was with a doctor who examined my breasts in under 30 seconds, while chattering mindlessly in what was probably some awkward attempt to put me at ease," says a 37-year-old survey respondent from Boise, Idaho.

Why are so many doctors doing short exams? "It's partly because of time constraints," says S. Eva Singletary, M.D., chief of breast surgery at the University of Texas M. D. Anderson Cancer Center in Houston, "and partly because doctors haven't been well-trained in breast exams. Medical schools spend very little time teaching breast exams. They're more focused on treatment than prevention."

Your Breast Health Primer

Doctors need to take time and care to examine all the territory that is vulnerable to breast cancer.

Ninety-five percent of women who responded to the survey said that their doctors examined the nipples and breasts. But significantly fewer respondents got what experts call a "complete and thorough" exam. A mere 37 percent were examined to the bottom of their rib cages; 56 percent were examined on their upper chests, above the breasts; and 63 percent report that their armpits were examined.

All these areas should be felt carefully during an office breast exam. The lymph nodes located in the armpit and lower neck are particularly important, explains Dr. Singletary. "Sometimes that's the first way breast cancer presents itself. You might not be able to find a lump in the breast, but you can feel swelling in the lymph nodes."

To make matters worse, most doctors are not examining women in the three positions that experts say are essential to a thorough exam: upright, with hands overhead; upright, with hands pressed to waist; and lying down. Only 9 percent of the women in the survey said that they were asked to assume all three positions. The majority (65 percent) said that they were only examined while they were lying on their backs.

The lying-down position is useful mainly to thin out the bottom half of the breast for manual examination, explains Jeanne Petrek, M.D., director of surgery at the Evelyn Lauder Breast Center at Memorial Sloan-Kettering Cancer Center in New York City. That is important, but more is needed.

A woman should also be upright for the doctor to properly feel the lymph nodes in her armpit. "If you're lying down, the lymph nodes will fall backward, making them more difficult to palpate," says Dr. Petrek. The upright position, with hands pressed to waist or hip, is useful for a different reason, she explains. "That tightens the muscles under the chest, so any malignant attachment between the muscle and the breast would show up as skin dimpling or flattening."

An A-Plus Checkup

A complete breast exam should be both visual and manual, says Dr. Kopans. It should explore the breasts from various angles. And it should cover the entire breast area from the collarbone to the rib cage and from high in the armpit across the chest to the breastbone.

The visual exam can be done while you're standing or sitting and involves placing the arms in a variety of poses that may make you feel like a contestant in a "Miss Body Builder" contest: arms at sides, hands on hips (shoulders forward), hands on hips flexing pectoral muscles and arms overhead (leaning forward).

These positions enable the examiner to observe breast contour and symmetry and note any irregularities or changes, such as skin dimpling or retraction; nipple discharge or rash; and bumps or discoloration in the supra-

<table>
<tr><td>

Breast

Cancer

Answers—

And

More

Questions

</td><td>

Losing a mother or sister to breast cancer brings not only grief but fear, since breast cancer is a family-linked disease in as many as 10 percent of cases.

Thanks to new research, scientists finally know why.

The mother lode is a gene they call BRCA1, a natural stoplight for breast cell growth. When a woman's BRCA1 gene contains an error, tumors can grow unchecked. Sometimes, the faulty code is planted among the branches of her family tree.

New revelations show that breaks in the BRCA1 gene may be prompted by dietary, lifestyle or environmental factors as well, triggering nonhereditary breast cancer. Identifying an enemy, however, doesn't mean victory is at hand.

"We're looking for a single break or a single mistake in a huge gene," says John Glaspe, M.D., associate professor of medicine at the Jonsson Comprehensive Cancer Center of the University of California, Los Angeles.

Gene therapy—replacing faulty BRCA1 genes with healthy ones—is still five to ten years away. And so even in families where the defect is known, women who learn that they may carry the ominous gene can only continue to be vigilant for now—by having regular breast exams and mammograms and by eating a healthy diet packed with fruits and vegetables, says Dr. Glaspe.

</td><td>

HEALTH FLASH

</td></tr>
</table>

Get with the Program

When you get your breasts examined is important. The American Cancer Society suggests that women ages 20 to 40 who have no family history of breast cancer should have a clinical breast exam performed by a health care professional every one to three years. Beginning at age 40, women should have clinical breast exams performed annually.

If you are at high risk because of a family history of breast cancer, the rule of thumb regarding annual screening is that clinical breast exams should begin at an age "at least five years younger than the age of the youngest relative when she was diagnosed," says Julie Abbott, M.D., chairperson of the Division of Preventive and Internal Medicine at the Mayo Clinic in Rochester, Minnesota.

In other words, if your mother had breast cancer at 32, you should, at the age of 27, begin getting regular clinical breast exams—and possibly regular mammograms. Says the National Cancer Institute (NCI): "Routine screening every one to two years with mammography and clinical breast exams can reduce breast cancer mortality by about one-third for women ages 50 and over."

For women between 35 and 40, clinical breast exams may be crucial because that is the age when cancer increases. While the NCI's current guidelines don't suggest mammograms for this age group, other medical organizations suggest screening to include mammography by age 40.

Experts also recommend that all women examine their breasts monthly at home.

clavicular (the gully between your collarbone and neck) and armpit areas.

Note: None of these is necessarily a sign of breast cancer, but if one is present, you should be examined.

For the manual part of the exam, the health care provider should examine your breasts and the supraclavicular and armpit areas while you are sitting or standing and lying down using three fingers of one hand.

"Lying down is the most important posture," advises Dr. Kopans. "With the arm extended on the side being examined and the breast flattened out," he continues, "you can get a good systematic coverage of the breast tissue."

During the exam, you should feel three levels of pressure—superficial, middle and deep—one for each tissue layer.

In Your Own Hands

When women across the country reported on their own breast self-exam "training" for the *Prevention* survey, the picture looked bright—at first.

Nine out of ten said that their doctors recommend monthly breast self-exams. Yet while doctors may be recommending breast self-exams, they need to be better teachers of the technique.

"It's not enough for a health care provider to tell a woman to do breast self-exams," says Dr. Singletary. "If the doctor doesn't make sure that the woman knows what she's doing when she examines her own breasts, she really hasn't done a very good job."

As a bewildered 37-year-old woman from Boise, Idaho, notes, "I've been told how, but never has anyone ever shown me how to do breast self-exam.... I'm not sure I would recognize an abnormality if I felt one."

In fact, 12 percent of the women who responded to the *Prevention* survey said that they got no training whatsoever in self-exams. And, while most reported that their doctors provided some form of instruction, only 17 percent got what experts consider to be the "best" training.

You can't learn to play the piano by watching someone else play. Neither can you learn to do a breast self-exam by reading a brochure, viewing a video or watching a doctor demonstrate the technique on you. Searching for lumps on a special breast exam training model has definite shortcomings, too; these breast facsimiles can't duplicate the unique, natural bumps and contours of your own body.

To do a self-exam correctly and confidently, experts say, you must practice on yourself in the presence of a capable teacher. A doctor, nurse or midwife should always watch a woman examine her own breasts to make sure that her technique is correct and to confirm what her fingers are feeling. "A woman needs to know exactly what's normal in her own breasts," says Dr. Singletary.

Don't Forget Your Mammogram

Almost all survey respondents over age 40 said that their doctors had advised them to get mammograms. Happily, while the survey did not specifically ask women to rate their doctors' human-relations skills, many wrote in comments suggesting that their health care providers excelled in this area as well—reporting back on mammogram results promptly.

"My doctor called me at home on a Saturday morning to tell me my test results, which I didn't expect until Monday. He didn't want me to worry all weekend," notes one 40-year-old from Wheeling, West Virginia.

"Very impressive," says Amy Langer, executive director of the National Alliance of Breast Cancer Organizations.

Doctors should always report mammography results back to women—and as quickly as possible. While four out of five women in the survey were notified of the results last time they had mammograms, it's absolutely inexcusable that all were not.

"My mammography films—showing a lump—lay on the radiologist's desk for more than three weeks before I was told of the results. And this was at a major medical center," says an outraged 50-year-old woman from Minneapolis.

Getting the Best Care

How can women improve the quality of breast health care? The experts suggest the following:

Have a plan. Initiate a planning session with your doctor to establish a breast cancer early-detection plan. Every plan should include annual clinician exams, monthly self-exams and regular mammograms. Mammogram schedules should take into account your age as well as family health history and other factors that may put you at higher-than-average risk for breast cancer. All women can benefit from regular mammograms beginning at age 40 (and annual mammograms starting at age 50).

Talk with your doctor. Be frank and specific with your doctor about the aspects of your breast medical care that need improvement. "A woman will be helping all of her doctor's patients if she discusses her concerns about the thoroughness of the clinical exam or ineffectiveness in teaching breast self-exam," says Dr. Singletary.

Request training. Ask at every clinical breast exam that the doctor also watch you examine your own breasts. Have her critique your technique and answer any questions that you may have about what it is you're feeling.

Stay alert during the exam. Be aware and ask questions. A skilled health care provider may not only give an excellent exam but offer tips on how to improve your own self-exam skills.

Know your own breasts well. Dr. Petrek also suggests that the night of your clinical breast exam, and every night for the next ten nights, you spend ten minutes feeling your breasts, memorizing where the tissue is thick or thin, irregular or smooth.

Then you'll know that some of those lumps are always there and you'll do breast exams better.

Don't let suspicious lumps wait. If your screening measures uncover a new or suspicious lump, don't accept a doctor's "wait and see" attitude. Every unusual mass should be promptly and aggressively explored—no matter what your age. And the only way to know for sure that a lump is not cancer is with biopsy. A mammogram cannot distinguish between benign and cancerous lumps.

Consider switching to a breast center. If your doctor's performance is unacceptable, don't hesitate to seek a more qualified breast health care provider—such as a doctor at a breast care center. These centers only do breast evaluation. So they generally have doctors, nurses and technicians on staff who are well-trained and experienced in doing breast exams.

Call in an expert. Another alternative is to schedule an exam with a breast surgeon. "They really know about breasts and only care for breasts," explains

Langer. Be forewarned, however: Unless you have an existing problem, a history of breast cancer or are considered at high risk, the surgeon may refer you elsewhere for routine screening.

Take responsibility for your own breast health. Adopt a high-fiber, low-fat diet; exercise regularly and maintain a healthy body weight. Most important: Be sure to vigilantly follow your breast cancer early-detection plan.

As one 55-year-old told the survey, "I don't expect my doctor to keep track of everything. I mark mammograms and checkups on my yearly calendar. In fact, that's the first New Year's resolution I take care of. In January, I make my appointments."

20 Take Control of Your Checkup

You jump down from the exam table and toss aside that unflattering flypaper gown. You have made your annual trip to the gynecologist, so you can relax, right? Maybe not. A new poll found that many women don't get a thorough exam.

Roughly 60 percent of those who depend on a general practitioner for all of their health care miss out on Pap tests and/or pelvic exams. But gynecologists also make mistakes—skipping breast exams nearly a quarter of the time.

And that is not all: Even if your M.D. covers the basics, the basics may not cover you. A Pap test, for instance, doesn't detect most sexually transmitted diseases. "It's simply a test for cervical cancer," says Linda Alexander, Ph.D., director of women's health at the American Social Health Association in Research Triangle Park, North Carolina.

The good news is that you can turn your annual visit into a remarkably comprehensive checkup. But don't wait for your doctor to make all the suggestions. You'll get more from the exam (and more for your money) if you speak up.

The Essentials

Here are the essentials that experts say you should ask for.

A clothes-on consultation. Request a private meeting with your doctor before you undress for the exam. This isn't always standard procedure, yet it's intimidating and distracting to talk to your doctor while sitting exposed and vulnerable in a drafty room, and if there's something you want your doctor to be on the lookout for, an après-exam chat is too little, too late.

One survey found that 65 percent of women under age 25 were afraid to point out genital sores or bumps to their doctors.

Unfortunately, women still feel stigmatized by sexually transmitted diseases, says Eddie Sollie, M.D., a gynecologist at Margot Perot Women's Hospital–Presbyterian Medical Center in Dallas and author of *Straight Talk with Your Gynecologist.* "They're more likely to reveal embarrassing symptoms if they've established a rapport first," she adds.

During your pre-exam chat, tell your physician if she's your only doctor, so she'll tune in to as many aspects of your health as possible.

A review of your list. A study at the University of Dayton in Ohio found that patients who wrote down a list of questions to ask their doctors left their appointments feeling less anxious than those who didn't.

"A list helps you focus on finding the answers instead of on remembering your questions," says Teresa Thompson, Ph.D., one of the study researchers. Remember that your doctor isn't a mind reader, so it's up to you to steer her toward your concerns.

Advice from the nurse. "Nurses are knowledgeable about health promotion and disease prevention areas of medicine that doctors often don't take time to practice," says Cheryl Walker, M.D., assistant professor of obstetrics and gynecology at the University of Chicago.

When the nurse weighs you and takes your blood pressure (she should do this at every visit), ask questions about your lifestyle: How much calcium do I need? Am I exercising enough? Will the nicotine patch help me quit smoking?

A breast exam and a self-exam lesson. The American College of Obstetricians and Gynecologists recommends that women have their breasts examined by a physician once a year. But many women miss out: "Until the mid-1980s, teaching breast exams wasn't part of the mandatory curriculum

State-of-the-Art Pap Tests

When it comes to getting a Pap smear, it's good if you like and trust your doctor (you'll be more apt to make your annual appointment). But it's even nicer when she has state-of-the-art tools on hand to increase precision. Here's what you may soon be seeing (if you haven't already) at the office.

The Cytobrush. To get an adequate cell sample, the doctor must collect cells from outside and inside the cervix. A recent study compared the two methods of collecting the harder-to-reach endocervical cells. The traditional cotton swab collected an adequate sample only about 40 percent of the time; the newer Cytobrush (which looks like a mascara wand) had a 93 percent success rate. More good news. There's usually no extra charge for the use of this gizmo.

A speculoscope. During a Pap smear, your doctor can also inspect your cervix with this magnifying device, which shines a bright light on possible abnormalities. Studies show that more than twice as many problems are identified with a Pap smear plus speculoscopy than with the Pap alone. Cost: between $10 and $20; insurance may cover.

A cervicography machine. Your doctor can snap a picture of your cervix with this special camera. The film is developed by a lab and sent to technologists, who identify lesions. A cervicography diagnosis is accurate more than 95 percent of the time. The cost, about $25, is often covered by insurance.

in gynecology, so some doctors feel unskilled or uncomfortable doing it," says Dr. Walker.

Your physician should perform the exam and show you how to feel for lumps so you can do it once a month. "If you already know how, have your doctor check your technique," says Dr. Walker.

Tests for chlamydia and gonorrhea. Experts at the Centers for Disease Control and Prevention in Atlanta recently recommended routine chlamydia testing for all sexually active women under age 20 and for older women in nonmonogamous relationships. But a survey by the Campaign for Women's Health and the American Medical Women's Association found that 40 percent of women under age 25—the highest risk group for sexually transmitted diseases—weren't offered tests.

"If you've ever had unprotected sex, ask for both tests," says Dr. Walker. These infections can be virtually symptomless and, if not treated, can lead to infertility.

A Pap test, of course—and the lowdown on the lab. Scary reports surface from time to time about the quality of labs that analyze Pap tests. To help slide-scanning cytotechnologists maximize accuracy, schedule your exam for

---

Cervical Cancer on the Rise

Alarmingly, cervical cancer is making a comeback in the United States, with a record-high 15,700 new cases expected by 1997, according to the National Cancer Institute.

One reason? More women aren't getting regular Pap screenings because they're "too busy," have not been feeling sick or are uncomfortable thinking about cancer, according to a study from the Mayo Clinic in Rochester, Minnesota.

That's tragic, says Edward Trimble, M.D., head of the surgical section of the Cancer Therapy Evaluation Program of the National Cancer Institute. "Here's a cancer we can prevent," Dr. Trimble says. "The Pap smear has been a success story: quick, not very expensive, easy to perform and very effective."

Having a Pap smear doesn't rank in any woman's Top Ten list of most pleasurable things to do. But how can you argue the wisdom of a test that can detect and help you entirely prevent cervical cancer—a disease that once killed more American women than any other form of cancer?

If your doctor doesn't suggest an annual Pap smear, bring it up yourself, advises Dr. Trimble. If your insurance won't pay, buy yourself peace of mind. At a cost of about $100, isn't your life worth the price?

HEALTH FLASH

two weeks before your period, so that you won't be menstruating at the time of your appointment. Avoid douching for several days before the exam (it's best to avoid douching altogether, unless your doctor recommends it), and don't use vaginal medication or spermicide for 24 hours beforehand (having sex is okay).

Finally, ask your doctor some questions. Sonya Naryshkin, M.D., a cytopathologist at Mercy Hospital in Janesville, Wisconsin, says that most doctors will consider it no big deal if you want to know the following: What does the lab charge? (If the fee is $10 or less, be suspicious—the lab probably concentrates on high volume and fast turnaround.) What's the screening load? (Most states require that a cytotech screen no more than 100 slides per day, but a lab that sets a lower ceiling—say, 80—will probably have a better accuracy rate.) Does the lab use Papnet? (Many labs now use this new computer system, which double-checks a cytotechnologist's diagnosis.)

Your test results. "Request that a copy of the lab report be mailed to you," says Dr. Sollie. That way, you can verify your name and Social Security number to rule out mix-ups. On your Pap-test report, you should also look at the "specimen adequacy" listing to see that your doctor got enough cells for a reliable reading. (If she didn't, call for a repeat test. The cost, usually about $25, is often covered by insurance.) If you prefer to get results by phone, say so. Your doctor should call if your Pap is abnormal.

"She alone has the expertise to answer your questions and discuss further tests that might be needed," says Dr. Sollie.

Info on abnormal results. If your Pap shows signs of a possible problem, book a follow-up visit on the spot and request educational brochures that explain the meaning of the results.

A recent study conducted at Toronto Hospital found that 75 percent of women who received printed information made follow-up visits and completed treatment; without the material, only 45 percent did so.

Smoking: Why Women Need to Quit

If you're one of the 22.2 million women who are still smoking cigarettes, it may seem as if the whole world is against you.

Once, smoking was glamorous. Just remember the power of the smoke-filled room, the allure of the smoky jazz club, the cool sophistication of actress Bette Davis, a plume of smoke rising from the cigarette resting between her long, elegant fingers.

Today, it's a quick puff outside the office door, a hurried drag before you enter a restaurant, or a cigarette in your backyard—not your living room. Even your nonsmoking friends and relatives may be asking you to "please smoke outside" more and more often. Smoking, it seems, is definitely out. The list of places where it's taboo continues to grow, particularly as the health dangers of secondhand smoke to adults and children are better documented by researchers—and better known to the public.

There's reason to be hopeful. Perhaps due to smoking's bad reputation, more women are quitting. But we have a long way to go still. Although the number of women who smoke has been steadily decreasing, the rate of decline has not been nearly as sharp for women as for men. In 1965, 52 percent of men and 33 percent of women smoked; this year, the rate is about 28 percent for men and 24 percent for women.

How Cigarettes Spell Trouble

There are no grounds for complacency about smoking trends in women, says researcher Ellen R. Gritz, Ph.D., chairman of the Department of Behavioral Sciences at the University of Texas M. D. Anderson Cancer Center in Houston and former director of the Division of Cancer Control in the Jonsson Comprehensive Cancer Center at the University of California, Los Angeles.

Although more adult women may be quitting, teenage smoking rates—as measured among high school seniors—have not declined appreciably since 1984. "Smoking is a really serious health problem for women," says Diana DeCosimo, M.D., director of the Division of General Medicine and Geriatrics in the Department of Medicine of the New Jersey Medical School and medical director of the Women's Wellness Center, both in Newark. "Some 2,000 girls start smoking every day. It's so tied up with looking good and staying slim. It's very seductive."

The American Cancer Society calls smoking the most preventable cause of premature death in America, adding that tobacco use is responsible for more than one in six deaths in the United States. That's more than 400,000 deaths a year.

The most deadly of smoking-related illnesses is lung cancer, which strikes more than 74,000 women in a typical year. The vast majority— about 90 percent—are linked with smoking, according to the National Cancer Institute.

In addition, smoking causes up to 90 percent of emphysema cases in women, says Norman Edelman, M.D., consultant on scientific affairs to the American Lung Association. Smoking is also a major cause of heart disease and has been linked with everything from gastric ulcers and colds to chronic lung diseases such as bronchitis, as well as cancers of the mouth, pharynx, larynx, esophagus, pancreas, kidneys and bladder.

More Risks for Women

Smoking has additional consequences for women. It has been implicated in miscarriage and lower birth weights, as well as bleeding during pregnancy and fetal deaths. And a study by the National Institute of Environmental Health Science in Durham, North Carolina, found that the fertility of women smokers declines by approximately 30 percent in any given menstrual cycle. One new study has found that the chemical by-products of smoking are definitely passed from mother to unborn child.

Additionally, women smokers over 35 who take oral contraceptives increase their risk of heart attack by 20 times.

Studies show that the risk of sudden infant death syndrome is two to four times higher among newborns whose mothers smoked during pregnancy than among infants whose mothers did not smoke. Also, breastfeeding mothers who smoke tend to produce less milk.

Female smokers also face an increased risk of certain forms of cervical cancer, along with urinary incontinence and cataracts.

And that's not all. "On average, women smokers go through menopause four to six years earlier," says Terry Pechacek, Ph.D., associate professor of medicine at the State University of New York at Buffalo and former chief of smoking research at the National Cancer Institute in Bethesda, Maryland. "Earlier menopause means damage to the bones and an increased likelihood of osteoporosis," he says. Also, with early menopause comes increased risk of heart disease, further elevating the risk for women who smoke.

To add insult to injury, just as smoking subtracts years from your life span, it adds them to your looks. Smoking reduces the oxygen that reaches the skin and leads to skin damage from the poisonous chemicals, explains Dr. Pechacek. Plus, smoking damages the ability of skin cells to repair themselves. "This leads to more rapid drying and aging of the skin."

Why Quitting Is So Hard to Do

Chances are, if you're a smoker, you've tried to quit. But of the 17 million women and men who try each year, only 10 percent make it stick for longer than six months. And the success rate has been lower among women than among men.

One reason for this may be that women report more depression when they quit smoking—and studies show depression makes it more likely that you'll resume smoking.

If you've tried to quit before but haven't yet made it, be assured that it's never too late. "Persistence seems to be the most important determining factor," says Gary DeNelsky, Ph.D., head of the Department of Psychology at the Cleveland Clinic Foundation in Ohio and director of the clinic's Smoking Cessation Program. "Each time you slip, don't view it as a failure but rather as a learning experience."

According to the Office on Smoking and Health at the Centers for Disease Control and Prevention in Atlanta, female smokers who quit in their late thirties add an average of three years to their lives. Even if they quit in their late sixties, they'll add a year to their lives.

Call on Your Friends

When you do decide to quit, be prepared for some challenging times. But don't let your fears stop you from acting. "Withdrawal symptoms can be highly individualistic," says Dr. Pechacek. "Asking others what is going to happen is not realistic. The only way to know is to quit yourself."

The woman who is most likely to quit is the woman who uses both a doctor and a program simultaneously, according to the American Cancer

Society. Your doctor should be able to refer you to stop-smoking programs in your area. Or you can check with your local hospital's social services department or the local chapter of the American Cancer Society, the American Heart Association or the American Lung Association to find the stop-smoking program nearest you. A good program is one with a quit rate of 20 percent, according to the American Cancer Society. Anything higher and they're probably fooling around with their numbers.

The American Cancer Society also recommends that you call your doctor to talk about whether you're a good candidate for nicotine gum or the nicotine patch. Both of these can help gradually reduce your physical addiction to nicotine.

Nicotine gum usually contains two milligrams of nicotine, and you may chew as many as 30 pieces a day. Your physician will give you the proper precautions, but make sure you've completely stopped smoking before you start chomping. Otherwise, you'll be putting too much nicotine into your system. While some successful former smokers credit nicotine gum, others cite one

Even Light Smokers Are Addicted

H E A L T H F L A S H

Light smokers, beware: According to a new report from the Centers for Disease Control and Prevention (CDC) in Atlanta, even puffing fewer than six cigarettes a day can lead to nicotine dependence among women—making it potentially difficult for even a light smoker to quit.

"Women shouldn't fool themselves that smoking just a few cigarettes is harmless and that quitting will be easy," says Corinne G. Husten, M.D., a medical officer in the CDC's Office on Smoking and Health.

Smoking raises your risk of fatal heart disease, lung cancer, lower respiratory-tract infections and a host of other cancers. In fact, the prevalence of cigarette smoking among women is the primary reason that lung cancer has recently edged out breast cancer as the number one cause of cancer deaths among American women.

For women, smoking is also associated with early menopause. Smoking during pregnancy may lead to increased risk of low-birth-weight babies, premature births, sudden infant death syndrome and respiratory problems in newborns.

"Greater awareness of the toll that cigarettes are taking on women and a heightened realization that smoking is truly a women's issue are needed," Dr. Husten says. Quitting not only benefits women but also protects their loved ones from the ill effects of cigarette smoke. If you don't smoke now, "Don't start," says Dr. Husten. "Or if you have already started, quit."

What Really Happens When the Puffing Stops

Stories about what smokers go through when they try to kick the habit are legendary—and sometimes made-up. Here's the truth about what could happen to you, so you'll know what to expect.

The burning desire. Crave, you will. Nicotine levels drop rapidly. Within two hours you'll develop the desire for a cigarette, says Mitchell Nides, Ph.D., a psychologist and researcher at the University of California, Los Angeles. "Emotionally, you may long for your 'friend,' the cigarette. You may even dream of cigarettes. You have to realize that will happen."

The bad mood. Physicians call it dysphoria. You—and your spouse, children and friends—will call it other, less formal names. "You'll be more on edge and irritable, more likely to snap or be hostile to other people," says Terry Pechacek, Ph.D., associate professor of medicine at the State University of New York at Buffalo and former chief of smoking research at the National Cancer Institute in Bethesda, Maryland. And you may feel depressed or anxious. The good news is that the number of dark days should be no more than ten, with the first few being the worst.

The extra weight. It's true that you'll probably gain a little weight, since smoking works to suppress the appetite. Here, too, your fears may be exaggerated: The average gain is about five pounds, and even this weight can be managed.

drawback: the taste, which some women find unpleasant.

The patch provides larger doses of nicotine—anywhere from 7 to 21 milligrams—over longer periods of time, from 16 to 24 hours. You'll likely use the patch for 12 to 16 weeks. It's also dangerous to smoke when you're wearing a patch because you can overload your body with nicotine, so make sure you've stopped completely.

Neither of these aids should be viewed as a magic bullet, says Dr. Pechacek. "They only deal with half of the addiction, the physiological side." You're responsible for learning the other half: dealing with emotional and situational challenges like stress, anger, boredom and alcohol.

First, Think Smart

Before embarking on any program to stop, be realistic about the challenge of quitting an addictive habit. Here are some tips to help ease the pangs.

Pay attention. Identify the times when you find smoking particularly enjoyable, Dr. Pechacek suggests, because that's when you are most likely to relapse. Be on the lookout for ritual and social cues, like smoking with that first cup of coffee. Firm up your resolve during those times and find something else to do—like chewing gum or avoiding the situation altogether.

Know why you want to quit. "Most smokers primarily want to quit for health reasons," says Mitchell Nides, M.D., a psychologist and researcher at the University of California, Los Angeles. Other smokers feel increasing social pressure to snuff out their cigarettes, he says, adding, "it's the reverse of the pressure they got as kids to begin smoking." Whatever your reason, make sure it's clear in your mind, so you can call on it when times are tough.

Get ready. "Make sure that you're picking the right time, that you've told all of your friends and have gotten rid of all of your ashtrays and cigarettes," Dr. Nides suggests. Ask your friends and family to support your effort by not smoking in your presence or by helping you occupy yourself with other pursuits.

Use the "four Ds." Michael Cummings, Ph.D., director of the Smoking Cessation Clinic at the Roswell Park Cancer Institute in Buffalo, New York, suggests that smokers use the four Ds: Delay, deep breathe, do something else and drink water.

If you can delay the urge to smoke for a few minutes, that gnawing feeling in the pit of your stomach will subside. The same with deep breathing and distracting yourself when you become bored, a time when many people light up simply for lack of anything better to do. Drinking a glass of water whenever you have the urge to smoke will flood your system and cleanse it of nicotine and other chemicals.

Ditch cig souvenirs. Get rid of all cigarettes, matches, lighters and ashtrays in your home and office. Also, have smoky clothes cleaned professionally or have your tobacco-assaulted teeth polished by the dentist.

Eat your fruits and veggies. People who get very little beta-carotene in their diets have two times more lung cancer than people who get plenty of it, says Harvey Simon, M.D., associate professor of medicine at Harvard Medical School, founding member of the Harvard Cardiovascular Health Center and author of *Conquering Heart Disease*. The best sources of beta-carotene are brightly colored fruits and vegetables such as carrots and red peppers, as well as dark green, leafy vegetables. "Every little bit helps, so munch away," says Dr. Simon.

Lose weight later. "Don't be discouraged about weight gain while you're quitting," Dr. Cummings cautions. "Most smokers gain a few pounds after quitting, but it doesn't have to be excessive." On the other hand, don't try to reward yourself with an extra scoop of ice cream every time you reach a milestone, such as one month of not smoking.

Stay upbeat. Try to view your withdrawal symptoms as recovery signs, says Dr. Nides. You should talk to your doctor about what withdrawal symptoms you may experience and how to interpret them. "If you have an increased cough," he says, "that's a way of the lungs clearing themselves."

Diabetes: Avoid It Now

At 34, worried by the prospect of diabetes, LaMyra J. began to overhaul her diet. Sugar-free iced tea replaced her favorite apple juice. Low-fat margarine debuted on her toast, and cornflakes—not sugar-frosted flakes—landed in her cereal bowl.

"My doctor told me I had a 50-50 chance that I'd get diabetes later in life," says LaMyra, a mother of three. "Of course, I don't want to get diabetes. So I changed my eating habits."

Few of us women realize that, for most of us, diabetes is now one of our most pressing health threats. Often, it is a silent threat. This year, more than 8.4 million women will have this disease, yet only half will know it. Even more are at risk for developing this debilitating problem—a problem that can often be controlled when a woman takes control of her food choices and steps up her activity levels.

LaMyra was considered at risk for four reasons: She is slightly overweight, has a family history of diabetes, is African American and had gestational diabetes, a temporary condition that can occur during pregnancy. Each factor raised the odds that someday LaMyra would have diabetes permanently.

If that happened, LaMyra's body would be unable to make or properly use insulin, a hormone that allows blood sugar (glucose) to enter the cells of the body and be used for energy. In the short run, a woman with diabetes may feel tired or thirsty or find that she must urinate frequently.

In the long run, she is at greater risk for heart disease, kidney ailments, blindness and circulatory problems. In fact, the risk of heart disease is two to four times higher among women with diabetes than among those without it.

So LaMyra was smart to take steps against diabetes early in the game.

Warning Signs

Diabetes affects women differently than men in some ways. A few women, like Susan Thom, R.D., a certified diabetes educator in Cleveland, notice that their bodies need more insulin in the week and a half before menstruation begins. Birth control pills can affect blood sugar levels, yet since women with diabetes are at higher risk for infection and intrauterine devices (IUDs) can lead to infections, most cannot use the IUD.

Despite warning signs ranging from excessive thirst and hunger to blurred vision, fatigue and the frequent need to urinate, fully half of the women with diabetes don't even know they have it.

"Too many people walk around with undiagnosed diabetes," says Richard S. Beaser, M.D., assistant section head for internal medicine at the Joslin Diabetes Center and a staff physician at New England Deaconess Hospital and Harvard Medical School, all in Boston. "Anyone who's at risk should be tested."

Learn Where You Stand

Researchers hope that before long, they will develop a way to help prevent Type I diabetes—also called juvenile-onset diabetes—which strikes when your pancreas stops making insulin. This type of diabetes usually develops before a person is 20 years old. But for the much more common Type II diabetes, also known as adult-onset diabetes, experts already know steps that you can take to lower your chances of developing the disease.

The first thing to do is assess your risk of getting Type II diabetes. Here is what doctors recommend.

Take a cue from your folks. Having a family history of Type II diabetes places you at increased risk for the disease, says John Bantle, M.D., of the Division of Diabetes, Endocrinology and Metabolism at the University of Minnesota in Minneapolis. "If you have a parent with diabetes, your risk goes up." Chances are about 1 in 3 that you will develop the disease if one parent had it. If both did, your chances are about 50-50.

Watch for clues. An estimated half of those who have Type II diabetes don't know it. Often, that is because there aren't any symptoms. But sometimes there are symptoms; watch out for unusual thirst, frequent urination and unexplained weight loss, says Dr. Bantle. If you experience any of these, be sure to tell your doctor.

Get screened. Since you can also have "silent" diabetes, find out for sure by asking your doctor to check how your pancreas is performing. This can be done with a blood sugar test. This test measures the amount of glucose in your blood to determine whether you might have the disease. If you have diabetes in your family, it is important to have your blood sugar checked once a year.

Watch that waist-to-hip ratio. There is evidence to suggest that the waist-to-hip ratio, and particularly, the waist circumference, are important in determining whether you're likely to get Type II diabetes, says Gregory Dwyer, Ph.D., exercise physiology professor at Ball State University in Muncie, Indiana.

Women who carry their weight around their waists are a prime target for the disease, he says. To determine your waist-to-hip ratio, take the measurement of your waist and divide it by the measurement of your hips. If the result is 0.86 or higher, then you are at high risk, says Dr. Dwyer. For example, if your waist is 28 inches and your hips measure 34 inches, your waist-to-hip ratio is 0.82, so you're on the safe side. If you let your waist size swell to 30 inches, however, the ratio becomes 0.88—which may be asking for diabetes trouble. Time for a weight-loss plan.

What You Can—And Should—Eat

There was a time when people thought that eating too many sugary foods caused diabetes, and therefore all you had to do to control diabetes was avoid sugar. Well, dietary control is pivotal, but it is not quite that simple. The goal is to achieve blood sugar levels that are as normal as possible, which is accomplished by looking at the whole diet, not just sweets.

"How you eat is one of the cornerstones for preventing and controlling diabetes," says endocrinologist Kathleen Wishner, M.D., Ph.D., associate clinical professor of medicine at the University of Southern California in Los Angeles and president of the American Diabetes Association.

Experts such as Marion Franz, R.D., vice-president of nutrition at the International Diabetes Center in Minneapolis, advocate a three-point plan for diabetes control to curb the risk of heart disease while tackling blood sugar and holding the line on body weight.

Instead of focusing on sugar, the emphasis is on nutrient-dense, high-fiber carbohydrates and low-fat proteins.

"In 1994, the American Diabetes Association recommended that people with diabetes get 10 to 20 percent of their calories from protein, less than 20 percent from saturated and polyunsaturated fats and 60 to 70 percent from carbohydrates and monounsaturated fats, because of the latter's beneficial effect on heart health," notes Franz. "Beyond that," she says, "individual diets will vary with a person's weight goals, activity level and whether they're trying to reduce their cholesterol levels or not." So experts no longer offer one diabetic diet for all, says Franz.

Here are some specifics.

Plan your carbohydrates. While everyone needs a certain quantity of carbohydrates for energy, in women with diabetes, too big a dose can send blood sugar soaring, notes Franz.

"Most women with diabetes can eat three to four servings of carbohydrates at a meal, but not more," she says. "A serving is about 15 grams of carbohydrate—the amount found in a glass of milk, a small- to medium-size fruit, a half-cup of pasta or three-quarters cup of cereal, for example. Keeping the amounts under control helps keep blood sugars even." Which carbs are best? "The least processed," Franz notes. "That means whole grains, fruits or vegetables. If you have the choice of a cookie, a glass of orange juice or an orange for dessert, choose the orange."

Snack early and often. For better blood sugar control, spread breakfast, lunch and dinner over five small meals or snacks throughout the day, suggests Franz. "You may not manufacture enough insulin to handle a large meal, but you may make enough for many small ones. The trick is to not overeat."

To eat more frequently without overeating, plan ahead. Franz suggests saving your breakfast fruit for a midmorning pick-me-up. At lunch, save bread or crackers and some low-fat cheese, yogurt or another piece of fruit for a nosh during the midafternoon slump. Carry dried fruit with you, says Thom. Hold off on that glass of milk at dinner and enjoy it at bedtime with a final carbohydrate food such as crackers or bread, suggests Franz.

Fit in the fiber. Nutrition experts no longer believe that fiber slows the absorption of sugar into the bloodstream, says Dr. Wishner. "You would need a

Diabetes' Threat Bigger Than Breast Cancer's

HEALTH FLASH

Ask any woman to name her most-feared disease, and it is likely that her answer won't be diabetes. But perhaps it should be.

A new report from the Centers for Disease Control and Prevention in Atlanta shows that diabetes is a greater threat to women's lives than breast cancer. Among women ages 25 and over, the most recent statistics show that while around 47,000 women died of breast cancer, 109,000 deaths were attributable to diabetes.

But there is even more reason for concern: This low-profile peril can also rob the quality of your life.

"Diabetes is a leading cause of blindness, amputations and heart disease," says Philip Cryer, M.D., director of the Division of Endocrinology, Diabetes and Metabolism at the Washington University School of Medicine in St. Louis, Missouri, and president of the American Diabetes Association.

The best way to protect yourself against diabetes? First, realize that it can happen to you. Then, get regular screenings to check your blood sugar levels—particularly as you get older, Dr. Cryer suggests. Early detection gives you a better shot at controlling diabetes through food choices and exercise.

Eat Mediterranean

Fruity olive oil. Pungent garlic. Crusty whole-grain breads and a riot of brilliantly colored vegetables. Italian, Greek and other Mediterranean foods are a pleasure for the eyes and taste buds.

And now researchers at the Center for Human Nutrition at the University of Texas Southwestern Medical Center in Dallas say Mediterranean food may be the best of all possible meal plans for women with diabetes.

In a recent study, 42 women and men with diabetes ate one of two diets for six weeks each. One of the diets supplied 55 percent of calories from carbohydrates and 30 percent from fats; the other provided fewer carbs and more fat—40 percent from carbs and 45 percent from fats. In the second group, the added fat came, in part, from healthy monounsaturated fat like olive oil and avocados—simulating the nutritional makeup of a Mediterranean diet.

The results? Both diets lowered low-density lipoprotein (LDL) cholesterol, the kind implicated in the development of coronary heart disease. But the regimen that was rich in olive oil had added benefits: blood sugar, triglyceride and VLDL (very low density lipoproteins, which help form LDL) levels were lowered, while levels of "good" high-density lipoprotein (HDL) cholesterol (which lowers the risk of heart disease) were maintained.

What's more, another study based at the same research center discovered that by consuming a diet rich in olive oil, patients with diabetes required nearly 13 percent less insulin.

"We think this is a plan that those with diabetes and their families could follow easily and enjoy, and it would be healthy," says lead researcher Abhimanyu Garg, M.D., associate professor of internal medicine at the Center for Human Nutrition. Other foods typically featured in Mediterranean cookery—whole grains, lots of fruits and vegetables, legumes like white beans and small amounts of meat—can be easily worked into meal plans, he notes.

"The beauty of the Mediterranean diet is that it contains lots of fiber and lots of complex carbohydrates, which are good choices, within bounds, for those with diabetes," Dr. Garg says. "The key to the whole thing is watching your calorie intake. Yes, you'll gain weight if you eat too much olive oil. So you have to be careful."

One mainstay of Mediterranean meals—wine—should remain off-limits if you have diabetes, cautions Dr. Garg. "Alcohol adds calories and can lead to obesity," he notes. "It increases triglyceride levels and can raise blood pressure. It's better to steer clear."

huge amount, well beyond the 30 grams recommended for the American diet," she notes. "People with diabetes should eat fiber for the same reasons everyone else does—to stay regular, reduce the risk of colon cancer and maintain healthy cholesterol levels to fight heart disease."

Quench your thirst. "I have clients whose blood sugar seems to get higher when they don't get enough fluids," notes Thom. Her best advice? Consume two to three quarts of sugar-free fluids a day—water, diet soda and so forth—and only moderate amounts of coffee or tea.

Bypass salt. Salty foods can raise blood pressure, notes Thom, and women with diabetes are two to three times more likely to develop high blood pressure. "The combination of high blood pressure and high blood sugar is a time bomb," she says. To prevent problems, the American Diabetes Association recommends limiting sodium to no more than 3,000 milligrams a day—less if you already have diabetes and high blood pressure. When buying prepared foods, read labels—they give the sodium content in milligrams. When cooking, remember that 3,000 milligrams of sodium is equal to about 1½ teaspoons of salt.

Skip dessert. Some women with diabetes can tolerate a small sweet dessert such as a cookie or a small scoop of frozen yogurt, but others cannot, says Franz. Even desserts sweetened with fructose, which seems to raise blood sugar less dramatically than sucrose, can be a problem, says Dr. Wishner.

Walk off excess pounds. Losing just 10 to 20 pounds can substantially improve diabetes control. Exercise helps those with diabetes to lose weight, increases the body's ability to use blood sugar for energy and builds lean muscle that helps the body expend more calories, says Dr. Wishner.

23

Eating Clear of Cancer

S weet, juicy peaches. Fresh spinach spiced with garlic and a glisten of olive oil. Tart, sun-bronzed apples. Fragrant whole-wheat bread. The menu for a romantic alfresco lunch? Yes, and now it is also much more.

An increasing body of research has been suggesting what nutritionists, cancer experts and natural healers have suspected all along: Fruits, vegetables and whole grains can play powerful roles in preventing cancer, the second leading killer of women in the United States.

Switch on your television, browse at the newsstand or listen to the radio, and you'll hear plenty about cancer-preventing foods and diets. The one place where you may not hear much at all about them is at your doctor's office.

"The American medical system is still oriented toward fixing cancer, not preventing it," says Daniel W. Nixon, M.D., associate director of the Division of Cancer Prevention and Control at the Hollings Cancer Center of the Medical University of South Carolina in Charleston. "Soon, your doctor's office will become a prevention center as well as a treatment center. But for now, the focus is still on treating cancer—even though it can be expensive and painful and often doesn't really work."

A Strong Link

While no diet can cure cancer, the link between special diets and cancer prevention is well-established.

"We've found in large population studies that people who eat more fruits and vegetables have a lower risk of cancer," says Susan Mayne, Ph.D., director of cancer prevention and control research at the Yale University Cancer Center. "We know that fruits and vegetables contain antioxidants and other substances that in laboratory studies block or suppress cancer growth."

While no diet can cure cancer, what you put on your plate can have a far-ranging impact on whether or not it occurs, says Dr. Nixon. More and more research bears this out. Consider the evidence.

- Half of the nation's colon and rectal cancers, one-fourth of all breast cancers and one out of six cancers of the endometrium and gallbladder would be prevented if Americans switched to diets that are low in fat and high in fruits, vegetables and whole grains, says Dileep G. Bal, M.D., chief of the Cancer Control Branch of the California Department of Health Services in Sacramento.
- When University of Toronto researchers followed the eating habits of 56,837 Canadian women, they found that those who consumed the most fruits and vegetables rich in vitamins A and C lowered their breast cancer risk by 30 percent.
- The typical American diet—one that is high in fat, bereft of fiber, high in calories and skimpy on fruits, vegetables and whole grains—is thought to play a contributing role in about one in three cancer cases in the United States. Some experts put the number even higher, saying that as many as 60 percent of cancers in women and 40 percent in men may be linked to nutrition.

"Our eating habits are the major preventable cause of cancer," says Dr. Bal. "But people don't want to think it's as simple as eating a lot of fruit and vegetables and whole grains, reducing fat in the diet and exercising every day. They are more inclined to blame something like fast-food restaurants or even genetics."

Power Foods That Rein In Risk

In recent years scientists have begun exploring a host of powerful compounds with names like beta-carotene, sulforaphane, phytosterols and isoflavones. These and similar compounds are plentiful at every produce stand and supermarket—and, says Dr. Bal, they appear to be one of your best hopes for winning the cancer war. The following are some other powerful cancer-fighters found in food.

Flavonoids. Present in almost all fruits and vegetables, this class of compounds is able to keep potential carcinogens out of cells, where they do their damage.

Indoles and isothiocyanates. These compounds are responsible for the biting taste of broccoli, cauliflower and other cruciferous vegetables and also help keep harmful substances out of cells.

Isoflavones. Found in soybeans and soybean products like tofu, isoflavones provide multiple benefits. They act like antioxidants and also help block tumors from getting started.

Organosulfur compounds. Found in garlic and onions, these appear to play a powerful role in helping to block the formation of tumors.

Monoterpenes. Occurring in citrus fruits, monoterpenes help protect cells by interfering with the harmful action of carcinogens.

Even some well-known nutrients like folate and calcium now appear to have larger cancer-fighting roles than researchers previously thought. "There is compelling evidence from both animal and human studies that suggests that folate may prove to be an effective nutrient in our fight against colon cancer," says Joel B. Mason, M.D., assistant professor of medicine and nutrition at Tufts University School of Medicine in Boston. Calcium, he adds, plays a protective role by disarming the toxins that can lead to colon cancer.

The Right Menu

Regardless of the protective power of individual nutrients, a diet that is high in fruits, vegetables and whole grains provides what scientists call synergy—protective powers that may be greater than the sum of the individual parts. "We don't know exactly which nutrients are most important for people," says Dr. Mayne. "I suspect it's a combination."

The National Cancer Institute and the American Cancer Society have formulated simple dietary guidelines that, if followed by more people, could save literally thousands of lives a year. Perhaps it is not surprising that these modern guidelines really aren't very different from the basic, good-health diets people have traditionally followed for thousands of years.

"No one fruit or vegetable will prevent cancer," says Carolyn Clifford, Ph.D., chief of the diet and cancer branch of the National Cancer Institute and co-author of the institute's diet guidelines. "What we do know is that a low-fat, high-fiber diet containing fruits and vegetables is associated with less cancer. We don't yet know all the reasons why. But as a plan, it seems to work."

In a nutshell, here is what experts advise.

Pile your plate. Eat at least five servings of different fruits and vegetables every day. A serving is a half-cup of cut vegetables or fruit, a cup of raw salad greens, one-quarter cup of dried fruit or a hand-size piece of fresh fruit.

This is one area in which most of us can use improvement. According to the Centers for Disease Control and Prevention in Atlanta, only one in four women and one in five men eat five or more helpings of produce a day. Most of us manage about three.

With today's busy schedules, it is not always easy to eat the way you would like. An easy way to boost your fruit and vegetable quotient is with a glass of 100 percent pure juice or a piece of fruit at breakfast. Or simply pick up a lunchtime salad or take an extra helping of vegetables at dinner.

"There's more to fruit and vegetables than science ever realized," says Dr. Clifford. "This is such an active area of research right now that I sometimes make the analogy to the 1940s and 1950s, when all the essential vitamins were being discovered and named. Now we're looking into the potential of preventing chronic diseases like cancer."

Eat by the colors. Try eating fruits and vegetables of at least three different colors daily. Each color means that you're getting a different type of protective nutrient. Be sure to include cruciferous vegetables like broccoli, cabbage, cauliflower and bok choy. Get plenty of citrus fruit and dark green, leafy vegetables as well.

"No one food item can provide all of the essential nutrients," notes Dr. Clifford. "So you need a variety. Green, leafy vegetables are good sources of B vitamins and carotenoids. Yellow and orange vegetables are also good sources of carotenoids and other important compounds."

Focus on fiber. One of the easiest—and most important—ways to keep yourself healthy is to eat foods with an abundance of dietary fiber. High-fiber diets have been linked to a lower risk of colon and breast cancer.

Selenium: The New Defense against Cancer

In a recent study from Finland, researchers found that women and men with adequate selenium in their bodies had a 60 percent lower risk of cancer.

Selenium may be a helper in activating one of the most potent cancer-fighting antioxidants, called glutathione peroxidase. This antioxidant discourages free radicals planning on damaging DNA, the genetic code that governs how cells grow. As a sort of healthy two-for-one bonus, the same antioxidant also seems to protect from heart disease.

In the Finnish study, researchers looked at the blood selenium levels of 2,600 women and men. They found that those with about 103 micrograms of selenium per liter had a 60 percent lower risk of heart disease or cancer than did people who were getting only about 60 micrograms.

Concentrations of selenium in food depend on how much selenium is in the soil. In Finland selenium is low. America, in contrast, is believed to have fairly good selenium status already. But if you want to maximize your intake, be aware that this element is highest in seafoods, grains, muscle meats and Brazil nuts.

If you are taking a multivitamin, aim for one with 70 to 100 micrograms of selenium (a safe range recommended by experts). A separate selenium supplement is not recommended because the toxicity level and the safety level are very close, explains study leader Li Li, M.D., at the University of Southern California.

The take-home message? To fill up on the recommended amounts of selenium, stick to food sources.

HEALTH FLASH

"Fiber is important," says Charles B. Simone, M.D., founder and director of the Simone Protective Cancer Center in Lawrenceville, New Jersey, and a former National Cancer Institute researcher. "It acts like a sticky substance, pulling fats and carcinogens and sugars out of the body with it. It also speeds the movement of food through the intestines, giving the bacteria there less time to produce carcinogens."

Although cancer experts advise raising fiber intake to about 30 grams a day, most of us eat less than 13 grams a day. To make up the difference, enjoy five servings of fruits and vegetables a day, along with four or more servings of whole grains. It sounds like a lot, but consider that one slice of bread or a half-cup of pasta each counts as one serving.

Cut back on fat. Most Americans get at least 34 percent of their daily calories from fat, which experts say is way too high. Research suggests that reducing your daily fat intake to 30 percent or less of total calories could substantially lower your risk of colon, breast, prostate, rectal and endometrial cancer. "Fat is carcinogenic," says Dr. Nixon. "It works several ways, including promoting the growth of cancer cells."

Studies have shown, for example, that diets high in fat and calories are associated with a higher risk of rectal cancer, especially in men. In addition, a major analysis of data from 59 countries showed that those who eat more animal fat and meat have higher risks of oral and esophageal cancer, while those who eat more fruit and cabbage have lower risks.

There are many ways to eat lean. Select the leanest cuts of meat or choose fish or skinless chicken, suggests Dr. Bal. Forgo gravies and sauces. Don't go overboard with creamy, high-fat desserts—select fresh fruit instead. Go light on salad dressings, and use low-fat or nonfat types. You could even try topping a salad with naturally fat-free salsa. Switch from whole-fat milk, yogurt and cheese to low-fat and nonfat varieties.

Curb the calories. Being overweight or taking in more calories than you burn each day may contribute to cancers of the colon, breast, prostate, endometrium, kidney, cervix and thyroid. One of the most dramatic anti-cancer steps that you can take is to restrict calories and maintain a lean body weight, according to the National Cancer Institute.

When you take in extra calories without increasing exercise, experts say, the cargo that accumulates in the form of body fat may increase cancer risk. "Fatty tissues may promote cancer, especially the hormone-related types such as breast and prostate cancer," says Dr. Bal.

Go easy on party fare. Foods that have been barbecued, smoked or pickled have been linked with some cancers of the stomach and esophagus. "When foods are overheated by frying or grilling, cancer-causing chemicals form," explains Sidney Weinhouse, Ph.D., professor emeritus of biochemistry at the cancer center of Jefferson Medical College of Thomas Jefferson University in Philadelphia and co-author of the American Cancer Society dietary guidelines. Pickled substances, he says, tend to be high in salt, which may encourage stomach cancer. "Foods prepared that way taste good, but they aren't good for you."

Be a moderate drinker. Heavy drinking has been shown to weaken the immune system, which can give cancer cells the "breathing space" they need to get a head start. Excessive drinking has been linked to some cancers of the rectum, mouth and esophagus, and even moderate drinking has been linked to an increased risk of breast cancer. When drinking is combined with cigarette smoking, there is a higher risk of lung cancer as well.

Low-Fat Anti-Cancer Diets

When it comes to fat, is lower always better? While cancer researchers debate how much fat we can safely eat, some argue that we should be getting considerably less than the amount recommended by the National Cancer Institute.

"I personally try to get just 20 to 25 percent of my calories from fat," says Dr. Mayne. "While the government recommends 30 percent or less, there's a large debate about whether that's low enough. My personal feeling is, the lower the better, within reason. In parts of China, people eating a diet that provides 12 percent of calories from fat are very healthy and have low rates of chronic disease."

When Dr. Simone counsels women at his New Jersey cancer center, his message is "Lower is better." Less fat, he maintains, means less cancer risk.

"Really rigorous research shows that protection against cancer begins when fat is in the 20 percent range," says Dr. Simone, who outlines his low-fat, high-fiber eating plan in his book *Cancer and Nutrition*. "People who think they're protected by eating 30 percent of calories from fat are misleading themselves."

Other experts counsel women concerned about breast cancer to go even lower—to a diet that gets just 10 percent of calories from fat.

Studies suggest that there is a strong link between a high-fat, low-fiber diet and breast and colon cancer—and there is also some evidence that dietary fat is linked to prostate cancer. But not all researchers agree about the interpretation of the evidence.

For instance, population studies suggest that women who eat more fat have more breast cancer. Yet a major Harvard University study of 89,494 nurses found no difference in cancer rates between women who got more than 49 percent of their daily calories from fat and those consuming less than 29 percent of calories from fat. Critics argue, however, that the Harvard study didn't go low enough—that cancer prevention doesn't occur until the percentage of fat in the diet falls to much lower levels, say, below 20 percent.

"I have no doubt that fat causes cancer," says Dr. Simone. "Eating less is important for two reasons—it helps control your weight, and it gets carcinogens out of your diet."

24

Arthritis, at Your Age?

For the last couple of months, your 38-year-old walking partner has had trouble with her knee. Some days, she takes the elevator instead of the stairs or drives to the local convenience store instead of walking.

It turns out that she has arthritis, a joint disease shared by a growing number of women. This year, two-thirds of the 40 million Americans with arthritis will be women—and most will be bothered by a type called osteoarthritis.

Researchers aren't sure why osteoarthritis is more common in women, but preliminary research has uncovered one clue, the female hormone estrogen, which has been found in arthritic cartilage. The role it may play, however, remains unclear.

Osteoarthritis develops when certain structures that make up a joint—the ligaments, tendons and cartilage—are damaged and the joint shifts out of alignment. Abnormal weight distribution on small areas of cartilage can cause inflammation and eventual joint destruction.

More Clues

Body weight is another factor, says Cody Wasner, M.D., assistant clinical professor at the Oregon Health Sciences University in Portland and a spokesperson for the Arthritis Foundation in Atlanta. If you looked at 100 women, he says, the heaviest 25 would be at three to four times greater risk for arthritis than the women who weighed less. Lab studies show that lowering body weight can decrease the severity of arthritis, says Dr. Wasner, in part, because joints are better able to stay in place if they're carrying less weight.

Injury is another major cause. This is because damage to the joint can cause misalignment and subsequent arthritis, says W. Joseph McCune, M.D., associate professor of internal medicine at the University of Michigan in Ann Arbor.

Arthritis in women ages 30 to 45 usually strikes in the knee, Dr. Wasner says, and arthritic knees are more prevalent in women than in men by a ratio of two to one.

The hands are another arthritis flash point for women, with the usual targets being the joints nearest the fingernails. "This kind of arthritis is associated with bumps at those joints," says Dr. Wasner, and women often start developing problems in their thirties and forties. The bumps are known as Heberden's nodes, and women are at ten times greater risk for developing them than men are.

Part of the reason for that, says Dr. Wasner, is genetics. The gene linked to Heberden's is more often passed from mother to daughter. "There's nothing to prevent that from happening," he says. This problem sometimes develops earlier in women who go through early menopause, he notes. While women can't prevent it, early treatment can help them maintain function in their hands.

Another area where arthritis commonly develops is the hip joint, but there the disease strikes men and women at about the same rate.

Arthritis is difficult to diagnose, Dr. Wasner says. That is because early arthritis, say, in the hip may first be noticed as pain in the groin area. Doctors don't realize that the problem is in the hip until the disease becomes serious.

Investing in Joint Preservation

Arthritis is a condition that you may be able to prevent. Here's how you can start protecting your joints.

Avoid injury. Condition yourself properly for whatever activity you're doing, warm up, stretch, cool down and wear the proper equipment, particularly footwear, Dr. McCune says.

Watch your weight. Since heavy people are at greater risk for arthritis, says Dr. Wasner, try to achieve your ideal weight. Consult with your physician about how to combine exercise and healthy low-fat eating to accomplish this goal.

Stay in shape. Muscles work to stabilize your joints, so the stronger they are, the less susceptible to injury and arthritis they will be. Patients with underlying joint problems should consult with a physical therapist, exercise physiologist or an individual trained in exercise science about appropriate exercises and techniques.

Fighting the Pain

If you think you have arthritis, here's what you can do to cope with the pain.

See a doctor. The longer you wait, the more damage can be done to your joints and the harder it will be to treat. A rheumatologist specializes in the treatment of arthritis and can either care for your disease herself or refer you to a physical therapist or to an orthopedic surgeon if your disease is severe enough to warrant joint replacement. To find a rheumatologist in your area, contact your local chapter of the Arthritis Foundation.

Ice down the pain. For the pain and swelling of arthritis, apply ice, says Dr. Wasner. Ice reduces inflammation because it causes blood vessels to constrict, reducing blood flow and fluid buildup. Ice for 20 to 30 minutes after you exercise or after any strenuous activity in which you've placed excessive demands on your joints, he says.

You can buy an ice pack at your pharmacy or make one yourself by putting ice in a plastic bag and wrapping it in a towel so that the ice doesn't harm your skin.

Warm up. If you have joint stiffness, heat can help, says Dr. Wasner. Sit in a hot bath for 20 minutes or apply a heat pack or hot towel for 20 minutes to the joint that is bothering you.

More Women Headed for Achy Joints

If you—or your friends—are complaining more and more about stiff, achy joints, you're not alone. Arthritis is the number one chronic condition among American women, according to the latest statistics from the Centers for Disease Control and Prevention (CDC) in Atlanta.

The CDC estimates that nearly 23 million of us now have arthritis, and the number will increase to 36 million by the year 2020. For reasons not yet clear, women with arthritis outnumber men by a margin of three to two.

"There may be a number of factors influencing that statistic. For starters, women live longer than men," says Doyt Conn, M.D., a rheumatologist and senior vice-president for medical affairs for the Arthritis Foundation in Atlanta.

As the baby-boom population ages, the number of women with arthritis will likely increase naturally, says Jaya Rao, M.D., a rheumatologist at the Richard L. Roudebush Veterans Affairs Medical Center in Indianapolis, Indiana, who worked on the CDC study.

What can women do to prevent this condition? Both doctors advise that early diagnosis, maintaining a healthy weight and pursuing a lifetime of exercise can help delay or limit the impact of arthritis on women's lives.

HEALTH FLASH

When Knee Joints Protest Too Much

Arthritis caused by wear and tear can also affect the knee joint. Damage to structures in the knee can cause the joint to shift out of alignment, which in turn leads to degeneration of the bone. Irritation and pain are the result.

You can reduce the risk—or even prevent it—by taking a few sound steps.

Be shoe-smart. Wearing well-fitting shoes in good condition can help keep your knees healthy. If your foot is out of alignment or improperly supported, that can translate right up to your knee and cause problems there, says Pekka Mooar, M.D., assistant professor of orthopedic surgery and chief of sports medicine at the Medical College of Pennsylvania and Hahnemann University School of Medicine in Philadelphia. Be sure to pick a shoe that is wide enough for your foot and made for the activity that you're doing—a walking shoe for walking, a tennis shoe for tennis and a running shoe for running.

Buy your shoes from somebody who understands your needs, Dr. Mooar says. If you have a friend who's into walking, ask her if she has found a shoe store with a knowledgeable staff.

Travel lightly. Even if you don't have arthritis now, you may be at risk for it later on if you're carrying extra body weight, says Gerald Eisenberg, M.D., director of the arthritis treatment program at Lutheran General Hospital in Park Ridge, Illinois. To help preserve knee health, keep your body weight under control with low-fat eating and plenty of exercise.

Cross-train year-round. The women who think that the only way to get exercise is to power-walk or run all the time are headed for trouble, says John Feagin, M.D., associate professor of orthopedics at Duke University Medical Center in Durham, North Carolina.

Cross-training—doing a variety of different types of exercises—can help prevent the wear and tear that comes from doing the same old exercise over and over. To add some variety to your exercise routine and give your joints a little relief, try step aerobics, aqua-aerobics (done in a pool) and plyometrics—exercises that involve jumping, hopping and bounding.

Exercise carefully. Not all leg-strengthening exercises are good for the knees, says physical therapist Mark Taranta, director of the Physical Therapy Practice in Philadelphia. Some exercises, such as squats and knee extensions, can accelerate arthritis. The best are straight-leg raises, because they help strengthen your thigh muscles without straining your joints.

Do stairs properly. Stairs place substantial stress on your knees. Practice the following technique when going up and down: Going up, lead with your "good" leg; this makes that leg carry most of the weight and do most of the work. On the way down, lead with your "bad" leg; this again allows your good leg to absorb the most stress, says Taranta.

Replace doorknobs. Rotating handles and doorknobs can be difficult for arthritic hands, so replace the ones in your home with lever- and latch-type devices, says Dr. Wasner.

Help your hands. If you have arthritis in your hands, says Taranta, ask your doctor about splints that can hold your wrists and hands in a comfortable position.

Chomp on the Bone Builder

Calcium is an essential building block for maintaining strong bones. It also helps prevent osteoporosis or bone loss, which takes its toll when the bone around a joint begins to crack or deteriorate.

Aim to get between 1,000 milligrams and 1,500 milligrams of calcium a day, says Angela Smith, M.D., assistant professor of orthopedics at Case Western Reserve University School of Medicine in Cleveland. Take calcium supplements if you don't get all the calcium that you need from food.

At the same time, don't block that bone builder. Both caffeine and nicotine are believed to interfere with calcium absorption, says Emil Pascarelli, M.D., professor of clinical medicine at Columbia-Presbyterian Medical Center in New York City. So do your best to give up smoking and cut back on caffeinated beverages such as tea, coffee and colas. Chocolate also contains caffeine, so sometimes it's advisable to have something else for dessert.

Pick up a cane. Using a cane can help ease hip pain by lessening stress on the hip. It may also prolong the time before you have to resort to more serious treatment such as surgery. It's hard for people to even consider using a cane, says Dr. Wasner. Just remember that you may get more mileage out of your hip if you do, he says.

Just a Twinge?

If you're getting mild complaints from the joints around your body, here's what doctors recommend for easing discomfort.

Take to the high road. It's good for your joints to have weight-bearing, low-impact exercise at least three times a week, according to Emil Pascarelli, M.D., professor of clinical medicine at Columbia-Presbyterian Medical Center in New York City. Translated, this means that you should take a good, long walk at least several times a week or use that time for step aerobics or a low-impact exercise routine, he adds.

There is no evidence that running is bad for the joints, says Angela Smith, M.D., assistant professor of orthopedics at Case Western Reserve University School of Medicine in Cleveland. If you have an injury already, running may aggravate it. Also, errors in training (for example, increasing distance or speed too rapidly for the body to adapt properly) can cause injury in any sport—even swimming, she adds.

Stretch for the future. Stretching is excellent for the joints, says Dr. Pascarelli, since tight muscles put unnecessary pressure on them. Any kind of stretching is good as long as you don't bounce, which can pull a muscle. Hold a slow, steady stretch for 15 to 20 seconds, then relax and repeat.

At Last, Relief for That Splitting Headache

B lame it on our unique hormones, our special brand of stress or the foods we love: Women still get three times as many migraine headaches as men do.

We'll also endure plenty of tension headaches—a brand of brain pain that doctors say often is little different from a migraine.

Now, researchers are discovering even stronger links between these debilitating headaches and the foods we eat. Oven-fresh bread, aged Cheddar cheese and a goblet of red wine. A romantic picnic? Maybe. But for a migraine-prone woman, this classic repast could be a surefire recipe for agony.

"I'd been getting migraines for years," notes Sarah, an accounting supervisor at a computer firm. "When I stopped eating cheese and drinking red wine, I got far fewer painful headaches."

What's going on? From Brie to bologna, chocolate to coffee, lima beans to pickled herring, dozens of foods contain natural substances or added ingredients that can ignite headache pain. These substances alter brain chemistry and prompt blood vessels that service the brain on the outside of the skull to swell, pressing on sensitive nerves, explains Frederick Freitag, D.O., associate director of the Diamond Headache Clinic in Chicago.

"Whether you get migraines or tension headaches, the basic mechanism is the same—a central nervous system disorder," says Ninan T. Mathew, M.D., director of the Houston Headache Clinic. "The pain can be mild or severe, and it can be triggered by many things. Dietary factors can account for one attack out of five."

Women can be especially sensitive to food. No one is sure why women are more migraine-prone, but doctors say reproductive hormones are often the culprits. Half of all women with migraines report the most attacks around the time of menstruation. In one study, 50 percent of women with migraines said that they had more severe or frequent headaches while taking birth control pills.

For many, food becomes a powerful player in the headache equation at particular times, such as on the days just before and at the start of a menstrual period, says Dr. Freitag. Plus, the consequences of a busy lifestyle—notably, missed meals, irregular sleep habits and stress—not only can cause a pounding headache or a migraine but may also leave you extra-vulnerable to one triggered by food.

Was It Lunch?

At times the food/headache connection can be downright puzzling. On Monday you devour an entire chocolate bar and feel no ill effects; on Friday one bite makes your cranium feel as though it is about to explode.

"There are well-established connections between certain foods and headaches, but people usually report that it only happens sometimes," notes Dr. Freitag. One reason, he says, is that the amount of headache-causing chemicals can vary dramatically in different brands of the same food due to differences in processing, preparation or storage.

The best way to identify your own food triggers is to keep a diary, says Joel Saper, M.D., clinical professor of neurology at Michigan State University and director of the Michigan Head Pain and Neurological Institute, both in Ann Arbor.

"Eliminating foods that hurt your head won't cure the reason you get headaches, but it could make you more treatable or less likely to experience an attack," says Dr. Saper. "The tendency for headaches will still remain.

"Look for the obvious foods initially, then expand if you don't come up with anything at first," suggests Dr. Saper.

Avoid These Food-Trigger Traps

Certain foods contain vasoactive substances, chemicals that prompt your blood vessels to either constrict or swell, causing pain. If you're sensitive to such substances, eating foods that contain them can trigger a headache. Here's what to watch out for, say migraine specialists.

Tyramine. This naturally occurring substance—found in strong aged cheese, pickled herring, chicken livers and the pods of lima, fava and other broad beans—acts on brain chemistry and makes blood vessels swell. Women sensitive to tyramine may lack an enzyme that breaks this substance down, so it keeps circulating in the body, says Dr. Freitag.

Similar, though less common, headache reactions can be caused by phenylethylamine (found in chocolate) and synephrine (found in citrus fruit and juices).

Histamine. When researchers from the University of Vienna in Austria asked 45 headache-prone women and men to stop consuming histamine-containing foods such as cheese, sausage, pickled cabbage and wine for four weeks, nearly three out of four reported fewer headaches. Vinegar (except white vinegar), fresh-baked yeast products, onions, bananas, figs, bacon, avocados and soy sauce all contain similar vasoactive amines that create headaches in the same way.

Nitrates, nitrites and monosodium glutamate. A hot dog at the ballpark or the lunch special at a Chinese restaurant could leave you with a splitting headache, too.

How? Nitrates and nitrites (used to preserve the color of cured meats like bacon, ham, salami and hot dogs) can alter brain chemistry and dilate blood vessels. So can monosodium glutamate (MSG), found in some restaurant

Old Tennis Balls Offer New Pain Relief

HEALTH FLASH

Here's a new "sports maneuver" that just may help you ease a headache: Grab two tennis balls and stuff them into a clean tube sock (or kneesock).

Now, turn them into a homemade neck massager by tying the end of the sock tightly so that the balls can't move. To use it, lie on your back on the floor, positioning the tennis balls under your neck—directly below the spot where your skull meets your neck. Remain there until those neck muscles relax.

While this trick—reported in a recent issue of the journal *Patient Care*—is unlikely to thwart migraines, it is useful for people whose headaches hover in the back of the head, often as a result of cradling the phone on the shoulder all day, driving long distances or falling into bad posture at the computer, explains Karl B. Fields, M.D., sportsmedicine physician and director of the family-practice program at Moses H. Cone Memorial Hospital in Greensboro, North Carolina.

The muscle tightness created by too much use or unfamiliar use may cinch the nerves at the base of the neck. Doctors sometimes numb these nerves with injections. Sometimes, direct pressure does the same thing. The pressure may also act like a massage, draining the muscle tension that is at the root of the headache.

food as well as in packaged items, from party dip to TV dinners.

Aspartame. Diet drinks and sugar-free foods—from yogurt to desserts—that contain the artificial sweetener aspartame may cause headaches in patients prone to migraines, says Dr. Mathew. "It's a controversial issue, but we strongly believe aspartame can cause headaches in migraine sufferers," he says. "Many patients report it to us."

Caffeine withdrawal. Caffeine in coffee, tea and cola drinks actually makes blood vessels narrow, but hours after the last cup, you may develop a rebound headache as vessels expand. Doctors think caffeine withdrawal explains why some people get headaches on weekends or holidays, when routines vary and the office—or kitchen—coffeepot isn't constantly beckoning.

Enjoying Life, Headache-Free

Start a diary to zero in on likely culprits, says Dr. Saper. Then try the following tips.

Stick to small helpings. "For some, a small amount of a problem food is okay," Dr. Mathew says. "Experiment to see if you can tolerate small amounts."

Avoid and conquer. If as little as a sip of red wine or a bite of Brie, navy beans or anything else brings on a headache every time, write it off. "If your headaches are triggered primarily by foods, you can make a very big change by removing the offenders," says Dr. Freitag.

Switch brands. If one brand of cheese leads to a migraine, try another. The same goes for other tyramine-rich foods. "You may find that you may not necessarily have to write off a food entirely," says Dr. Freitag. "There's a wide variance in the amount of tyramine by brand," he notes. "Many of my patients find that they can tolerate a different one just fine."

Explore substitutes. Love chocolate, hate the headache? Try substituting carob, suggests Dr. Saper. Fresh-cooked roast beef and turkey are delicious substitutes for processed lunchmeats, although he recommends avoiding meat whenever possible.

Looking for a "safe" cheese? Stick with processed types, such as American and loaf cheeses like Velveeta, as well as farmer cheese, cottage cheese and cream cheese, which are usually low in tyramine, says Dr. Mathew. Mozzarella, Havarti and other mild, soft varieties generally contain less tyramine than hard, crumbly, strong-tasting cheeses. For overall health reasons, look for low-fat varieties.

Read the label. Scan the ingredients list of any prepared product that you plan to eat for nitrites or nitrates and MSG, but beware, suggests Dr. Mathew. "Nitrites, nitrates and MSG may be listed only as hydrolized protein or natural flavor on a label," he says. "That could be the only clue you get."

Make it fresh. All food—particularly meat, fish and poultry products—

should be prepared and eaten fresh. Tyramine levels build quickly as food sits, even when refrigerated, so don't consume leftovers held for more than one day.

Talk about food with your party host. Sizing up party finger foods can break the conversational ice. "Ask about the food in a nice, nonoffensive, neutral way," suggests Dr. Freitag. "Comment on the cheeses and find out what they are. If you see a dip that may be safe to eat, make a simple inquiry like, 'Boy, where'd you get the dip?' If the answer is the local convenience store, it probably has MSG in it. If the answer is 'Well, I whipped it up myself,' it's probably fine."

Try calcium. At Mount Sinai Hospital in New York City, two women whose migraines were related to their menstrual cycles felt significantly better after taking calcium and vitamin D supplements for two to three months. One found that she could stop oncoming migraine attacks by taking 1,200 to 1,600 milligrams of calcium (in chewable form).

Think twice about alcohol. If you opt to enjoy an occasional glass of wine with a meal, consider white wines. Red wines like Chianti and sherry, as well as beer, burgundy and vermouth, contain more headache-promoting substances like esters, tannins and acids than do white wines.

As for hard liquor, if you're headache-prone, you may find that you're better off without it, says Dr. Freitag. Instead, try an alcohol-free "mock" cocktail or a white-wine spritzer, which is white wine mixed with club soda.

Consider the herbal route. The herb feverfew has proven abilities to reduce migraine pain and lengthen the period of time between migraines—provided it is taken daily, says Varro E. Tyler, Ph.D., professor of pharmacognosy at the Purdue University School of Pharmacy in West Lafayette, Indiana, and author of *The New Honest Herbal.* "The usual dose is a capsule or tablet with 380 milligrams of feverfew in it, but make sure the label says it contains two-tenths of 1 percent of parthenolide, the active ingredient," Dr. Tyler says. "It only works when taken regularly."

If you find that you can avoid headaches only by limiting yourself to a very narrow selection of foods, see a doctor. Severely restricting your food choices can leave you deficient in key nutrients, says Dr. Saper. Also see your doctor if, after trial and error, you can't detect any link between your headaches and food. Other nondrug tactics—like stress reduction or meditation—may offer help.

The New Tune-Up for Stress Incontinence

I n 1997, as many as two in five American women will be bothered by stress incontinence—the embarrassing condition that can bring a whoosh or trickle of urine each time you sneeze, laugh or exercise.

But you don't have to grin and bear it—or suffer in silence, as past generations of women did. From exercise tapes to special workout weights, and from at-home muscle-toning routines to sophisticated electronic aids available at the doctor's office, there's more help than ever for this annoying condition—help that's also more effective than ever.

What exactly is stress incontinence? First, imagine a hammock. When the hammock is new, it supports your weight easily. But then life takes its toll. For the hammock, that could mean wind, rain, snow and kids bouncing on it. One afternoon, you climb in with a couple of volumes from *The Decline and Fall of the Roman Empire* and—whoops! That hammock is history.

In a way, the same kind of thing can happen to your all-important pelvic-floor muscle, which stretches like a hammock from your pubic bone in the front to the base of your spine in the back.

Called the levator ani, this thick muscle is designed to support the bladder, uterus and rectum. Over time, however, normal wear and tear—coupled with neglect and giving birth to a bouncing baby or two—can damage nerves, weaken the muscle and compromise connective tissue and ligaments. But the weakness may not become apparent for years after the damage is done—usually when a woman is well into her forties.

Now many health professionals suggest that it may be possible to prevent—and even reverse—pelvic-floor damage if you take special precautions and commit to a unique kind of fitness program.

That "Sagging" Feeling

Most women walk around blissfully unaware of the engineering marvel in their laps. But consciousness is raised when the pelvic floor begins to sag.

"Women don't come to us and say, 'My levator ani feels weak,'" notes Stephen B. Young, M.D., a University of Massachusetts Medical Center (Worcester) urogynecologist (a gynecologist who specializes in disorders of the pelvic floor). "Instead they say, 'I'm losing urine when I sneeze.' Or, 'I feel a heavy achiness in my groin when I'm on my feet for a long time.'"

"Stress" incontinence—meaning urine is released during lifting, laughing, sneezing or exercising—is the most common sign that the pelvic floor is losing ground. "It's one of the secrets of motherhood. A third of women who deliver vaginally develop stress incontinence," says Chicago's Rush Presbyterian–St. Luke's Medical Center director of urogynecology Linda Brubaker, M.D.

Another symptom, says Dr. Brubaker, is "a heavy feeling of things dropping, but only when you're upright, not lying down."

What happens is, as pelvic muscles weaken from disuse or injury, the uterus, bladder and rectum begin to slip from their moorings.

Pulled south by gravity, the pelvic organs get squeezed into the lower regions of the pelvis. When push comes to shove, the bladder and rectum can bulge into the vagina or, in extreme cases, the uterus tumbles down into the vaginal canal.

"Genetics appears to be a factor," Dr. Brubaker maintains. "If your mother had problems related to pelvic-floor weakness—like stress incontinence or a prolapsed uterus—you may be more predisposed."

"Floor" Exercises to the Rescue

If you think you have a problem, don't hesitate to seek help, says Dr. Brubaker. Often, a simple "preventive" program, including pelvic-floor exercises, is all that's needed to stem the decline. Even if you're symptom-free, there's no better time to start such a program than now.

"Regular exercise of the pelvic-floor muscles is as important to all women as doing breast self-exams," says Dr. Brubaker. "After all, a woman's chance of developing incontinence during her lifetime is much greater than breast cancer. And what an impact on her quality of life."

The pelvic-muscle exercises Dr. Brubaker refers to are known as Kegels (pronounced KEE-guls). Developed back in the 1940s by California physician Arnold Kegel, they involve repeatedly squeezing the levator ani. For women, this can feel like clenching a tampon.

"They're not a cure-all," says Nicolette S. Horbach, M.D., director of the division of gynecology and urogynecology at George Washington University Medical Center in Washington, D.C. "But studies show that, when practiced correctly and faithfully, Kegel exercises do make a difference for most women with mild incontinence."

Neil Resnick, M.D., director of the Continence Center and chief of geriatrics at Brigham and Women's Hospital in Boston, concurs. "If you leak a little urine when you sneeze or cough, you have a 75 to 80 percent chance of benefiting from Kegels."

Identifying Pelvic Muscles

To benefit at all, you've got to know how to do Kegels correctly. For many of us, that's no small feat. "According to several recently published articles, as many as eight out of ten women are doing Kegels incorrectly. And these women received instruction from a doctor, nurse or physical therapist," says Dr. Resnick. So don't expect to be an expert after reading this article. Beyond proper instruction, mastering the technique takes time and patience. And practice.

Critical to the process is learning to isolate the pelvic muscle. The simplest way is to lie down, put a finger or two inside your vagina and squeeze as if you were trying to stop the flow of urine. If your fingers feel pressure from the side vaginal walls, that means you're using the levator ani.

Another way to identify the pelvic muscle is while urinating. See if you can stop or slow the flow of urine by squeezing, says Dr. Young. (This should be a one-time test only; repeatedly interrupting urination can aggravate urinary problems.)

If you have any doubt about where this muscle is, enlist your gynecologist's help during your next exam.

But squeezing the right muscle is just half the job. For some women, the really difficult part is not contracting other muscles.

"It's very common that patients are puzzled when I tell them to 'squeeze,'" Dr. Brubaker continues. "They'll squeeze their arms and lift their buttocks off the table, or bring their knees in. They substitute other muscles and bear down." Tightening the abdomen is particularly bad; it can actually increase pressure on the pelvic floor and, if you're prone to it, bring on urine leakage.

Mastering the Squeeze

That's why it's so important to learn how to exercise your pelvic muscle correctly. To do this, you can buy a self-help audiotape. But your best bet is to sign up for a hands-on demonstration by a trained health professional.

Your doctor may be a willing teacher but most likely will refer you to a nurse, nurse practitioner, midwife or physical therapist who specializes in teaching pelvic-floor exercise.

The advantage to personal instruction is the availability of certain aids to make learning easier. In fact, studies show that, properly used, these devices can increase enormously the success rate of Kegels. Perhaps the biggest boon comes from computer-assisted biofeedback.

A pressure probe is placed into a woman's vagina, with a wire leading to a computer monitor. When she squeezes, her contraction is instantly registered by a rising line on the screen. The stronger her contraction, the higher the line goes.

Meanwhile, other electrodes connected to her abdominal muscles track whether she's squeezing the wrong muscles. A smaller chart at the bottom of the screen shows that line.

"I tell women, 'You want to see the line on the top graph rise and the smaller one stay smooth,'" says Jane Marks, R.N., clinical coordinator for

Kegels Go High-Tech

Barbells for your pelvic muscles? It's true: Women who need extra help strengthening their pelvic-floor muscle can now take advantage of special new exercise equipment and instructional tapes.

The tape, put out by the National Association for Continence, is a gentle but thorough workout for your pelvic-floor muscle. To order, call 1-800-BLADDER, or contact the association at P.O. Box 8310, Spartanburg, SC 29305. The tape costs $8, plus $2 for shipping.

If you need more help, your doctor can help you determine whether or not you'll benefit from using "cones," special tampon-like vaginal weights, or a "perineometer," which measures muscle strength.

Cones come in sets of five, of varying weights. To keep the cone from slipping out of the vagina, you must squeeze your pelvic muscle continuously for several minutes—a version of muscle-strengthening exercises called Kegels.

"The weights are very convenient," says Linda Brubaker, M.D., director of urogynecology at Rush Presbyterian–St. Luke's Medical Center in Chicago. "You can pop them in when you're showering and blow-drying your hair. After 15 minutes, you've done your pelvic-floor exercises for the day!" (For more information on the cones, contact your gynecologist.)

Another device for scoring a "10" on your pelvic exercises is a perineometer. You place this thin, air-filled cylinder in your vagina and a numbered gauge registers the strength of exercise contractions by the amount of air displaced.

You may be able to purchase a perineometer directly from your physician, or she can order one for you from North American Distributors (1-800-995-0510; in Canada, call 1-714-553-0263) or Milex Products, 5915 Northwest Highway, Chicago, IL 60631.

HEALTH FLASH

the continence program at Johns Hopkins Geriatric Center in Baltimore.

This kind of training isn't a one-shot deal. The woman must return for three or four sessions over the next few months. Women who cannot contract their pelvic muscles at all can benefit from another training device, which delivers electrical stimulation to the pelvic muscle, causing it to contract.

Success Secret: Practice, Practice, Practice

How many Kegel reps you can do depends on many factors, says Dr. Brubaker. "For prevention purposes, I typically have women do a set of ten (holding each contraction for about ten seconds), three times a day."

That's not a prescription for everyone, she adds. "A frail 80-year-old who can't contract her pelvic floor very well needs to start with fewer contractions, held for a shorter period. Or she may need to begin doing Kegels while lying down so she's not fighting against gravity." The point is, do what's comfortable for you. Don't overdo it.

"If you overdo Kegels, you can develop pelvic-floor spasms and pain. It's a moderation issue," says Dr. Horbach. The easy thing about this kind of fitness program is you can do it anywhere without special equipment. Nor will you break a sweat.

Since many women are advised to do pelvic exercises three times a day, Marks suggests practicing them either before or after meals.

"I tell women to do them in the shower," says Seattle-based urogynecologic physical therapist Kathe Wallace, P.T. "Or standing at the sink while brushing their teeth.

"Here in Seattle it rains all the time," says Wallace, "so some of my patients do pelvic-floor exercises in conjunction with the windshield wipers—ideally set on 'delay.' The wipers swish, and then they hold until the next swipe." Whatever works for you. The bottom line: Just do them.

In most cases, a gynecologist, urologist or geriatrician can treat pelvic-floor disorders. If you feel you need to consult with another specialist, ask your physician to refer you to a urogynecologist; or write to the American Urogynecologic Society, 401 N. Michigan Avenue, Chicago, IL 60611, for the name of a urogynecologist in your immediate area. These physicians usually have additional expertise in conditions affecting the pelvis.

Pelvis Protectors

Beyond exercise, some other actions to preserve the integrity of your pelvic floor are:

Drop excess weight. Data suggest overweight women may have more pelvic-floor weakness and prolapse than their slim sisters.

Don't smoke. "Smokers have been found to be predisposed to problems with pelvic weakness," says Nicolette S. Horbach, M.D., director of gynecology and urogynecology at George Washington University Medical Center in Washington, D.C.

Lift with care. Straining to lift a jammed window or schlepping a stack of encyclopedias to the attic can create "incredible stresses" on your pelvic floor, says Linda Brubaker, M.D., director of urogynecology at Rush Presbyterian–St. Luke's Medical Center in Chicago.

"When you lift a heavy object, you momentarily push the pelvic muscle down very forcefully beyond its normal range of motion," she explains. That's called an increase in intra-abdominal pressure. And the cumulative effect of years of repetitive motion that creates this kind of pressure can certainly take its toll. Don't be shy. Ask for help if you need to hoist anything heavy. Or contract your pelvic muscle and hold it as you lift.

Go low-impact. Doctors are the first to admit they're just not sure how dangerous jogging and high-impact aerobic exercise are to the pelvic floor. But, most agree, why risk it? The trauma of repetitive jolting may damage the nerves and muscle of the pelvic floor.

There are better ways to burn calories and challenge the cardiovascular system. Walk. Bike. Swim. Or, if you really want to get your heart pumping, work out on a stair-climber or rowing machine. Or sign up for a low-impact aerobics class and pump those arms.

Keep regular. "Early research suggests straining due to chronic constipation may damage pelvic muscles as well as the nerves that supply those muscles," says Dr. Horbach. Best bets: Adopt a high-fiber diet, get regular (low-impact) aerobic exercise and drink six to eight glasses of water a day.

YOUR PERFECT WEIGHT

Part 5

Enjoy your food. Denying yourself can lead to eating more calories later.
—nutritionist Connie Roberts, R.D.

Female Advantage

Why Big Hips Are Less Risky for Your Health

If television's *NYPD Blue* stars Andy Sipowicz and Donna Abandando made a wager over which was better—Sippy's big belly or Donna's amply padded hips—guess who would win?

If you put your money on Donna's hips, you're about to pocket some change. We may curse it, but a woman's tendency to store fat on her hips is actually a health advantage. (Remember that when bathing-suit season rolls around!)

Although an excess of body fat is dangerous regardless of its location, abdominal fat is riskier than hip fat. Why is this so? Abdominal fat is metabolically more active than fat in the hips or thighs, says JoAnn E. Manson, M.D., co-director of women's health at Brigham and Women's Hospital in Boston. It's constantly breaking down and rebuilding itself and sends out by-products that travel directly to the liver and raise the risk for disease.

Hip fat, by contrast, is a quieter fat. It just sits there, less active, and so doesn't increase the odds for health problems as greatly as does belly fat.

The hormone estrogen may play a role in determining whether women carry fat on their hips—a "pear" shape—or around their middles—an "apple" shape, says Dr. Manson.

The next time you squash your hips into too-tight jeans or squeeze into those control-top panty hose, count yourself lucky. Here are three reasons why belly fat would be worse.

◗ Promotes heart disease. The more tummy fat—especially when packed around internal organs—the greater the risk of heart disease. Belly fat can lead to higher levels of dangerous blood fats called triglycerides and to lower levels of heart-healthy blood fats called high-density lipoprotein (HDL) cholesterol, says Susan Fried, Ph.D., associate professor of nutritional sciences at Rutgers University in New Jersey.

◗ Leads to diabetes. Belly fat releases fatty acids into the bloodstream that seem to set off a chain reaction, causing insulin resistance in the liver, increased production of sugar by the liver and rises in blood sugar levels, experts say.

◗ Raises blood pressure. Experts have pinpointed a clear link between tummy blubber and high blood pressure. Again, insulin resistance—which causes changes such as increased salt retention—is responsible, adds Dr. Manson.

Fill Up to Slim Down

In a new study from the University of Sydney in Australia, researchers found that some surprising foods have the power to satisfy your hunger now—and for hours to come.

Call them "bargain foods," edibles that pack a lot of satisfaction, not a lot of calories. The best news is that these power foods aren't expensive or exotic—you can get them right in the supermarket. In fact, you probably eat them already but haven't been aware of just how much they can do for you.

By including more of these bargain foods in your daily eating plan, you can easily save enough calories to finally lose the 10, 20 or 30 pounds that you want . . . without ever going hungry.

The Sweetest of All

A rose by any other name may smell as sweet, but 240 calories of apple is two times sweeter to your appetite-control system than 240 calories of ice cream. That is just one surprise to come from this food study from the land Down Under.

In the study, students were asked to come in each morning and eat 240-calorie portions of a specific food. Then they rated their feelings of hunger or fullness every 15 minutes. At the end of two hours came the ultimate test of how satisfied the students really were: They were allowed to hit a buffet table and eat as much as they liked, while researchers took copious notes.

A number of foods were tested, and when the crumbs settled, it was very apparent that equal caloric portions of different foods do not equally satisfy hunger. Basing their ratings on a scale that assigned white bread an automatic score of 100, the researchers discovered that some foods are only half as satisfying as bread while others are actually three times more filling.

At the bottom of the Aussie list (in the middle of a grease stain) were croissants. With a rating of 47, they were barely more satisfying than air.

The star performer at the top of the scale was the not-so-modest potato. With a way-out-in-front rating of 323, it gave them the most bang for their caloric dollar, filling them up faster and on fewer calories than any other food tested.

Weight-Loss Magic

Before we take a longer look at which foods make your stomach the happiest on the fewest calories, let's look at how they work this minor miracle.

Obesity Gene Holds No Weight-Loss Magic—Yet

Recently, newspaper headlines told the story of the Ob Mouse—a rodent whose outrageous plumpness was the result of a broken obesity gene. When researchers injected this pudgy critter with the newly discovered substance leptin, the mouse slimmed down.

The news has left Americans hoping for a breakthrough in the battle of the bulge. Unfortunately, leptin seems to hold no immediate weight-loss miracles for humans.

Why? First, experts aren't sure if leptin functions the same way in overweight mice and overweight people. Second, even if an obesity-regulating substance is discovered, having a safe and effective drug on the market may be years away.

In the meantime, obesity experts note that even if you're genetically programmed to be overweight, two old-fashioned strategies—careful food choices and an active lifestyle—are still the best strategies for keeping pounds at bay.

"I don't care what your genetic predisposition is," says David Allison, Ph.D., assistant professor at Columbia University College of Physicians and Surgeons and an associate research scientist at New York Obesity Center at St. Luke's–Roosevelt Hospital, both in New York City. "If you don't eat, you won't become obese."

Accepting your unique body shape will also help. "There's far too much condemnation," notes Dr. Allison. "Work to accept yourself as fit, worthwhile and even beautiful, independent of your weight."

HEALTH FLASH

"The whole question of what makes a food satiating (satisfying to the appetite) is a complex one, and there are still many factors we haven't sorted out," admits Barbara Rolls, Ph.D., Guthrie chair in Nutrition at Pennsylvania State University in State College. "In some cases, a food satisfies because we believe it will satisfy. In other cases, it may be the taste, how quickly it is digested or the hormones it triggers."

But there does seem to be one constant we can take to the bank. "Foods with a low energy density are less likely to be overeaten than those with a high energy density," says Dr. Rolls. What is energy density? Simply the scientific terminology for how many calories a food packs for its weight. So your favorite chocolate bar has a high energy density because it weighs very little but delivers a whole bunch of calories . . . much to your dismay. On the other hand, a piece of apple of the same weight has a great deal fewer calories, giving it a lower energy density.

Looking back at the potato and the croissant, the mystery of why one is more filling than the other becomes a whole lot less mysterious once the weight of each is taken into account. Two hundred and forty calories of potato weighs in at about 13 ounces, while 240 calories of croissant weighs just over 2 ounces.

"The more weight or volume of food for a given amount of calories, the less likely you are to eat more calories than you need," says Dr. Rolls. "First of all, if you see more food on the plate, you automatically expect to be more satisfied. Second, it takes longer to eat, making the experience more substantial." A greater portion of food also stimulates various receptors around your gastrointestinal tract—receptors that eventually tell your body that it has had enough to eat.

And finally, eating more food distends your stomach, literally filling it until you either need to stop eating . . . or unhook your pants. But the weight-loss trick here is to find the foods that accomplish all of this for the fewest number of calories.

Foods That Won't Let You Down

To find the foods big on bulk but short on calories, let's get back to that Australian study.

The foods tested were arranged in six groups: bakery products, snacks and confectionery, breakfast cereals, protein-rich foods, carbohydrate-rich foods and fruits. Right off the bat, researchers found that certain food groups as a whole are more filling than others on an equal-calorie basis.

Fruits are number one with an average satiety index of 170. That means a fruit calorie is 70 percent more filling than a bread calorie. Next come carbohydrate-rich foods and protein-rich foods, which tied in a close second at 166. The third most filling group, at 134, is breakfast cereals, then snacks and confectionery at 100. The least satisfying of the bunch were

Weight-Loss Friends and Foes

Stomach growling? Here is how foods rate when it comes to satisfying hunger pangs. Choosing a food from the top of the list (high satiety-index scores) can fill you up while providing the fewest calories.

Food	Satiety-Index Score
Potatoes	323
Fish	225
Oatmeal	209
Oranges	202
Apples	197
Pasta, whole-wheat	188
Beefsteak	176
Grapes	162
Popcorn	154
Bran cereal	151
Cheese	146
Crackers	127
Cookies	120
Bananas	118
French fries	116
Bread, white	100
Muesli	100
Ice cream	96
Potato chips	91
Peanuts	84
Candy bar	70
Doughnut	68
Cake	65
Croissant	47

baked goods, turning in a poor rating of 85 on the satiety index.

But each group had its star performers, as well as a few duds. Apples and oranges came out on top in the fruit category. Their satiety-index scores of 197 and 202 make them twice as appetite-fulfilling as bread (which, if you remember, had a score of 100). Not surprising, considering a 240-calorie portion of orange weighs nearly 1½ pounds. Low on the fruit-basket totem pole were bananas with a satiety index of 118—not much better than bread. Again, no surprise since 240 calories of banana buys you only less than half the bulk you get with an orange.

In the carbohydrate-food category, we already know the winner—good old Mr. Potato Head, whose score of 323 mashed all competitors. The next best: whole-wheat pasta, though it placed a distant second with a rating of 188. In last place was potato again, but this time as french fries. Thanks to their swim in oil, fries contain about four times the calories as an equal weight of boiled tater.

For a low-cal but more filling food in the protein category, you can't beat fish, which gets a healthy score of 225. Yes, it even beats beefsteak, which rates at 176. The fact that these protein foods are so satisfying is something that your own experience has probably taught you. And research agrees, says Dr. Rolls: Protein definitely knows what buttons to push in your appetite-control system.

The most filling snack you can reach for is a handful of popcorn. At a rating of 154, it is still 50 percent more satisfying than white bread. But from there, the whole snack category goes downhill fast. Ice cream rates only a 96, followed by potato chips at 91, peanuts at 84 and a candy bar at 70. The problem in this category is clear: Too much fat or sugar makes these foods so calorie-dense that a few mouthfuls may blow your weight-loss budget.

Finally, you can forget about filling up without filling out when it comes to baked goods. The most satisfying food here is crackers at 127, followed by cookies at 120, doughnuts at 68, cake at 65. . . and the previously mentioned croissant in dead last place of all the foods at 47.

No-Hunger Slimming

The simple fact of the matter is that if you want to lose 10 pounds by this time next year, you'll need to cut about 100 calories a day (or cut 200 a day for 20 pounds, 300 for 30 pounds). The foods we have just explored can help, and here's how.

If instead of eating 300 calories of french fries you ate 100 calories of baked potato, not only would you feel just as full, but you would have also cut 200 calories right there. Reach for an apple at breakfast instead of a croissant, and again you'll feel fuller but save yourself more than 100 calories. Or try oatmeal instead of a doughnut. It will get you through the morning with fewer calories.

For late-night munchies, opt for popcorn over potato chips. You'll feel more satisfied and slash nearly three-quarters of the calories.

And here's another bonus. These filling foods don't just satisfy you at the moment. They can continue to satisfy you for up to two hours after the meal.

Remember the Australian experiment? At the end of two hours, the students could hit the buffet table and eat all they wanted. But the ones who ate the more-filling foods ate less.

While the current research has only just begun identifying specific foods that fill you up for less calories, you can find some on your own. "Look for foods low in dietary fat," says Dr. Rolls. "They tend to provide more bulk for the calories. Also go for high-fiber foods like vegetables and fruits—again, they will fill you up for fewer calories."

New Lessons from the *Real* Weight-Loss Experts

N ationwide surveys say that on any given day, one out of every three women is trying to lose weight. We fast, skimp on calories, count fat grams, join weight-loss programs, take supplements, pop diet pills and run, walk, bounce and swim in our quest for svelte and healthy silhouettes. And we do lose weight—sometimes even lots of weight. Some of us lose it permanently, but many regain those dreaded pounds within a few months or years.

Why do some women succeed where others don't?

Those who report lasting success at weight control used various action plans—from limiting fats in their diets to exercising regularly or making subtle changes in the way they viewed food. In fact, many credit their success to a combination of very simple but surprisingly effective strategies.

Their triumphs over yo-yo weight patterns conform to what experts are finding about long-term weight loss. Strategies that succeed seem to have seven elements in common, according to John P. Foreyt, Ph.D., director of the Nutrition Research Clinic at Baylor College of Medicine in Houston, and G. Ken Goodrick, Ph.D., assistant professor of medicine at Baylor.

These elements are:

▸ Realistic weight goals
▸ "Normalized" eating routines
▸ Exercise

- Social support
- Focus on health rather than appearance
- Enhancement of overall self-esteem
- Control of binge eating (sometimes through therapy)

More and more, diet experts are asking women how they have lost weight—learning lessons from real life. Here some techniques that have worked, with commentary from weight-loss experts.

A Social Life, Not Another Cookie

Lorraine, age 50, lost 40 pounds

Lorraine says that when she was a child, "my rotund Italian Grandma would pinch my cheeks and ask my mother in dismay, 'Don't you feed her?'"

Lorraine abhorred becoming a "skinny, flat-chested teenager" (as she described herself), and she responded by eating rich, fat-laden foods that gave her voluptuous curves. But at size 16, she found herself unhappy and unhealthy.

"In terms of food addiction, I bottomed out after a holiday binge and a big-time New Year's depression," Lorraine notes. She found a support system in the form of a friend named Jerry who had already lost weight and gave Lorraine much-needed pep talks on the telephone.

Why it works: Lorraine is to be commended for taking control of a difficult problem, says Peter D. Vash, M.D., Ph.D., assistant clinical professor of medicine at the University of California, Los Angeles.

For many women, says Dr. Vash, weight is an issue deeply rooted in childhood, entwined in genetics and firmly bound to family expectations and heritage. Lorraine set out on her own path, re-educated herself about food and managed to avoid turning to food for comfort when things got tough. In Jerry she found a role model she could emulate, rather than slipping back to food, her family's solution to every problem.

"To cope with your problems, start by confronting them directly," Dr. Vash says. "To solve problems, think them through. Food never solves anything."

Shape Up!

Regina, age 40, lost 35 pounds

"I've lost my fat from being on a low-fat diet (15 percent of calories coming from fat) and exercise, exercise, exercise," says Regina.

Why it works: When it comes to maintaining weight loss, the evidence in favor of a low-fat diet plus a regular exercise plan is overwhelming. One reason, of course, is that you decrease the calories you eat and increase the calories you burn.

But researchers suspect there is an additional factor at work: Scientists at the University of Pittsburgh speculate that the magic may be in the flexibility of a diet/exercise regimen. A woman who slips up on her diet can compensate by stepping up her exercise regimen.

Establish New Habits

Michelle, age 32, maintains a healthy weight

"My diet changed dramatically for the better when I had a roommate who only cooked healthy foods," says Michelle. "I adopted her diet and found my body preferred it to the diet I had grown up with (lots of meat and a few overcooked vegetables). I eat a low-fat, low-sugar, high-carbohydrate diet to maintain consistent energy levels and to fuel my sports-intensive lifestyle. I eat small, frequent meals throughout the day."

Why it works: By moving into a new household, Michelle snipped the ties

The Key to Successful Weight Loss

The most important factor in successful pound-paring isn't simply diet or exercise. According to a new study from the University of Rochester in New York, it's self-motivation.

When the researchers tracked the weight-loss histories of 128 extremely overweight women and men, they found that dieters pressured by friends or family members did not keep the pounds off. The same was true for women and men who pressured themselves to lose weight through guilt or humiliation.

The dieters all took psychological tests to determine if their efforts were self-driven or simply encouraged by others. Then, researchers checked with them two years later. Folks who were self-motivated by positive reasons, such as a healthier lifestyle, were most likely to succeed—regardless of age, gender or starting weight.

"Those who were the most self-motivated or autonomous lost the most weight and maintained the greatest weight loss over a two-year period," notes researcher Geoffrey C. Williams, M.D., Ph.D., assistant professor in the Departments of Psychology and Medicine and part of the Human Motivation Research Group at the University of Rochester in New York.

The bottom line? The researchers say the best time to attempt weight loss is when you are truly ready—not when you do it because of pressure from yourself and others, however forceful. Where there's a will, there may well be a way. But the will has to come from within.

HEALTH FLASH

to her family's poor eating habits, says Maria Simonson, Ph.D., Sc.D., director of the Health, Weight and Stress Clinic at Johns Hopkins Medical Institutions in Baltimore. "Habit accounts for a great deal of poundage," she says. Michelle's roommate led her to an eating plan that makes scientific sense. Similarly, a roommate who has faulty eating habits can influence a woman for the worse, says Dr. Simonson.

Researchers in Britain found that carbohydrates act powerfully on people's perception of how full they feel. Adding a carbohydrate to your breakfast, for example, is likely to curb your hunger for two to three hours and reduces the likelihood that you'll crave a midmorning snack. Eating the same amount of a high-fat food with your breakfast won't produce the long-term feeling of fullness, called satiety.

Low-Fat Spells Success

Carol, age 47, lost 20 pounds

"I don't buy foods that aren't healthy or low-fat," says Carol. "Then when I raid the refrigerator or cupboards, at least my choices are healthier. Now if I eat a high-fat food—like a cheese steak, for example—my digestive system lets me know it. My mind and taste buds want it, but my body doesn't."

Why it works: Scientific evidence is mounting in support of the theory that it may be the amount of fat a person eats, not the amount of total food, that makes the difference in weight loss. A variety of studies have shown that people can lose weight by cutting fat, even when they are eating the same number of calories. Intriguing research from the University of Minnesota hints that avoiding specific foods (hot dogs, beef, sweets, dairy products and french fries) may result in more impressive weight reduction than avoiding fats in general.

Carol is right, by the way, when she notices that heavy, fatty meals don't sit well with her anymore, says Robert Kushner, M.D., director of the Nutrition and Weight Control Clinic at the University of Chicago. Eating a lower-fat diet with little or no meat has conditioned Carol's stomach to expect healthy, reasonable portions, he says. When she suddenly eats a big beef sandwich, "her stomach gets distended because it's not accustomed to the high-fat load."

Portion Control Was the Key

Jean, age 41, lost 15 pounds

"After years of failed attempts to control my weight and eating habits, I consulted a nutritionist, who taught me the difference between a normal portion and what I was eating," says Jean. "I'm Italian. I come from a background where we eat large amounts of pasta, for example. It was a shock to me that a half-cup of spaghetti is considered a portion. So I started measuring everything.

"The nutritionist also showed me that what I was eating could use some improvement," says Jean.

Why it works: Experts have observed that people who carefully monitor their food intake—actually measuring their food portions and counting fat grams, for example—have greater success in dieting than those who guesstimate or do not keep track of quantities. And Jean's misjudgment of portion sizes is all too common.

In a study conducted at St. Luke's–Roosevelt Hospital and Columbia University in New York City, people who said that they were unable to lose weight even on restrictive diets were carefully monitored by researchers for two weeks while keeping their own records of their diets and activity levels. Unwittingly, the people who felt that they were "diet-resistant" underreported the amount of food they ate by an average of 47 percent. They also overestimated their physical activity by 51 percent.

If you really want to lose weight, seeing a professional, as Jean did, is one way to go, says Dr. Simonson. Many times a professional, such as a registered dietitian recommended by your doctor, can point out hurdles to progress that you can't see in yourself, she says.

Never Say Diet

Joyce, age 46, lost 45 pounds

"A few years ago, I was depressed and sought counseling," says Joyce. "One of my problems was poor self-image. The therapist suggested that I stay away from the scale and start walking for 10 minutes a day. As I walked, I did a lot of thinking. My 10-minute walks increased to 20, 30, then 40 minutes.

"I thought, why not try to eat healthy and see if I could reduce my cholesterol level? I read a pamphlet on controlling cholesterol and followed the suggestions. My cholesterol level dropped 84 points. As an added bonus, I lost 45 pounds!" says Joyce.

"Walking compensates somewhat for my indulgences," she notes. "I don't think of myself as being on a diet, because then I'd think 'failure' and put myself down. My goal is to get healthy, mentally and physically."

Why it works: Joyce got good advice from her counselor, says Dr. Foreyt. "Regular physical activity improves well-being, self-esteem and a sense of control. All of those components helped her stabilize her eating habits and put food in its proper perspective in her life. Exercise works, not only because of the calorie expenditure. It's the psychological component, changing your outlook," he says.

Joyce is also doing herself a favor by avoiding a "diet mentality," since experts say that "going on a diet" implies short-term deprivation that tends to give way to old eating habits. In fact, a study conducted at the University of Minnesota found that over a two-year period, women who were dieting gained weight, as compared to co-workers who weren't actively trying to lose weight.

A Food Routine

Barbara, age 55, lost 60 pounds

"Every morning, I eat a half-cup of cooked oatmeal with a half-cup of skim milk," says Barbara. "I eat three prunes and drink a cup of green tea on my way to work. For lunch, I eat a salad—usually spinach—with onion, tomato, black olive slices, grated carrots and broccoli pieces. I dip my fork in the dressing and then stab the salad. I also eat about half a can of tuna in water, drained and mixed with several spoonfuls of low-fat cottage cheese and chopped onion. For dinner," says Barbara, "I have either pasta and a vegetable or meat and one vegetable."

Why it works: Like Barbara, many women manage to lose weight by eating the same foods each day, ordering the same foods at lunch and putting the same things in their grocery carts each week. Experts call this strategy "sensory-specific satiety."

If a rigidly structured diet is based on the food guide pyramid—emphasizing grains, fruits, vegetables and beans and going easy on meat, sugar and fat—it probably can be followed without unhealthy consequences, says George L. Blackburn, M.D., Ph.D., associate professor of surgery at Harvard Medical School and chief of the Nutrition/Metabolism Laboratory at New England Deaconess Hospital, both in Boston. "And it can unquestionably lead to short-term weight loss," he says. "That's because it's very boring. Food loses its appeal, so you don't overeat."

The New ObesityDrugs: Are They Right for You?

I f you've ever tried—and failed—to get slimmer, you've probably fantasized about a magic pill that would solve your weight problems for good. Well, it's not available yet—but researchers think they've taken a step in the right direction.

That's heartening, given that some of the latest diet news has been grim: How much you weigh, scientists have revealed, seems to be based as much on who you are as on what you eat. Weight problems appear to be programmed into our genes, hard-wired into our brain chemistry. But these findings may be a blessing in disguise: They are finally putting an end to the depressing notion that plumpness is simply a sign of lousy willpower.

They are also leading scientists to develop new (and potentially more effective) ways to attack fat. Here is a look at some promising methods.

Better Dieting through Chemistry

Recently, researchers at Rockefeller University in New York City announced that they had discovered an obesity gene in plump mice and that a similar gene, along with a handful of others like it, may be responsible for up to 60 percent of weight problems in humans.

Scientists hope ultimately to screen people for defects in the obesity gene, then prevent weight gain by replacing flawed specimens with a perfect version.

At Amgen, a Thousand Oaks, California, biotech company, researchers are already working on a method of supplying overweight people with more of the protein produced by the obesity gene. They've been experimenting with giving doses of the protein to overweight mice.

"It appears to be working," says company spokesperson David Kay, although it's too soon to tell which overweight people will benefit from the protein. "It could be only people who are severely obese—or it could be everyone," says Kay.

The New Weight-Loss Prescription

Not all the new fat-fighters are so far in the future. Prescription diet pills, disdained for decades, are getting a second look. One, dexfenfluramine (Redux), was approved by the U.S. Food and Drug Administration (FDA) last spring—the first new weight-loss drug to win approval in more than a decade.

But before that, some doctors were helping patients lose weight with a combination of two existing prescription appetite suppressants, fenfluramine (Pondimin) and phentermine (Adipex-P). The downside: The drugs stop working when patients stop taking them, and little is known about the health effects of using them for more than a few months.

The antidepressant fluoxetine (Prozac) is also sometimes prescribed, though studies have not yet demonstrated that it helps keep weight off for the long term.

No one knows exactly how these drugs diminish appetite, but the buzz is all about a brain chemical called serotonin, which seems to promote a sense of satiety. Fluoxetine, fenfluramine and dexfenfluramine are thought to curb the desire to eat by increasing levels of this chemical. (Serotonin-boosting drugs have also been studied for their ability to dampen cravings for other unhealthful forms of satisfaction such as cigarettes.)

And more prescription diet drugs are on the horizon: The FDA has indicated that it will make it a top priority to evaluate other new diet drugs that are awaiting approval.

"Mind-Altering" Milk Shakes

At least one researcher is trying to find a nonpharmaceutical way to lift serotonin levels.

Judith Wurtman, Ph.D., a biochemical nutritionist at the Massachusetts Institute of Technology in Cambridge, believes that overeating is often an attempt to increase serotonin levels with carbohydrate-rich foods. (Consuming carbs leads to a serotonin surge.)

Dr. Wurtman is developing a drink made from extracts of high-carb foods, such as potatoes, that would naturally boost serotonin levels—and squelch cravings. It is currently being tested on women who overeat when they are under stress.

Is High-Tech Weight-Loss Right for You?

Some overweight people are leery of these futuristic diet strategies, recalling past diet drugs that were highly addictive and didn't keep weight off permanently. It's true that the new therapies, though probably more effective in the long run, won't be risk-free.

For example, one study found that dexfenfluramine caused brain damage in monkeys. And a small percentage of patients taking the fenfluramine-phentermine combo have suffered short-term memory loss.

Even those in favor of the experimental approaches are quick to point out that the treatments should be reserved for people who are truly overweight and for whom other weight-loss methods have failed. (In other words, they're not for someone who just wants to drop a few extra pounds.)

But should overweight people who appear perfectly healthy try the therapies as they become available? What about the people who aren't fat now but

Dieter, Beware of New "Thin" Pill

The U.S. Food and Drug Administration (FDA) recently approved dexfenfluramine, a new prescription anti-obesity drug that sells under the trade name Redux, for treating obesity—a decision that has intrigued millions of women who see themselves sailing into a size six and staying there forever.

But let the dieter beware: the FDA cautions that Redux is no magic fat-melter. An appetite suppressant, it is intended only to boost the results of a doctor-supervised program of diet, exercise and behavior modification.

Many unanswered questions surround Redux. Could you take it forever? And if you don't, will the pounds stay off once the prescription runs out? No one knows for sure.

And you can pretty much forget Redux if you're hoping to shed five to ten pounds. The FDA advises doctors to consider it only for obese patients or those with special risk factors such as diabetes or high blood pressure.

While some diet medications are used just at the beginning of a weight-loss program, Redux has been tested on dieters who used it for up to one year. The results? According to the FDA, its most serious side effect is a rare lung disorder called primary pulmonary hypertension. Other side effects such as dry mouth, sleep disturbance and diarrhea are mild or short-lived.

Still, the FDA says that you should be under a doctor's supervision while using this appetite-suppressing drug.

HEALTH FLASH

worry that they may be in the future? Opinions differ, even among experts. After all, there's the danger that these treatments will be offered to people who don't need them—and will be used to promote thinness rather than health.

Yet hope remains that for genuinely overweight people, science will soon produce the first fat-fighting treatments that actually work.

A New Look at Drugstore Diet Pills

New findings about prescription diet pills have sparked an interest in the over-the-counter variety—already a $125-million industry, with women ages 18 to 29 among the biggest consumers of these nonprescription appetite suppressants.

The active ingredient in over-the-counter appetite suppressants is similar to phentermine. Both medications create a temporary energy boost that helps some people overcome hunger; however, the nonprescription varieties are less potent.

Drugstore diet aids may work for a few days or weeks, but can be ineffective if used long-term and dangerous if taken at higher-than-recommended doses.

And "as soon as you stop taking the drugs, the weight comes back on," says Richard Atkinson, M.D., director of the Obesity Program at the University of Wisconsin Hospital and Clinics in Madison. "That's why those taking this type of drug should be followed by a doctor."

Over-the-counter diet pills are taboo if you have diabetes, high blood pressure or heart problems, and they shouldn't be mixed with caffeine. Like any diet method, they should be combined with healthful eating and exercise—and used with caution.

Break the Emotional Eating Cycle

Jane's children are tucked in bed. The last fiery argument with her husband is extinguished. As she has on many previous nights, Jane huddles at the kitchen table, eating all night long. Chocolate. Homemade bread. Leftover spaghetti.

"I ate whatever there was," recalls Jane, 56. "I could never get enough."

Likewise, Sue's self-esteem was as fragile as a porcelain teacup. Sharp words and imagined slights sent her racing to the freezer for ice cream (lots of it). "I was eating to push down anger and depression," Sue, 50, a photographer's assistant, says. "I thought I needed a goody, a treat. Years later I realized that eating was really a punishment—I was making myself fatter."

Barbara, 47, a busy manager at a utility company, roars up to a convenience store after work. She has just finished a big project, and once again, it's treat time. She picks a hefty slice of cheesecake.

"It feels good at the time," Barbara says. "But the next day when your skirt won't button anymore, you say, 'Oh my God, why did I do that?'"

Emotional Numbing

Like Jane, Sue and Barbara, most of us turn to food once in a while to satisfy emotional needs—to fulfill a hunger of the heart or quell what Sandra Campbell, a doctor of psychology and director of the Eating Disorders Program at the Brattleboro Retreat in Vermont, calls a hunger of the soul.

It's not that our stomachs are growling. We may be angry, depressed, anxious or sad or feel that our self-esteem has been punctured. We may be avoiding intimacy. We may eat during lulls in our hectic schedules—like when we walk through the door after work. And sometimes munching goes along with procrastinating, so we eat to avoid paying the bills or making a decision. Or we may even be pleased with ourselves and, like Barbara, celebrate the occasion with a treat.

"Emotional eating is a way to manage overwhelming feelings," says Dr. Campbell. "Some women literally fill themselves up with food, and it becomes an emotional anesthetic."

Who is most vulnerable? Studies show that so-called restrained eaters—women who diet or strictly control food intake to maintain a low weight—seem especially susceptible, responding to strong feelings by reaching for something to eat. Yet no one is immune.

Solace by the Spoonful

If you're feeling particularly blue on occasion, there is no real harm in taking solace in a pint of soft double-chocolate-chip ice cream—if it happens once in a blue moon. Eating in response to emotional cues can release tension.

The key is to not overeat, which in itself can cause guilt. "By overeating and then feeling guilty about it, you create another tension. This is how a vicious cycle develops," says Connie Roberts, R.D., manager of nutrition consultation services and wellness programs at Brigham and Women's Hospital in Boston.

Routinely using food to distract yourself from, disguise or detour around inner feelings has definite physical and psychological downsides, says Mary Anne Cohen, director of the New York Center for Eating Disorders and author of *French Toast for Breakfast: Declaring Peace with Emotional Eating.*

The downsides? Guilt and shame about enjoying food and an empty, never-satisfied feeling because needs for love, passion, independence, self-confidence, achievement, freedom or a sense of belonging are not being truly satisfied.

"Emotional eating is like a red flag going up, telling you that there's something deeper you need to attend to," says Dallas physician Frank Minirth, M.D., co-author of *Love Hunger: Recovery for Food Codependency.*

The upside? Breaking patterns of emotional eating will leave you free to experience your true feelings, to more easily reach and maintain a healthy weight and to savor food to the fullest—even the occasional goody—without guilt or shame.

"The range of foods that a person likes tends to increase as they stop compulsive overeating and become healthier with food," says Hoyt Morris, Ph.D., director of the Oklahoma City Center for Eating Disorders. "The sense of taste tends to become more pronounced. Foods taste better."

Trigger Points

When Ronette L. Kolotkin, Ph.D., a clinical psychologist and director of behavioral programs at the Duke University Diet and Fitness Center in Durham, North Carolina, asks women in her weight-control classes to describe how food satisfies them, the answers are rarely about nutrition. Food, they say, is: A best friend. Unconditional love. Comfort. Escape. A pick-me-up. Sexual fulfillment. A tranquilizer.

When Dr. Kolotkin asks which emotions would make them stray from a well-balanced diet and regular exercise program, two are at the top of almost every list: anger and stress. "Yet few women are aware of the connection between what we eat and how we're feeling, unless they really look for it," she says.

Here's what you can do to unveil this often-ignored connection.

Keep a food/mood diary. Angry and stuffed? Write it down. Uncovering those connections is the first step toward curbing problem eating and satisfying buried emotional needs, says Edward Abramson, Ph.D., professor of psychology at California State University in Chico and author of *Emotional Eating*.

"Carry a small notebook or three-by-five card in your pocket or wallet," he says. "Then, if you find yourself eating unnecessarily and it seems related to an emotional experience, write down what you ate and what you were feeling or thinking and note your location and who was around you."

After you've monitored emotional eating for a week or so, patterns may begin to emerge. Perhaps you eat when you're depressed or anxious or angry or bored or lonely. In some cases, food can even be a substitute for sex and intimacy.

Ask yourself why you reach for food when you do. "Maybe you're anxious because you're getting ready to host a big party on Saturday night. You worry that there won't be enough food and everyone will dislike you, that no one will come and you'll be a social failure, that no one will talk to each other and you'll feel awkward," says Dr. Abramson. "These thoughts can contribute to a stressed or anxious feeling. If you can teach yourself to be a little more realistic, the feelings don't have to be quite so intense and negative."

Identify the triggers that make you eat. Using your food/mood diary—or mentally reviewing your personal emotional eating patterns—pick out recurring interactions with people or situations that send you running to the candy machine, suggests Dr. Minirth.

Eat regularly, not impulsively. Dr. Kolotkin says that you can also uncover triggers by eating on a regular schedule.

"An unaware emotional eater is probably popping something in her mouth often," she says. "But if you eat on schedule, then find yourself wanting food an hour after lunch, you can say, 'Wait. This isn't necessary. What's going on here?'"

Halting a Feeding Frenzy

Overcoming emotional eating can be especially challenging for women who are faced with conflicting messages about food, weight and body image. "How do we make sense of a culture that promotes slenderness, yet advertises seeking comfort through food?" asks Dr. Campbell.

Still, you can sort it out—even when the desire seems overwhelming, say experts. If you feel drawn to the candy machine or the refrigerator when you know that you are not hungry, experts suggest the following on-the-spot rescue techniques.

"Lite" Chocolate Might Satisfy Your Cravings

There's a brand-new choice at the candy counter: Instead of the gooey, crunchy, creamy, nut-studded chocolate bars you grew up with, you can now reach for sweet treats that are lower in fat.

Call them "choco-lites." From Hershey's Sweet Escapes Chocolate Toffee Crisp Bar to M & M Mars's Milky Way Lite (and there are plenty more), these confections weigh in with five to eight grams of fat apiece—33 to 50 percent less fat than the average amount found in leading chocolate brands. But chocolate fans, take note: The new reduced-fat bars aren't calorie-free—they weigh in with about 150 to 190 calories apiece.

And if the candy makers are to be believed, these "low-guilt" chocolates have the same soul-satisfying qualities as higher-fat varieties, too. But can they help you quell a chocolate craving without padding your hips? Actually, you can eat any type of chocolate without gaining weight—provided that you remember to cut fat elsewhere and indulge in moderation, says nutrition consultant and dietitian Connie Diekman, R.D., of St. Louis, Missouri.

A reduced-fat bar may make the job a little bit easier, "but you have to be honest with yourself," she says. "If what you really want is a block of solid chocolate, a reduced-fat bar may not satisfy you. Then, you run the risk of eating more fat and calories afterward, until you're satisfied."

Ask yourself what it is about chocolate that meets your needs, she suggests. Is it the creamy, rich texture of the candy or just the chocolate flavor?

If it's simply the chocolate flavor, you may be satisfied with a low-fat hot chocolate drink or a fat-free brownie. But if it's a candy-bar experience that you crave, then try a light bar with attributes that match your needs. "I haven't heard anyone say that they can tell the difference between a regular bar and a reduced-fat bar," Diekman says.

HEALTH FLASH

Talk to yourself. "Tell yourself, 'This feeling will pass whether I eat or not,'" says Cohen. One reason some women cannot tolerate discomfort is that they are sure the discomfort will last forever. You need to realize that feelings have a beginning, a middle and an end, explains Cohen. You must understand that your depression will end.

Solve the problem. What is prompting you to reach for food at the moment? A tight work deadline? A conflict with a spouse? A crying child? Try to focus on solving the problem, rather than avoiding it with food, suggests Dr. Minirth.

Take a time-out. For ten minutes, resist the urge to nosh and ask yourself what's going on. Take the opportunity to figure out what's behind that craving, says Dr. Campbell. And make it a habit to tune in to your inner feelings at these times.

Reach out and call someone. A brief phone call to a friend or relative may distract you and provide the emotional connection you really crave, says Roberts.

"You don't have to tell them you were about to eat four chocolate cupcakes," she says. "Just chat. It helps."

Delay. In advance, come up with a list of alternative activities to do when the eating mood strikes, suggests Dr. Abramson. At work, tack the list to your calendar. Distractions that usually work include reading your mail or flipping through the newspaper.

At home, sew a button on that skirt that's been out of commission for months. Polish your navy blue shoes. Repot your favorite fern. Do one small thing—but make it an activity that can compete with eating. (Cleaning the oven probably won't cut it.)

Enjoy new treats. Celebrating a personal achievement? Had a good day at the office? Lost five pounds? Indulge in a manicure, pedicure or facial; take a bath in your favorite bath salts; relax with a new book; sign up for a low-fat cooking course.

"I suggest women try things that they used to like as kids, or just try new things," says Dr. Kolotkin. "One woman started horseback riding again. Another joined a soccer league for enjoyment."

Practice safe snacking. We all need an emotional pick-me-up once in a while. Try satisfying your need with tasty foods that don't load on the calories. This approach also keeps you from fearing the foods you desire.

"I have patients practice buying one chocolate truffle and enjoying it to the utmost," says Roberts. "Sometimes denying yourself the one thing you want can lead to eating more calories somewhere else."

Plan. If you must eat, tell yourself in advance what snacks you'll turn to when emotion-driven episodes occur, says Roberts. Possible examples, she says, include a muffin with jelly or air-popped popcorn. Picking and choosing what you do instead of eating anything in sight reminds you that you are still in control.

Nourishing Your Heart and Soul

After keeping a food/mood diary for a couple of weeks, says Dr. Abramson, you'll probably be able to identify specific feelings that make you eat. Here's how to deal with them.

Don't beat yourself up. Pay close attention to your inner voice and give yourself positive messages, not self-criticism.

"We think 450 to 1,200 words a minute. If you turn your thoughts against yourself, it's like a laser beam on the heart that will literally destroy you," says Dr. Minirth. "Be realistic. If you make a mistake, ask yourself what you can learn from it. If you're having a difficult time, don't say, 'I'm done for.' Instead, tell yourself, 'This is tough on me right now, but things will work out.'"

Confide in others who are supportive. Talk with friends and family or join a support group for problem eaters, such as Overeaters Anonymous. "Many emotional eaters feel ashamed of their feelings and thoughts," says Dr. Kolotkin. "It's so helpful to have supportive friendships, people who can say, 'Oh, I know what that feels like, too. You aren't alone'"

Listen to your anger. You may have grown up hearing that anger is not polite or fearing an angry parent. As a result, you may not recognize your own anger.

Try using time-outs before eating to see if, in fact, you are angry. Then what should you do? Talk it out with a friend—a neutral third party—before confronting the object of your anger, suggests Sheryl Russell, R.N., Ph.D., a psychotherapist in Knoxville, Tennessee, who studies women's eating issues. Why should you do that? It may keep you from blowing up.

Make time for self-reflection. If you're always busy meeting the needs of your spouse, your children and your boss, when do you meet your own? Make time to ponder, to keep a journal, to clarify your goals and priorities— to respond to your inner self.

"If you don't stop and reflect, you're going to ignore a lot of emotions," notes Dr. Kolotkin. "And if you ignore emotions when they're mild, they'll only get stronger and hit you over the head. But if you monitor your emotions regularly, they won't loom so large."

Learn—and look ahead. One emotional eating episode is not the end of the world, says Dr. Russell. Learn from it. Recognize your vulnerable states and anticipate trigger events, she advises. Then take steps and seek support to do things differently next time.

The Seven-Meals-a-Day Diet

I nstead of stuffing yourself at two or three meals a day, it makes far more sense to eat less at each meal and eat more often, according to new research published in the *New England Journal of Medicine* and the *American Journal of Clinical Nutrition*.

Sounds hard to believe, yet it's true. Eating healthful, low-fat between-meal snacks increases your energy and metabolism, triggering an energizing process that produces heat and burns calories. Eating these snacks—or mini-meals—also reduces the urge to overeat, especially at night.

During the day when you go for four to five hours at a stretch without eating, your blood sugar levels drop and your energy wanes. It may take a strong dose of willpower just to get out of your chair, let alone exercise.

According to new studies, moderate-size meals plus small between-meal snacks may help lower blood cholesterol levels, reduce body fat, enhance digestion, lessen the risk of heart disease and increase metabolism. In one study, researchers found that people who ate more frequently had lower cholesterol levels than those who ate just a few big meals. Furthermore, their cholesterol levels went down even though the more frequent eaters consumed more food during the day.

The Three-Plus-Four Eating Plan

There are many good scientific reasons why it is time for most of us to change not only *what* but also *when* and *how much* we eat.

The large, traditional American meals that stimulate excessive insulin production essentially build up the body's strongest pro-fat hormone. A burger and french fries—or any high-fat variations on this theme—promote fat storage. Such meals also speed the conversion of sugar to body fat.

In contrast, moderate meals and between-meal snacks promote a steadier production of sustained energy. This eating plan also promotes fat burning and tends to produce a smaller, healthier insulin response.

It is important to note that this eating plan still allows for the normal and necessary storage of some body fat, which is vital to health. Yet the plan is targeted to prevent the storage of needless, excess body fat.

The plan changes that by altering not just when and how much you eat but also what you eat. If you follow this plan, keeping your calorie intake moderately low for each snack and meal in the Three-Plus-Four Eating Plan, you'll satisfy your appetite while stoking your energy system at just the right intervals.

Eat Seven Times a Day

"Eat three square meals a day" was the old advice, but it came from another era. Today you're much better off eating three low-fat meals and three or four low-fat snacks every day. Research now points to the conclusion that this pattern—not the three-square plan—will help you turn on the fat-burning power, keeping your body fat to a comfortable minimum.

How do you do it? Keep mealtime calories to less than 500—with a maximum of 25 percent of those calories from fat. But in addition to the three meals, you should treat yourself to at least two—and up to four—snacks during the day, at two- to three-hour intervals. All snacks should be lower in calories, and therefore lower in fat, than the meals. If you space your meals and snacks and stick to the recommended calorie levels, you'll help keep the calories stored as excess fat to an absolute minimum.

Snack Time's the Right Time

There are many other good reasons for snacking. Since ancient times, people have instinctively and traditionally taken a pause several times a day to make tea and consume a favored serving of food. Then, while enjoying each sip and every bite, they look out at the horizon or share a warm conversation or reflect on the path just traveled. It is through these simple actions that the day—and life—remains in a bit better perspective, and one of the simplest and healthiest of human pleasures is not forgotten.

Few choices provide greater rewards, no matter how fast the world seems to be moving. So here are some guidelines for taking low-fat snack breaks—yes, even in the rush of twenty-first-century life.

Scatter your snack attacks. Snacking on low-fat foods throughout the day has considerable weight-loss advantages, observes Dean Ornish, M.D., assistant clinical professor of medicine at the University of California, San Francisco, School of Medicine and president and director of the Preventive Medicine Research Institute in Sausalito, California.

By eating low-fat snacks at midmorning and midafternoon, you're less likely to stuff yourself at main meals or lapse into stress-related eating binges in the evening.

Keep favorite snacks nearby. Adults make an average of 20 to 30 food decisions a day, according to George L. Blackburn, M.D., Ph.D., associate professor of surgery at Harvard Medical School and chief of the Nutrition/Metabolism Laboratory at Deaconess Hospital, both in Boston. Therefore, it is critically important to have low-fat snacks readily available to make your between-meal food choices as easy as possible.

If the only food on hand is a monster soda and a bag of chips or a huge candy bar, you may end up consuming 50 to 60 grams of fat or 1,000 calories all at once, just because you grabbed what was convenient.

Make teatime your snack time. Many, if not most, people are better off with low-fat snacks at midmorning and especially at midafternoon, says Richard N. Podell, M.D., director of the Overlook Center for Weight Management in New York City.

As the day wears on, what and when you eat take on increased signifi-

Variety Lengthens Life

Does a boring diet limit your life span? When researchers at Queens College of City University of New York looked at the diets of 10,337 women (and men), they found that people with the most monotonous diets also had the shortest life spans.

Women who scored low for "dietary diversity" were usually skimping on the fruits and vegetables. Putting these foods back in the picture may simply be a matter of thinking about fresh produce first when planning a meal, says study leader Ashima K. Kant, Ph.D., professor of nutrition at Queens College.

In other words, instead of saying to yourself, "I have this wonderful cut of meat, what can I serve with it?" start with something like, "I have this beautiful broccoli and these nice grapes, what can I serve with them?" Dr. Kant suggests.

How varied must your food choices be to get the longevity edge? Going way out isn't necessary—diets with variety don't have to be filled with chervil, jícama or emu fillets (unless you want them). But do go beyond eating, say, apples and pears every day.

"It will help to eat foods from all food groups every day," Dr. Kant says.

HEALTH FLASH

cance, because metabolism gradually starts falling off. An afternoon snack helps to boost the glucose supply that you need for energy, according to Dr. Podell. "Eating at this time helps you handle the midafternoon blood sugar dip," he notes. "Also, an afternoon snack helps keep your blood sugar levels steady, so you won't become ravenous by the time you eat dinner."

In mid- to late afternoon the brain has a strong tendency to crave high-fat, high-sugar foods. It is important to head off the pattern of having a high-fat, late-afternoon snack or a high-fat dinner. That too-hearty dinner, especially, sets off signals that prime you to consume far more fat late at night.

Turn the fat down low. Generally, the snacks to choose have less than five grams of fat per serving—and an even better target may be three grams per serving. And if you're eating a packaged low-fat food, be sure to read the label carefully to find out exactly what is meant by a "serving." Remember, if you overeat snacks—even fat-free ones—you may end up converting existing calories into body fat.

Pare the calories. Though fat comes first, you need to keep an eye on calories as well. Even if you're eating nonfat food, the calories can increase quickly if you eat fast or go back for a second or third serving.

Dole out the dried fruit . . . slowly. The problem with dried fruit is that it's so tasty! This food is so easy to munch—and leaves you eager for more. Not only that, it seems so healthy. Just fruit that has been dried—what could be more naturally delicious?

Well, here is the surprise: If you munch about 20 pieces of dried fruit— which is easy to do—you may consume as many as 500 to 1,000 high-sugar calories. Even though the sweeteners in the fruit are natural, those handfuls of fruit can shift your fat-forming processes into overdrive.

"Fruit sugar causes significant increases in blood fats (triglycerides) in some people," explains internist John A. McDougall, M.D., founder and director of the McDougall Program at St. Helena Hospital in Santa Rosa, California. "These fats are the very ones stored in fat tissues. Fruit also stimulates insulin production, which stuffs these fats into fat cells."

Even fruit juice can be a problem when you consume lots of it. "Processing fruit into sauce or juice disrupts and/or removes fiber, increasing the speed of absorption and the amount of carbohydrate absorbed by the bloodstream," says Dr. McDougall. "Fruit puree such as applesauce raises insulin more than whole fruit."

Spurn the sly sweets. Studies suggest that synthetic sweeteners may reinforce your taste for sweet foods. "Artificial sweeteners may impede weight loss by increasing hunger," warns Dr. McDougall.

It is thought that in large quantities the fake sweeteners may decrease the level of serotonin, which is one of the chemicals that signals to the brain, "I'm full! Don't eat any more!" At the same time, the sweeteners may increase insulin, with the usual result of reducing fat burning.

Avoiding sweeteners, however, does not mean that you have to ban them completely. On occasion, you may want to have an artificially sweetened food or drink or use very small amounts of sucrose or table sugar.

Dodge the fake fats. Substitutes for fat are being tested all the time, and there is no telling when the next breakthrough will come.

"Fake fats may be a shot in the arm for manufacturers, but they are no answer to America's weight problems," warns Neil Barnard, M.D., faculty member at George Washington University School of Medicine and Health Sciences in Washington, D.C., president of the Physicians Committee for Responsible Medicine and author of *Food for Life*. "Not only is their safety in doubt, but these additives reinforce the taste for fatty foods rather than help you break the habit."

Snack for sharpness. Eating smaller, nutritious meals and snacks throughout the day helps to stabilize blood sugar levels, which in turn optimizes memory, learning and performance, according to psychologist and

Snacks That Attack Fat

One of the lucky things about the Three-Plus-Four Eating Plan is that so many low-fat snacks are included. At first, you may have to change your shopping patterns somewhat—and even visit a few new food stores—to gather an interesting range of tempting low-fat snacks, but there are many to choose from.

Here are some suggestions to help make up your list—and these are just for starters. Step into the fresh fruit and vegetable section when you're looking for snack food, and you'll find specials that change with the seasons.

The quantities given here are for one good, solid low-fat snack. For fresh fruits and vegetables, however, no quantities are given since it's almost impossible to go overboard with those foods.

▶ One thick piece of 100 percent whole-grain bread topped with nonfat cream cheese and 100 percent all-fruit preserves. Some favorite breads include Ezekiel Sprouted Grain Bread, Shiloh Farms 100, Shiloh Farms Sprouted Wheat Bread, Vermont Bread Company's 100 Percent Whole-Grain Bread and Wild's Whole-Grain Bread. Also be sure to try any locally made whole-grain breads carried by supermarkets, farmers markets and health food stores.

▶ A whole-rye cracker or bagel with nonfat cream cheese or nonfat cream cheese and a piece of fresh fruit

▶ A whole-wheat English muffin with all-fruit preserves and nonfat cream cheese

▶ A whole-wheat English muffin with nonfat mayo and a thin slice of part-skim cheese such as Jarlsberg light Swiss

▶ A Health Valley Fat-Free Whole-Grain Muffin or Snack Bar

▶ A low-fat, whole-oats granola bar

▶ One to three pieces of RyKrisp, Wasa Crispbread, Scandinavian-style bran crispbread or another whole-rye cracker with all-fruit preserves and/or nonfat cream cheese

▶ A whole-grain bagel with one teaspoon of Dijon mustard, one teaspoon of nonfat mayo and two slices of turkey breast

▶ A whole-grain bagel with one teaspoon of Dijon mustard, one teaspoon of nonfat mayo and two thin slices of part-skim cheese such as Jarlsberg light Swiss

chronobiology researcher Ernest Lawrence Rossi, Ph.D.

By taking a break to snack, you allow your mind and body to resynchronize, Dr. Rossi notes. "Oxidative waste products and free radical molecules that have built up in the tissues during preceding periods of high performance and stress are cleared out of the cells. The stores of messenger molecules so vital to mind/body communication are replenished, and energy reserves are restored."

Treat yourself on occasion. One of the great tastes to emerge from the new generation of light, lighter and lightest foods is low-fat or nonfat chocolate. Since it's available, why not have some once in a while?

On a cold winter's afternoon, make a cup of fat-free hot cocoa with skim milk—or for a summertime treat, add fat-free chocolate syrup to ice-cold skim milk. For true chocolate lovers, one or two chewy chocolate fat-free whole-grain brownies or cookies can be just as good as the real thing.

- A Nature's Choice Whole-Grain Fat-Free or Low Fat Snack Bar
- One to three whole-grain cookies such as Health Valley Fat-Free Cookies
- One to three fat-free rye or other 100 percent whole-grain crackers spread with fat-free bean dip
- One cup of nonfat plain yogurt with fresh, unsweetened frozen or canned fruit
- A half-cup of nonfat, old-fashioned whole-oats granola served with skim milk or yogurt
- One cup of low-fat or nonfat yogurt sweetened with fruit juice
- One cup of tomato soup, made with skim milk, and two whole-rye crackers
- One cup of old-fashioned oatmeal with skim milk and one teaspoon of brown sugar
- A quarter-cup of nonfat ricotta cheese topped with a handful of nonfat whole-oats granola
- Four ounces of nonfat frozen yogurt
- A half-cup of 1 percent low-fat or nonfat cottage cheese with fresh, unsweetened frozen or canned fruit
- Eight ounces of tapioca pudding, made with skim milk
- One cup of nonfat or low-fat bean, lentil or vegetable soup, such as Progresso, Pritikin or Healthy Choice products
- A variety of fresh-cut raw vegetable and fruit pieces with three whole-grain crackers, served with a nonfat dip or dressing
- One piece of angel food cake with unsweetened fresh berries
- One piece of whole-rye or whole-grain bread with one teaspoon of nonfat mayo and two ounces of water-packed albacore tuna
- Eight ounces of unsweetened orange juice with a small low-fat, whole-grain muffin. (If it is store-bought, read the label to make sure it is low-fat.)
- One celery stalk stuffed with one tablespoon of nonfat cream cheese or cottage cheese
- One apple or other fresh fruit with three whole-grain crackers
- Sliced fruit and berries mixed into a half-cup of nonfat plain yogurt or nonfat cottage cheese

If your taste buds whine for chocolate ice cream, you may occasionally choose a fat-free frozen chocolate fudge bar, which delivers the flavor but not the fat of chocolate.

Savor it all. The bottom line is if you want to burn off excess body fat and think, feel and perform at your best all day long and well into the evening, make it a priority to take a low-fat snack break at midmorning, midafternoon and midevening.

Use these minutes to stop what you're doing and step off the fast track. Look out the window, walk outside and find a quiet spot to lift your vantage point and savor some food and drink that you love.

As simple as it sounds, few of us make this choice. And we pay the price for it every day—not just in lessened fat-burning power but in our personal effectiveness, relationships, mental outlook and life satisfaction.

BODY SCULPTING

Part 6

To wage war against fat, you have to be a calorie-burning machine.

—exercise scientist
Bryant A. Stamford, Ph.D.

Female Advantage

That's Not Vacuuming, It's Aerobics

If you're worried that you'll slow down with age, relax. A new study shows that women in their fifties to mid-sixties are a more active bunch than their male counterparts.

When California researchers asked 357 women and men, all ages 50 to 65, to wear heart monitors round the clock for three days, they discovered that the women spent more time doing moderately intense physical activity. Women were active 17 percent of the day; men, 11 percent.

The women also sustained a mid-intensity level of activity longer— 20 minutes at a time, compared to 15 minutes for men, according to the study, called the Stanford/Sunnyvale Health Improvement Project.

"Based on our research, women were more active than men well into advanced middle age," says researcher Deborah Rohm Young, Ph.D., assistant professor of medicine at Johns Hopkins University School of Medicine in Baltimore.

Seemingly mundane household chores may play a role in keeping women on the go. In Dr. Young's study, just 67 percent of the women studied were employed outside the home, versus 87 percent of the men. That means that while there were fewer women going to work every day, a greater proportion exerted more physical effort—most likely performing common household tasks.

What's the health benefit of this activity? For starters, increased activity leads to higher levels of "good" high-density lipoprotein (HDL) cholesterol—associated with a decreased heart disease risk. That's good news since heart attacks are the primary cause of death for women.

Active women are also less likely to gain weight. And according to Dr. Young, people feel better about themselves after exercising, leading to an increased sense of well-being and accomplishment.

For those who don't have the time or inclination to work out at a health club, performing daily household tasks could help to attain those benefits. Here are five ways to get the activity edge at home.

- Vacuuming, strenuously for 30 minutes
- Walking up and down the stairs, continuously for 30 minutes
- Brisk walking around the house, perhaps dusting as you go
- Strenuous gardening
- Bicycling to and from the grocery store at a moderate pace

Walking: Everybody's Doing It!

Women love walking. In one new nationwide poll, 57 percent of women rated walking as their favorite physical activity. And that's good news. Fitness experts say that walking is a great way to firm up and slim down. But how can you turn a love for walking into a lifetime weight-loss plan?

The latest research not only shows that the land of thinness is reachable by putting one foot in front of the other, it also suggests how many steps away it is.

Of course, the research also shows that the journey is one that needs to be made regularly. You'll have to walk today, tomorrow, next year . . . and ten years from now. In other words, walking must become a permanent part of your life. And, as with anything in life, you can make it easy on yourself or you can make it downright impossible to maintain.

Let's go for easy, okay?

How Often, How Long, How Hard?

Research conducted over the past several years has consistently shown that walking is an excellent way to maintain weight loss. Now a recent study conducted at William Beaumont Hospital in Birmingham, Michigan, has given us an idea of just how much walking may be involved.

In the study, 45 obese people were put on a very low calorie diet and experienced an average weight loss of approximately 61 pounds. Two years later, this same group was not only reweighed but also questioned as to their daily exercise habits. As you might imagine, the people who were in the low-activity group (burning less than 850 calories a week in exercise) gained back much of the weight—72 percent of what they had lost two years earlier.

Surprisingly, the moderate-activity group (burning a more respectable 850 to 1,575 calories per week) fared even worse, regaining 75 percent of the weight. But here's the kicker: The high-activity group, burning more than 1,575 calories, gained back only 24 percent of what they had originally lost; and for those burning more than 2,000 calories, a mere 13 percent.

"The majority of the people we studied achieved these results by walking," says Charles Lucas, M.D., chief of the division of preventive and nutritional medicine at William Beaumont Hospital. "But the real story is the difference between the amount of weight regained by the moderate-activity group and the high-activity group. It suggests that there is a definite dose that's required to keep the weight off."

And the dose starts at around 1,575 calories burned a week. Let's call it 1,600 for good measure. How does it translate into time spent hoofing it? A person weighing 130 pounds burns about 320 calories by walking four miles in an hour. Walking at that pace five times a week adds up a grand total of 1,600 calories burned. So you have your target: an hour a day, five times a week, walked at four miles per hour. Or, to make it simple, walk 20 miles per week.

Read This Before You Slip into Your Sneakers

An hour a day? Five times a week? For the rest of your life? Who has that kind of time to spend meandering around the local park system?

"Well, just ask yourself this," says James Hill, Ph.D., associate director of the Center for Human Nutrition at the University of Colorado Health Sciences Center in Denver. "If you could make an extra $5,000 a week in only five hours, would you do it? You bet you would. So you do have the time . . . it's just a matter of seeing exercise as being every bit as valuable as that $5,000."

You can't start an exercise program that you intend to make permanent without doing a little thinking first. And as Dr. Hill aptly points out, one of the things that you need to think about is how to make exercise seem like something you just can't do without. So before putting on your walking shoes, consider the following:

Give it value. Sure, the real reason that you're going to start walking is because you don't want to have to lose the same 20 pounds over and over again. But exercise provides many other goodies as well. It can help lower your blood pressure and cholesterol levels. It can also reduce your risk of heart attack and stroke.

"And all the benefits are not strictly physiological," adds Dr. Hill. "Exercise can help you sleep better, feel more relaxed and even keep your moods on a more even keel."

Make it irresistible. Unfortunately, all the information in the world, both positive and negative, is not going to keep you exercising throughout your lifetime if you hate the activities that you're doing.

"In other words, you have to choose an activity that you really love to do," says Rod Dishman, Ph.D., professor in the Department of Exercise Science at the University of Georgia in Athens. "Weight maintenance is a long-term goal that, on a daily basis, is not strong enough to get you out of bed. But if you have fun doing what you're doing and it makes you feel good . . . and you miss it when you don't do it . . . that's what keeps you going back for more."

Give yourself a history lesson. If you're like most people, you've already had a past affair with exercise that for some reason or another ended in divorce. Why? Did you dislike the exercise you chose? Scheduling problems? Not enough support from friends and family? Figure it out fast because those who do not learn from history are doomed to repeat it.

Consider your environment. "When people talk about getting support for their exercise program, they mostly mean support from family and friends," says William McCarthy, Ph.D., director of science at the Pritikin

Move More, Eat Less

In a new study from the University of Chicago, weight-loss researchers have found that women who add a three-times-a-week workout to a reducing-diet program are less likely to indulge in diet-busting overeating.

The study compared 30 women on a 12-week weight-reduction diet. All overate once in a while. But the 13 women who did a 45-minute workout of their choice three times a week gave in to the munchies less often than the 17 women trying to slim down through diet alone. Plus, those working out lost an average of two pounds more.

Working out has long been associated with peeling pounds off your body. But this is the first time a study has suggested that getting to the gym may influence what goes on your dinner plate, says study leader Dale A. Schoeller, Ph.D., associate professor of medicine at the University of Chicago.

Motivation may have been fueled by the dream of getting into spandex at the gym. It could have been that exercisers had less time to spend staring at the fridge. In fact, it could have been nearly anything—more studies have to be done before the cause can be determined. But Dr. Schoeller speculates that greater likelihood of sticking to an eating plan probably has to do with the mood-boosting effects of exercise.

"The ability to stay on the diet could have come from the increased feeling of self-control that comes with exercising," he says. "Also, they're making a bigger investment in the program and thus may be willing to make a little more investment in terms of the diet."

HEALTH FLASH

Longevity Center in Santa Monica, California. "But your environment can also provide support . . . or a lack of it."

But your environment is not an insurmountable obstacle if you plan ahead, says Dr. McCarthy. "We encourage people who come to the Pritikin Center from northern climes to get a treadmill. That way, when bad weather hits, they're covered," he says. "Likewise, mall-walking is another good suggestion: It's safe and warm."

Get a backup. It's hailing golf balls. They are drilling for oil on your favorite walking path. Your cat just had kittens in your right shoe. In other words, you don't feel like walking today. "We always encourage people to have an alternative activity that they enjoy," says Dr. McCarthy. "That way, minor injury, boredom or unforeseen circumstances don't break the routine."

Make it a great big deal. Tell your family, your friends and the people you work with that a new exercise program is about to be born.

"The reason a lot of commercial and university weight-loss programs work is because the participants know they are going to be weighed and watched," says Dr. Hill. "It's called accountability. You want to make sure someone you know asks questions every so often to keep you honest."

Finally, keep it simple. One of the big mistakes that beginners make is being overly optimistic concerning their motivation. Are you really going to get in the car after dinner and drive over to that lovely park on the other side of town, take an hour walk and then drive home . . . every night? Probably not.

"The more steps you have to take to exercise, the less chance you will actually do it," says Tedd Mitchell, M.D., medical director of the Cooper Wellness Program at the Cooper Aerobics Center in Dallas.

From Zero to 20, Very Slowly

All right. It's time to pump some pavement to the tune of one hour a day, five times a week, four miles per session. And that's what you'll do right from the start no matter how much it hurts, right?

Wrong. You're going to be doing this for the rest of your life. So, what's the rush?

"It's been found that people who start out exercising moderately are twice as likely still to be exercising at the end of a year as people who start out at high intensity," says Dr. McCarthy. "We only suggest starting out at even a moderate level if it feels comfortable. The best way to make the best beginning is a step approach. Do what feels good and build from there."

Sensible advice. Here are a few more tips not only to get you going but to keep you going as well.

Take it by the numbers. "In any exercise program you want to first establish frequency, then duration and then intensity," says Dr. Mitchell. "In other words, the first thing you should do is try to walk five times a week, even if it is only for five minutes at a time," he says.

Trying for five small workouts makes sense for a number of reasons. "We are creatures of habit," says Dr. Mitchell. "You want to get yourself used to the idea of walking five days a week, incorporate it into your schedule and make it feel natural before taking on a more challenging workout."

Once you're walking five days a week, make each walk longer until you're doing an hour at a time.

Pamper yourself initially. "The first four to eight weeks is the critical time period that determines whether you quit or keep going," says Dr. Mitchell. "Conversely, it's also the period when exercise isn't quite delivering the rewards it will be down the road. You may feel tired. You may feel a little sore. It's less than motivating, so you'll want to pamper yourself a bit."

Get a calendar specifically for walking and give yourself a gold star on each day that you do it. Lay out your exercise clothes within easy reach at the beginning of the week so that there's no scrounging to do it at the last minute.

Don't fret about your progress. "The more time you spend worrying about whether or not you're walking fast enough or burning enough calories, the less time you spend enjoying the walk," says Dr. Hill. "Just get out there and do it. As your fitness level rises, you'll naturally find yourself walking farther, walking faster and burning more calories."

Do it in the morning. "We find that people who work out in the morning are more likely to have better long-term adherence than those who wait until evening," says Dr. Mitchell. It may be because morning schedules are a little easier to control than evening ones.

Do a little if you can't do a lot. There will be days when, for one reason or another, an hour-long walk seems as likely as a Beatles reunion. In cases like this, the best thing that you can do for yourself is to try for at least ten minutes—that way, you don't break the shape up habit.

Get yourself two pairs of walking shoes. The one thing that you'll want to avoid is having to take a few days off due to sore feet since there is always the chance that those few days will stretch into weeks, months and years.

A Routine to Shed a Size

One of the most important new fitness discoveries is that well-toned muscles serve a vital role in the distribution of fat. They act as fat-burning furnaces 24 hours a day, providing a remarkable metabolic boost.

"To wage war effectively against body fat, you need to be a good calorie-burning machine 24 hours a day, and having adequate muscle tissue is the only way to do that," observes Bryant A. Stamford, Ph.D., exercise scientist and director of the Health Promotion and Wellness Program at the University of Louisville in Kentucky.

Many of us seem to have accepted the "fact" that we have to fight a battle against waistline flab—and too often we view this single battlefield as the Waterloo of our campaign. To remain slim and fit, however, you will have to look past your abdomen to all the other major muscles in your body.

Here's why: Your body comes with a built-in warranty. If you consistently use all your muscle groups in adulthood—as well as when you're a child—those muscles will remain firm, flexible and well-balanced throughout your life. You'll look good, feel energetic and burn more calories, all the time.

Muscle loss begins in the mid-twenties. If you're sedentary, you have been losing muscle at the rate of about a pound a year since age 25 or so. And even if you have exercised regularly for many years, doing aerobic activities such as walking, jogging or cycling, you have still lost some valuable muscle since that time.

If your lean mass steadily decreases, so does your resting metabolism. As a result, your body needs fewer and fewer calories to function, and the excess calories are more easily stored as body fat.

Calorie Gobblers

By toning your muscles you raise your metabolic rate so you burn more fat, even when resting. And different exercises tone the muscles in different ways.

Taking the prize in most categories are the exercises involved in resistance training. This is any kind of training that involves lifting weights, even if they weigh just few pounds. (A big distinction: This is not Arnold Schwarzenegger–style muscle building—or anything like it.)

According to the latest guidelines from the American College of Sports Medicine, all it takes for solid, progressive strength-training results is a total of 15 minutes of strengthening exercises three or four times a week, using free weights, supported weight machines or body-weight calisthenic exercises.

Muscle-strengthening exercises are just as vital for women as they are for men, says Barbara Drinkwater, Ph.D., a research physiologist at the Pacific Medical Center in Seattle and past president of the American College of Sports Medicine, based in Indianapolis. "It's healthy that women are now accepting muscles as part of a normal human body."

Strength training confers other benefits on women, too, according to a study published in the *Archives of Internal Medicine*. Researchers reported that strength-training exercises for premenopausal women were associated with decreases in levels of "bad" low-density lipoprotein (LDL) cholesterol.

Strength Training Benefits Older Women

In a recent study, researchers at the University of Alabama at Birmingham found that even women past menopause gained strength, boosted muscle mass and lost fat when they raised a dumbbell or two.

In other words, you don't have to be young to benefit from a little strength training.

For this study, 14 women over age 60 worked out three times a week for one hour, doing 12 strength-training exercises. After 16 weeks, they had reduced tummy fat by 10 percent. That is important, because abdominal fat is linked to heart disease.

Participants found that the benefits extended into their day-to-day activities, providing added strength during recreation and family activities.

But there's more. "Strength training increased their metabolic rate, so they will be able to burn more calories and over time lose weight," says study leader Margarita Treuth, Ph.D., an exercise physiologist now at Baylor College of Medicine in Houston.

The good news is that you can get these benefits by exercising in one-hour sessions, three times a week, Dr. Treuth says. "If you stick with it," she says, "you'll see a change in strength in a month."

HEALTH FLASH

Getting Started

If you haven't done muscle-toning exercises before, it's easy to get into the swing of the routines. Here are some general rules to help you prevent injury and get the maximum muscle-toning, fat-burning benefit out of each routine.

1. Precede every strength-building session with some smooth, comfortable warming-up motions to increase blood flow and loosen your muscles and joints.
2. If you're using weights, you should know your one-repetition maximum (1RM) for each exercise and use weights that are 80 percent of that. One RM is the most weight you can lift with a single movement or muscle contraction. The amount of this weight varies from person to person, and it also varies as you become accustomed to the exercises. Once you know your 1RM, be sure to keep checking it every two to four weeks.
3. Listen to your body. If you feel any pain during a particular movement, stop immediately. Continue if the pain subsides, but only after reducing the amount of weight that you are lifting.
4. Use good posture and smooth, controlled movements and keep your breathing as even and steady as possible.

To maintain balanced posture throughout every movement, don't arch your back or use any twisting or turning motions that are not part of the exercise. Smooth movements are essential.

And never hold your breath while exercising, since that could cause an unhealthy rise in blood pressure.

5. Once you have worked up to it, go through two sets of five to ten repetitions of each exercise (a repetition, or rep, is the complete motion of an exercise).

The exercises take a total of about five minutes for each body part. It may be helpful to rest a few seconds between repetitions. If you have the ability, the desire and an extra few minutes, add a third set.

6. Cool down for at least several minutes after the exercise session. Keep moving as you ease back into your normal routine and let your heart rate and blood flow return gradually to their pre-exercise level.

Ab Solutions: How to Flatten Your Stomach

Okay, let's get to the waistline first.

Without a doubt, a slim, toned abdomen is the most sought-after symbol of success if you're trying to follow a healthy, low-fat eating and fat-burning exercise plan. When the abdominal muscles are strong and balanced, they flatten your waist and help hold your internal organs in place.

But you might not realize how much good it does your back to have well-toned abdominal muscles—or abs, as they're more often called. Strengthening the abs helps the back at a strategic point—the lumbosacral angle of the pelvis. Lower back pain often gets started or aggravated in this area, so the firming exercises could also help prevent future back trouble.

The following abdominal exercises are extremely effective. And as you'll see, a number of them can be done with variations. Whether you do all of them every day or repeat just a few is entirely your choice. Try all of them at first to get a feel for the ones that seem to benefit you the most.

Transpyramid Breathing Exercise

This exercise will help you build a toned, fit lower abdomen. It's called the transpyramid breathing exercise because of the two muscles it targets—the transversalis and pyramidalis.

1. Lie on your back with your shoulders relaxed and knees bent just enough that your feet rest comfortably on the floor. Place your hands on each side of your hips, with your fingers spread across your abdomen. The index finger of each hand should point to your belly button, but without touching it.

2. Take a deep breath and then exhale. As you breathe out, notice which way your lower abdomen moves. At the end of the exhalation you should feel your lower abdomen moving inward, toward your spine. This motion tells you that the transveralis and pyramidalis muscles of the lower abdomen are getting their workout.

3. Now inhale. Notice how your belly tends to "pop" outward against your fingers.

4. When you repeal, exaggerate to make a very clear distinction between these two motions—pulling your abdomen in and up during the exhalation, then "popping" your abdomen outward on the inhalation. (For muscle-toning, the key half of the movement is the exhalation phase.)

5. At the end of each exhalation, use the lower abdominal muscles to press

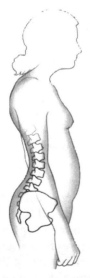

When you do sit-ups and leg lifts, the abdominal muscles may pull on the front of the lower spine, pushing out the lower abdomen.

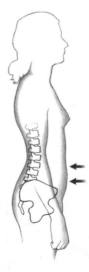

By doing the exercises in this chapter, you'll pull in your abdomen, flattening your belly.

that area inward even more. Then, on the next inhalation, consciously release the abdomen "out" against your fingers.

It's a good idea to learn this movement while lying on the floor in a comfortable position as shown. Once you have the exercise motion mastered, however, you can do it sitting or standing.

Variation: When you're seated and doing this exercise, you should be in an upright, straight-backed chair. Slowly exhale and, as you reach the place where you normally finish breathing out, smoothly and forcefully breathe out more, using the power of your lower abdominal muscles. At first you might use your hands to gently push up on the lower abdomen during the exhalation part of the exercise.

Repetitions: Work up to doing ten repetitions of this exercise each day. But they don't all have to be done at once. Fit them in wherever you can—one or two in bed before rising in the morning, several right before each meal or even at stoplights when you're running errands or driving home from work. They can also be done while standing up.

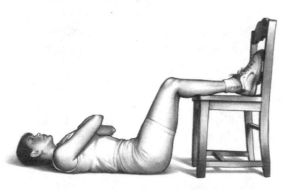

At the start of the abdominal roll-up, your upper body should be relaxed, with your arms crossed on your chest.

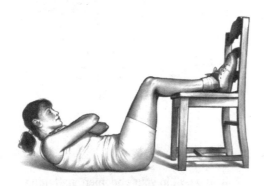

As you lift your head and shoulders, you'll feel the pull on your abdominal muscles.

Abdominal Roll-Ups

Also called crunches or curls, abdominal roll-ups are among the easiest and most effective exercises for toning your upper abdominal area. Here's how they're done.

1. Lie on your back with your knees bent, your calves resting comfortably on the seat of a chair and your feet free, as shown. (If you find that the chair seat isn't a comfortable height for supporting your lower legs, you can just bend your knees a little and place your feet flat on the floor.) Cross your arms on your chest.
2. With your middle and lower back still flat, slowly raise your head and shoulders off the floor about 30 to 45 degrees. During this movement, keep your lower abdomen flat. Make sure it doesn't "pouch out" during the upward movement.

3. Pause for a second at the top of the motion and then slowly lower yourself to the starting position.

When you're doing this exercise, make sure your legs and feet stay free. You might be tempted to secure your feet or legs under the edge of a sofa, but it's best not to do that. If your feet are held down, you're not doing the abdominal muscles much good: Instead, the hip flexor muscles take over the movement, and that can seriously stress your lower back.

Also be sure to keep your arms crossed in the position shown when you lift yourself. If they whip upward, the sudden motion may cause injury to the neck.

Repetitions: When you begin doing abdominal roll-ups, start very gradually. Do just a few repetitions, then take a break and see how you feel. As long as there's no serious discomfort or pain, over a period of weeks you can work your way up to 25 or more repetitions, three times a week.

Exhalation Roll-Ups

This exercise turns the transpyramid breathing exercise into a single abdominal-strengthening move. Have a look at the illustrations and then follow these guidelines.

1. Lie on your back with your knees bent and your feet flat on the floor. Your fingers should be spread on your lower abdomen with your index fingers pointing toward your belly button.
2. Do a roll-up exercise as shown, lifting only your shoulders and upper back from the floor.

3. At the top of the motion, gently force out an exhalation.
4. Pause for a two-second count before slowly returning to the starting position.

Repetitions: Work up to five or six repetitions, repeating the exercise at least three days a week.

To get into position for the exhalation roll-up, lie on your back in a relaxed position, breathing normally.

When you exhale and lift your neck and shoulders, the tension puts pressure on the abdominal muscles.

Reverse Trunk Rotations

Here is another proven exercise for abdominal fitness and good posture. This movement involves the external and internal obliques, a set of mid-section rotation muscles that help keep your abdomen slim and toned.

When you do reverse trunk rotations, you'll also strengthen the deep spinal muscles (multifidus and rotatores), the posterior spinal surface muscles (erector spinae) and an important lower back muscle, the quadratus lumborum. The full range of motion of this exercise builds both flexibility and strength in the waist and lower back, an ideal combination for helping to prevent injuries and back pain.

1. Lie on your back with your arms extended to the sides, as shown. Your arms should be perpendicular to your torso so that, if viewed from above, your body forms the letter T.
2. Bend your knees at a sharp angle, pulling your heels toward your buttocks with your knees together.
3. Maintaining the same angle at your knees, slowly lower your legs to one side until the outside of your lower leg lies flat on the floor.
4. Smoothly raise your legs to the starting position. Your arms and shoulders should remain in contact with the floor throughout the exercise to stretch and strengthen the internal and external obliques.
5. Repeat the movement, lowering your legs to the other side.

Variations: If your shoulders come off the floor as you lower your legs to the side, you may wish to have a friend gently hold them down as you do the exercise. If you still find the exercise difficult, use less knee bend. Or you might begin by having a partner support your knees as you gently lower them. With your partner helping, test both sides to assess your current strength and flexibility levels.

One rehabilitative medicine authority suggests another slight variation that could also make it easier. As you gently lower your legs toward the floor, let your knees come up

When you first try reverse trunk rotations, your heels should be as close to your buttocks as possible.

For the most benefit, try to maintain the same knee angle as you lower your knees to the floor.

toward your shoulders, suggests Rene Cailliet, M.D., chairman of the Department of Rehabilitative Medicine at the University of Southern California School of Medicine in Los Angeles.

As you get in great shape, you can pull in your heels more and more to raise your knees higher. The exercise becomes more difficult as your knees go higher, approaching a 90-degree angle to the floor.

Repetitions: Begin with very few repetitions and then gradually, over a period of weeks, work your way up to six to ten reps three times a week. Over time, gradually bend your knees more as you do the exercise.

Lower Back Muscle-Toning

Your posture and back strength can influence how much your abdomen protrudes and also whether or not you can safely, enjoyably perform other exercises without injury or tension-related fatigue. Here are a few simple exercises, each recommended by at least one medical specialist on back care, that can gently stretch and strengthen your back. If possible, perform these exercises two or three times a week on the days when you also do a five-minute set of abdominal-toning exercises.

A word of caution: It's best to do lower back muscle-toning only after you've warmed up with a brief walk or another form of low-intensity aerobics. Start with only one or two repetitions of each exercise. If you have a history of back problems or are currently experiencing back pain, consult your physician before doing these or any other exercises.

Single Knee-to-Chest Lift

This easy-does-it exercise helps stretch the muscles and connective tissues of your back and hip.

1. Lie on your back with both knees bent and place both your feet flat on the floor.

2. Lift one leg and raise the knee until you can grasp your thigh just below the knee with both hands.
3. Gently pull your knee toward your chest for a slow count of five. Relax.
4. Release your leg and slowly return it to the starting position.
5. Repeat with the other leg.

When you do the knee-to-chest lift, you should feel the stretch along your back and hip.

Repetitions: Six to ten with each leg.

Seated Lower Back Stretches

The advantage of these stretches is that you can do them almost anywhere—at home, in the office or even while you're waiting somewhere. Just don't try to do them too fast, wherever you are, since they really do stretch the lower back muscles to the max, and sudden movements can pull or strain them.

If you can't reach the floor with the palms of your hands, just stretch as far as you can—but don't bounce.

1. Sit in a firm-seated chair with your feet flat on the floor and your knees apart.
2. Slowly and gently bend forward, reaching down to place the palms of your hands on the floor.
3. Hold the down position for a five-second count.
4. Remember to breathe slowly and evenly.

Repetitions: Six to ten.

Pelvic Tilt Movements

This simple, relaxing exercise helps strengthen some of the front spine structures and stretch the back.

1. Lie on your back with your arms extended to the sides, your knees bent and your feet flat on the floor, as shown.
2. Gently press your lower back flat against the floor.
3. Hold for a few seconds.
4. Remember to use smooth, controlled muscle movements.

Repetitions: Six to ten.

By pressing the small of your back to the floor, you shift the position of your pelvis, which helps to align your back.

Chest, Shoulder and Upper Back Muscle-Toning

The muscles in your upper back and shoulder area are so closely inter-connected that it makes sense to work all of them in the same session. Three specific exercises—modified push-ups, chest and shoulder raises and chest crosses—are targeted to help strengthen and tone all the muscle groups. For best results, when you do one exercise for this area of your body, do them all.

Modified Push-Ups

This revision of a classic exercise strengthens muscles in your arms, chest, shoulders and back. Even if you can't lift your knees off the floor at first, you may be able to work up to regular push-ups gradually.

1. Lie facedown on the floor with your knees together.
2. Place the palms of your hands flat on the floor on either side of your chest, with your hands on the floor near the front of your shoulders.
3. Support the weight of your upper body on your arms and keep your knees in contact with the floor as you slowly raise your body.
  During this movement, keep your back as flat as you can.
4. Smoothly return to the starting position.

At the top of the modified push-up, your arms should be fully extended, but your knees remain on the floor.

Lower your upper body slowly, feeling the stretch in your shoulders and upper back.

Variations: To increase the strengthening effect on your upper arms and back, move your hands directly underneath your shoulders for the push-ups. If you want to increase the strengthening effect on your chest, move your hands slightly outward so they're positioned just a little wider than your shoulders.

Repetitions: 6 to 25.

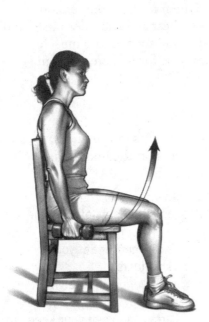

As you begin chest and shoulder raises, your arm should be relaxed and hanging straight at your side.

Keep your arm fully extended as you lift the weight, using the muscles in your shoulders and upper arm.

Chest and Shoulder Raises

For these exercises you'll need a small, handheld weight. Adjustable dumbbells come with small round plates that are weighted in two-, five- and ten-pound increments. But if you don't have dumbbells, you can start out by lifting a book instead. Another alternative is to pour water into a plastic milk or juice container that has a sturdy handle. Fill the container until it's the correct weight, then securely fasten the lid.

1. Sit upright in a chair with one arm at your side and the weight in your hand.
2. Keeping your elbow straight, slowly raise your arm forward and up.
3. Pause when your arm is fully extended almost above your head, but not quite perpendicular.
4. Slowly return to the starting position.
5. After you finish the repetitions on one side, do the same number with the weight in the other hand.

Repetitions: Six to ten. If you can't perform six correct repetitions without getting too tired to lift the weight, then it's too heavy and you should reduce it. If you can easily perform ten repetitions or more, however, you should gradually increase the weight.

Chest Crosses

Here is another exercise with weights that will give the muscles of the front part of your chest and shoulders an excellent workout.

At the start of this exercise, your forearms should be straight up and down, perpendicular to the floor.

Lower the weights slowly to the floor, keeping the tension in your chest and shoulders.

Lift your arms very slowly as you raise the weights, maintaining tension in your shoulder and chest muscles.

You can use a pair of equally weighted books or partially filled milk or juice containers if you don't have regulation adjustable weights.

1. Lie on your back on the floor with your knees bent and your feet in a comfortable position. Your lower back should be pressed firmly against the floor. Hold a weight in each hand above your chest as shown, with your elbows bent at 90-degree angles.
2. Extend your arms straight out, level with your shoulders, holding the weights in your hands with the palms up.
3. Keeping your elbows slightly bent, raise your arms very slowly and move them in an arc toward each other until the weights gently touch above the center of your chest.
4. Slowly move the weights apart and reverse the motion to bring them to the starting position.

Repetitions: Six to ten.

Upper Arm Muscle-Toning

The two toning exercises included here will help you work on both the front and back of your upper arm. For both you'll need weighted objects or dumbbells. The arm curls, however, can also be done with stretchy resistance cables, available in many sporting goods stores. As in other exercises that require weights, you'll need to experiment to find your ideal starting weight, then adjust upward as you get more proficient.

Arm Curls

This is a popular, easy exercise to strengthen the biceps muscle in the front of your upper arm and to help tone your forearms.

1. Sit on an armless chair or a bench.
2. Holding a weight in one hand, with the palm up, bring your forearm straight up toward your shoulder, keeping your elbow bent. At the finish of the motion, your palm should be facing your shoulder.
3. Slowly return to the starting position.
4. After finishing the repetitions on one side, move the weight to the other hand and do an equal number of repetitions.

Variations: In this exercise you can either lift both arms at once or alternate left and right. And you can vary the exercise by doing it with palms down.

There's also an isometric variation, which means pushing against an immovable object instead of lifting weights. The variation, which is easy to do at your desk, is recommended by Dr. Stamford. Sitting in a normal position, just push up against the underside or lip of the desk and exert pressure for six seconds. Repeated five to ten times, this isometric arm curl will aid muscle tone, according to Dr. Stamford.

Repetitions: 6 to 25.

At the start of an arm curl, your arm should be relaxed at your side.

You should feel the tension in your biceps as you bring the weight up to your shoulder.

Back-of-the-Upper-Arm Extensions

This basic exercise will help tone the triceps muscles at the back of your upper arms. You'll need a chair or bench to support your free hand when you lean forward.

1. Stand to the left of the support with your right foot slightly forward and your left foot back. Grasp a weight in your left hand and bend forward at the hips, placing your right hand on the support. Your torso should be almost parallel to the floor, with your back as straight as possible, as shown in the illustration.
2. Raise your left arm—the one holding the weight—until your upper arm is in line with your torso, with your elbow bent and your forearm hanging straight down. Your arm should be bent at nearly a 90-degree angle at the elbow and pressed lightly against your torso when it's in the correct lift position.
3. Slowly straighten your arm, lifting the weight backward until it's slightly above the level of your buttocks.
4. Slowly return to the starting position.
5. Move to the other side of the support. Put the weight in your right hand, place your left hand on the support and repeat the exercise with your right arm.

Repetitions: Alternate left and right, doing six to ten repetitions with each arm.

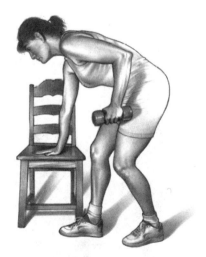 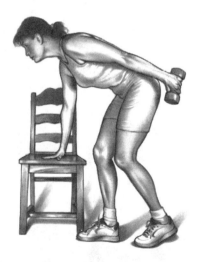

At the start of the extension, your upper arm should be close to your torso with your lower arm hanging straight down.

When you straighten your arm and raise it toward the horizontal, you'll feel the pull in your triceps muscle.

Thigh and Buttock Muscle-Toning

You can select any two or three of the following exercises, depending on how much time you have. Just be sure that whichever ones you choose, you go through each exercise correctly, without rushing. As you do these exercises, you'll feel the tension in the area that is getting the workout.

You can select the exercises that best target your personal muscle-toning needs.

Modified Knee Bends

This is a great do-it-anywhere leg-strengthening exercise. Although your thighs and buttocks get the biggest benefit, other leg muscles get a workout, too. For best results, you'll need to grasp the back of a stable chair, desk or counter for support, as shown.

1. Begin in a standing position, with your feet flat on the floor and shoulder-width apart.
2. Holding on to the support, slowly bend your knees and lower your body until your thighs are almost parallel to the floor. You should feel as if you're sitting in a chair.
3. Return to the starting position.
4. End the movement by raising your heels off the floor so that you're balanced on the balls of your feet.

Repetitions: 6 to 25.

Make sure you're standing erect—not leaning against the chair for support—when you begin to do modified knee bends.

As you bend your knees, keep your body aligned with your heels and your back as vertical as possible.

Seated Leg Extensions

For this exercise, you'll need a set of ankle weights, which are available in most sporting goods stores. Select a pair that is comfortably padded and easy to adjust to fit the diameter of your lower leg just above the ankle. Adjustable weights use small rectangular sacks of sand that slide into side compartments to increase the weight in half-pound or one-pound increments. If you have strong legs, you may want to use two ankle weights on each leg.

1. Put on the weights and sit on a chair or bench with your back straight and your feet firmly on the floor. Grasp the sides of the seat with your hands.
2. Raise one knee slightly to lift your foot off the floor. Raise and extend the lower part of your leg, straightening it until the entire leg is parallel to the floor. Hold for a count of four or five.
3. Hold the tension in your leg muscles as you slowly return the leg to the starting position.
4. Do one set of repetitions with one leg, then an equal number with the other.

Repetitions: 6 to 25.

Leg extensions can be done from a seated position on a chair or a bench.

You'll feel the tension all along the top of your thigh as you move your leg forward to a horizontal position.

Standing Side Leg Raises

You'll need some support when you do these leg raises. You can use a door frame or put your hand on a desk or tabletop for support. As your legs get stronger, you may use adjustable ankle weights. You can gradually increase the poundage on your ankle weights as your thighs get stronger.

1. Holding on to the support with one hand, raise the opposite foot off the floor and out to the side until you feel tension along the outer muscles of your thigh.
2. Hold this position for several seconds.
3. Slowly lower your leg a foot or so, but don't touch the floor.
4. Repeat the lifting movement.
5. After you complete a set of repetitions with one leg, switch positions and do an equal number of repetitions with the other leg.

Repetitions: 6 to 25.

When you're in the correct starting position, your upraised leg is straight and lifted off the floor.

Lean forward against the support as you bring your leg farther up and out to the side, putting tension on the thigh.

Hip Raises

This simple, effective exercise uses body weight and voluntary contractions to help tone the buttocks area. No weights are needed.

By the way, you can maximize your muscle-toning routine by performing hip raises, or other exercises from the thigh-buttocks strengthening set, three times a week—for example, on Tuesday, Thursday and Saturday. In the same workout, also perform abdominal toning, lower back toning and lower leg muscle-toning moves. Then, do back-strengthening and upper arm–strengthening routines on Monday, Wednesday and Friday. Try to fit transpyramid breathing in every day.

1. Lie on your back with your arms extended directly out from your shoulders and your palms flat on the floor.

   Bend your knees and place both feet flat on the floor. Your knees and feet should be slightly apart.
2. Slowly raise your hips and upper back while keeping your head, shoulders, hands, arms and feet on the floor.
3. Arch your lower back slightly and tense your buttocks. Hold for a few seconds.
4. Slowly return to the starting position.

   Repetitions: Six to ten.

At the start of the hip raise, your torso should be relaxed and flat on the floor.

Tighten your buttocks to lift your hips and your lower back all the way off the floor.

Lower Leg Muscle-Toning

You can easily tone the muscles in your lower leg with a single exercise—standing calf raises. You will need a piece of wood such as a two- by six-inch board (or two- by eight-inch) plus a pair of straight-backed chairs for support.

Standing Calf Raises

Place the chairs so you can hold the backs comfortably with arms outstretched. Stand between the chairs and hold onto the backs. Step up on the board so that your toes and the balls of your feet are positioned with toes pointed straight ahead. Your heels should be raised to the height of the board. Keep your back straight, knees slightly bent.

When you're positioned to begin calf raises, your back should be straight, your knees slightly bent.

1. Lower your heels as far below the level of your toes as is comfortable. Your heels don't have to touch the floor, but you should feel the stretch all along the back of your calf muscles. Make sure your heels don't roll outward.
2. Slowly rise as high as you can on the balls of your feet until your heels are elevated well above the level of the board.
3. Ease down to the starting position, with your heels lowered as close to the floor as possible.

Variations: Try doing the calf raises with one leg at a time.

To tone additional lower leg muscles, keep your knees straight rather than slightly bent. That will stretch a different group of muscles. (Keep up the repetitions until your calf feels too tired to continue.)

Or, alter the exercise by bending your knees during the downward motion. Then straighten your leg during the upward motion.

Repetitions: 10 to 50.

As you raise yourself on the balls of your feet, you'll feel the tension in your calf muscles.

The New Strategy for a Flat Stomach

Y ou lose a few pounds and do sit-ups until you drop—but your potbelly still looks like, well, a potbelly. In fact, it's as big and as noticeable as ever.

Sigh. No wonder that in one recent national survey, women named bulging tummies as the number one body part that they would like to correct. A flat stomach, it seems, matters more than sleek thighs, a firm derriere or trim upper arms. The frustrating thing is, a trim tummy seems so hard to get—no matter how many crunches you do.

The truth is that once you know a few secrets, you can achieve a flat, sexy stomach. You see, potbellies aren't just bumps on a log—they're complicated (and unsightly) phenomena made possible by several different factors. A few of those factors you can't control (like genetics). But most of them you can.

In addition to the obvious (like extra body fat and a high-fat diet that contributes to it), factors include the tone and strength of muscles in your pelvis, shoulders, chest, abdominal area and back. There are also the crucial variables of posture and the health of your spine.

Losing weight and doing sit-ups address only a small part of these factors. So what you need is a multifaceted frontal assault on the enemy.

Read on for the details. And be patient with your slowly shrinking belly: Experts say that it can take two to three months of concentrated effort to flatten a pot.

Posture Perfect

Anything that makes the spine curve can contribute to the pot by shortening the distance between your ribs and your hips. This pushes out your abdominal organs, launching a paunch. The longer your spine, the flatter your tummy. This principle operates on a temporary, day-to-day basis, but over time, good posture strengthens your back and abdominal muscles for longer-lasting results.

Stand tall. To elongate your spine, make like a marionette. Imagine a string tugging you from the top of your head toward the ceiling. Try to visualize this image often while walking and standing.

Use your chair as a throne. If you slump when you sit, you'll pouch out your paunch. For a regal sitting posture, a chair should fit your body. If your chair seat is too high to let your feet touch the ground without slumping, you're reinforcing a slack belly.

Find a footstool about four inches high. Placing a pillow in the small of your back helps bring you forward in your chair so that you won't have to slump to get your knees over the seat's front edge.

Suck in that gut. Simply staying conscious of keeping the abs tight acts as a steady exercise to keep them from slackening. This takes extra effort, so keep checking your form. As you tuck in your tummy, you elongate your spine, giving your abdominal organs more room inside the body so that they don't bulge forward.

Shrink Belly Blubber to Drop Blood Pressure

A new Japanese study offers evidence that women with an unhealthy "gut-to-butt" ratio—that's a big belly—don't have to take their excess risk for high blood pressure lying down.

Researchers from Toyonaka Municipal Hospital in Osaka, Japan, monitored the health of overweight women who lost fat in their midsections while on a 12-week low-calorie diet program. The women saw significant declines in their blood pressure, regardless of how many pounds they lost overall.

That's good news, because high blood pressure raises the risk of heart disease. And heart disease is the number one cause of death among women.

Deborah L. Wingard, Ph.D., professor of family and preventive medicine at the University of California, San Diego, School of Medicine notes that any woman who is shaped more like an apple than a pear would be wise to get regular blood pressure checks so that she can take steps to reverse it, if necessary.

"We know high blood pressure is controllable through diet, exercise—and sometimes, medication," she says.

HEALTH FLASH

Ab Toners

"The abdominal muscles are designed to contain our organs like a woven basket," says Willibald Nagler, M.D., physiatrist in chief at New York Hospital–Cornell Medical Center in New York City. "The rectus muscles run vertically, crossed by the obliques. As these muscles lose mass, they lose the force to restrain the gut."

The process accelerates in the decade after age 55, when women lose 15 to 20 percent of their muscle mass. But you can lose muscle tone at any age if you're not careful.

Dr. Nagler prescribes the following series of exercises to strengthen the abdominal muscles.

Do the head-to-knee crunch.

1. Lie on your back, knees bent, feet flat on the floor. Your arms should be straight, at your sides.
2. Bring your left knee up slowly toward your chest.
3. Begin to exhale slowly by counting to three as you lift your head and try to touch your forehead to your left knee. Hold this position as you count to six.
4. Return your head and foot to the floor.
5. Repeat with the right leg.

Repetitions: 12 with each leg.

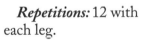

Try a double head-to-knee crunch.

1. While lying on your back, knees bent, arms at sides and palms toward floor, slowly bring both knees to your chest simultaneously.
2. Exhale and lift your head. Try to touch your forehead to your knees while counting to six.
3. Return head, then legs to floor.

Repetitions: 12.

Combine a crunch with a shoulder lift.

1. While lying on your back, knees bent, arms at sides, palms down, lift your right knee up toward your chest as you count to six.

2. Tuck your chin toward your chest, exhale, then lift your left shoulder off the floor, pulling it toward your right knee.

3. Return your left shoulder, head and then right foot to the floor.

Repetitions: 12 on each side.

Opt for an oblique crunch.

1. Lie on your back, knees bent, feet flat on the floor.
2. Rest your fingertips on your shoulders or at the base of your neck. (Be careful not to pull on your neck.) Breathe in through your nose.

3. Then, as you breathe out through your mouth, curl up and bring your left elbow toward your right knee, keeping your lower back on the floor.

4. Lower slowly.

Repetitions: Six on each side, alternating the right and left sides.

Do a pelvic tilt.

1. Lie on your back with knees bent, heels on floor with rest of foot up and arms on floor, stretched out away from your body. Press your lower back into the floor so that your pelvis tilts upward.

2. Maintain this tilt as you straighten your knees by slowly sliding your heels

along the floor. Stop when you can no longer hold a full tilt position.

3. Hold that position as you count to six.

4. Bring first one leg then the other back to the starting position, maintaining the pelvic tilt throughout.

5. Hold the starting position for six more counts. Relax.

Repetitions: 12.

Try the advanced pelvic tilt.

1. Sit on the floor with your legs outstretched in front of you.
2. Raise your heels off the ground as you bend your hips and knees. At the same time, reach forward with your arms like an oarsman.
3. Then bring your arms back toward your hips as you extend your knees and hips. (Don't try this exercise unless you have strong back muscles.)

Repetitions: Six.

Paunch Preventers

Ab-toning exercises alone miss another muscle group responsible for a prominent paunch: the hip flexors.

These muscles, which tip your hips, also help keep your tummy flat. As the hip flexors tighten, the hips roll back, making your paunch stick out. You must keep those muscles long and loose so your pelvis tucks neatly under your ribs.

Hug your knee.

1. Lie on your back with knees bent, feet flat on the floor.
2. Exhale as you bring both knees toward your chest.
3. Put your hands around one knee and clasp it tightly to your chest.
4. Slide the other leg down until it is flat against the floor, trying to touch the back of your knee to the floor. Hold while you count to six.
5. Slowly return to the starting position. Relax for a count of six.

Repetitions: Three with each leg, alternating the right and left legs.

Grab a foot and stretch.

1. Lie on your right side, resting your head on your arm, and bring your left heel toward the left buttock. Keep your bottom leg slightly bent.
2. Grasp the top part of your left ankle with your left hand and push the knee back, past the right leg. Do not arch your back.
3. Hold this position as you count to 15.

Repetitions: Three with each leg.

Body Straighteners

If your spine shortens—due to aging, osteoporosis, weak muscles, poor posture or any combination of these—it shrinks the back wall of your abdominal cavity, making your organs spill forward into an unsightly bulge. But you can help elongate the spine (and keep abs taut) by strengthening muscles in the shoulders, chest and back.

If you haven't been working out with weights, first try the exercises without using any. Then add a one- or two-pound set of dumbbells. Slowly increase the weight by a pound or two when you can easily complete the recommended number of repetitions.

Strengthen your shoulders. Your tummy sticks out more when your shoulders slope forward. Strengthening the shoulders helps keep them straight. Dr. Nagler's prescription is the overhead press.

1. Starting with dumbbells at shoulder height, sit on a straight chair or bench with your feet firmly on the floor.
2. Keeping your back straight, press the dumbbells to arm's length overhead, pause, then lower slowly to the count of six.

Repetitions: 12.

Build your chest. Strengthening your chest also helps keep your shoulders straight. Dr. Nagler recommends the bench press.

1. Lie on an exercise bench with knees bent, feet flat on the floor or on the bench.
2. Grasp dumbbells or a barbell with your hands slightly more than shoulder-width apart.

3. Slowly lower them to your chest to a count of six.
4. Press the weight up until your arms are fully extended, with elbows almost locked.

Repetitions: 12.

Try a power move for the upper back. Strong upper-back muscles keep your spine erect, tummy flat. Dr. Nagler recommends dumbbell bent rows to target a weak upper back.

1. Stand on your right leg, place your left knee and left hand on a flat bench (or chair) and lean so that you're facing the floor and your back is nearly parallel to the floor.
2. With your right hand extended toward the floor, pull the dumbbell toward your shoulder, hold momentarily and slowly lower to a count of six to the starting position (like starting a powered lawn mower, only slower and smoother).

Repetitions: 12 on each side.

Support your spine. This trunk raise strengthens the muscles that support your spine.

1. Lie on your belly with a towel rolled under your forehead.
2. Clasp your hands behind your waist and lift your head and shoulders, pinching the shoulder blades together.
3. Hold as you count to three. Relax.

Repetitions: Work up to ten.

Lift-up for a sleeker, stronger torso. Work those important torso muscles by lifting one arm and the opposite leg.

1. Lie on your belly with a towel rolled under your forehead.
2. Extend both arms overhead with elbows straight. Lift one arm. At the same time, lift the opposite leg from the hip. Be careful to avoid lifting so high that your body twists.
3. Hold as you count to three. Relax.
4. Repeat with the other arm and leg.

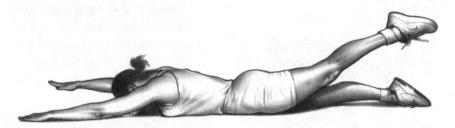

Repetitions: Work up to ten on each side.

Stop Making Excuses!

Y ou would love to work out, but day after day, you can't find the time. Your job goes into overtime, grocery shopping claims your hour at the gym or rainy weather calls off your weekend walk—leaving you without a free minute during the week to make up for it.

You're not alone. In a recent national survey of America's fitness habits, three out of four women told the President's Council on Physical Fitness and Sports that they would love to be more physically active—if they had more time.

But the truth is, the women who stay faithful to their exercise plans don't have any more hours in the day than you do. Or any more willpower. They don't need it. What they have is a habit. A routine. Exercise for them is like brushing their teeth. They don't spend a single brain cell making decisions about it. They just get up and do it.

And they feel great about it.

"It's been said that if you could put the benefits of exercise in a pill, it would be the single most prescribed medication in the world," says Kerry Courneya, Ph.D., assistant professor at the University of Calgary in Alberta and author of numerous studies on what makes people stick to an exercise routine.

No small part of those benefits is the effect of exercise on weight loss. Studies show that when people have lost weight and acquired an exercise habit, they're more likely to stay trim than are people who try to keep the pounds off through dietary changes alone.

Turning an exercise routine—and all its benefits—into a permanent resident in your life is a matter of housecleaning your priorities, setting up a schedule and toning up your motivation (until you're hooked, that is). Here is the plan.

Step #1: Make Fitness a Priority

Take a look at the priorities that are driving your calendar. Put exercise on that priority list. High on that list, right next to working and paying bills and watching Dan Rather.

"If exercise is my third priority and it's your fifteenth, you're not going to find the time to exercise, and I am," says Dr. Courneya.

"I often say that if you want to get to the top of the stairs, you must negotiate the steps," says time-management consultant Virginia Bass, who teaches people to organize their lives through the company Day Timers. "If you continue to put a lower priority on the task or activities required to reach your goal (exercising in the evenings, for instance) than on the goal itself (improving health, for example), then you're not going to make it."

Step #2: Find the Time

Try this: For about a week, write down where you have spent your time, as if minutes are checks that you're entering in your checkbook. This gives you a picture of how you're spending your time, says Bass.

Chances are, there are points that can be nipped and tucked to free a bit of time every day. Maybe you're on the telephone with a neighbor when you could both be walking around the neighborhood together. Maybe your Cable News Network addiction could be sated from the seat of a stationary bike.

If reshuffling this time inventory still hasn't yielded a full 30 minutes for exercise, wipe your schedule clean, reach for your priority list and highlight those activities of highest importance (including exercise) on your daily calendar.

Step #3: Assign a Time

As far as making exercise a habit, science is on the side of the early birds. People who work out in the mornings are much more likely to stick to their programs than people who leave it until later—when spur-of-the-moment meetings or family responsibilities can knock the best intentions off balance.

Your morning schedule might not even need much revising to include exercise. "I tell people to let their secretaries know that Monday through Friday, they're not going to be seeing people until 8:30 A.M. instead of 8:00 A.M. You get up at the same time, but you have your workout done by the time you get to work," says Tedd Mitchell, M.D., medical director of the Cooper Wellness Program at the Cooper Aerobics Center in Dallas.

No matter what time of the day you don your walking shoes, keep it consistent. "One way to make something a habit is to have the same environment, the same situation every time you exercise," says Dr. Courneya.

Step #4: Do It

So what are you going to do with your new fitness time slot? Let hedonism be your guide. Why do something that is no fun? Use your creativity to boost the fitness potential of activities like walking the dog that you might not even consider exercise.

Start by promising yourself 30 minutes of exercise per session (20, if you're new to exercise). Wimpy? Nope. Realistic is more like it. When you have a breakfast meeting every day and special dinners and meetings all week, you'll find a 30-minute workout manageable and a 90-minute one nearly impossible.

The point isn't to do light exercise. It's to shift your thinking from "This is what I'm going to have to do to get in shape" to "This is a habit that I have." If you have been sedentary for a while, even 20 minutes of exercise every day is going to have you feeling great in no time.

In the first few weeks, however, don't underschedule yourself. A 30-minute workout means 30 minutes of moving around. Not 5 minutes for finding your shoes, 1 minute for tying them and 15 minutes for looking for your shades, applying sunscreen and pulling yourself together afterward. So be realistic; schedule an hour if that's what you really need to accomplish a 30-

Shedding Pounds Can Lengthen Your Life

HEALTH FLASH

A new study of 28,388 women found that those who lost 20 pounds were 20 percent more likely to stay alive in the next 12 years than were women who didn't lose any weight.

Among 15,069 women in the study who had obesity-related problems (heart disease, stroke or diabetes, for instance), those who lost any weight also dropped their risk of dying from obesity-related cancers—such as breast, cervical and ovarian cancers—by half. Weight loss also reduced their risk of dying from diabetes by 30 to 40 percent.

"In spite of the prevalence of women trying to lose weight today (half of American women on any given day), there was no direct evidence until this study that intentionally doing so would improve your longevity," says study leader David F. Williamson, Ph.D., at the Centers for Disease Control and Prevention in Atlanta. Until now.

Benefits didn't belong only to those who turned tubby into twiggy. "You don't necessarily have to get down to an ideal body weight to get the benefits of intentional weight loss," says Dr. Williamson. "I'm starting to believe that losing just a few pounds may be very good for you."

Nonetheless, the women who were best off did lose their 20 pounds in a year. It may be that taking off that amount of weight in that span of time requires the kind of eating and exercise habits that are natural life-span extenders.

minute workout. Eventually, you'll get more efficient at preparation and re-entry, and you'll have more time to exercise.

Building a Habit

There is no magic number for how long it takes habits to take hold. But there are strong hints that it can happen in as quickly as six to eight weeks. "I always tell people that after the first few months, my job becomes very easy—I don't have to tell people to exercise anymore," says Dr. Mitchell. "Once they feel the benefits of it, they'll establish it as a lifestyle."

You'll soon see that a routine is anything but routine. It's simply a matter of following a format that makes you feel good; about making promises to yourself and keeping them.

"Making a change isn't really about deprivation," says Ronna Kabatznick, Ph.D., psychological and motivational consultant to *Weight Watchers Magazine*. "Sure, there are impulses that you're not going to follow. But you're making a decision on your own behalf that will improve your life."

The Stairway to Weight-Loss Heaven

S tuck on a dreary weight-loss plateau? Can't get firmer, can't lose those last annoying pounds? Then step up to your local stair-climbing machine and boost your buns off that weight-loss plateau they've been resting on!

In the gym or at home, stair-climbers remain one of the hottest pieces of exercise equipment today—thanks to their calorie-burning powers, their flexibility (you set the program to meet your needs), their easy-on-the-knees action and the fact that they're ready to go, rain or shine, day or night.

Now, add a new attribute: A stair-climber can be a booster shot for your fitness routine.

Burn Calories, Bust Flab

A mile of stair climbing burns 40 to 60 percent more calories than a mile of brisk walking. But how do you use that knowledge to your best advantage when waging the battle of the bulge? Not by dropping your walking routine and heading for the health club. Do *not* replace your daily half-hour walk with the same time on the stair-climber. That route to weight-loss heaven could easily lead you to a stair-stepper hell of sore shins, sore buns and burnout.

In fact, walking is *still* the exercise of choice for weight loss. Consistency counts, and walking is the easiest way to be consistent because of that anytime-anywhere factor. It's also pleasant, relaxing and stress-reducing to walk outside in a natural setting—something that's unlikely on a stair-climber. So stick with the great outdoors when you can.

Use the stair-climber judiciously to boost your total calorie burn. The idea is to add stair climbing to your current exercise schedule. Because stair climbing can be a very strenuous activity, we suggest you add it to your workout only after you've been walking briskly and regularly (three to five days a week for at least half an hour each) for about a month. That should give you sufficient stamina and conditioning to begin working at the intensity a stair-climber requires—without giving up after the first three minutes.

The Vertical Advantage

Why a stair-climbing machine instead of faster walking? Well, you could walk faster. Walking at a 12-minute-per-mile pace burns over 500 calories an hour compared with about 400 calories an hour for a 15-minute-per-mile pace. Speedwalking and racewalking are fun. But they take a fair amount of training, technique, coordination and mental effort to accomplish.

You could add a little jogging to your walks, but you'd be tripling the impact on your feet and joints. Stair climbing is very low impact, like walking, because your feet never leave the pedals.

On a stair-climber, just by virtue of the vertical lifting of your body weight, your heart rate accelerates rapidly. And the heavier you are, the more weight you'll be lifting and the higher your heart rate and calorie burn will soar. You don't have to learn how to do it or concentrate hard, it just happens.

Stepping Right

The stair-climber is one of the most popular exercise machines at health clubs, YMCAs and spas around the country. Assuming that you'll be using a club machine to introduce yourself to stepping, make sure you schedule your visits at times when you won't have to fight for one. (Many clubs give trial memberships for low fees or even for free.) Watching other people work out may feel exhausting, but the calorie burn for spectators is just a hair above sleeping.

Your first time on, have an instructor explain how to use all the special features. You may be able to choose a preformulated program or create your own. You can often set your time and intensity and vary the terrain automatically.

As exercise physiologist Doug Garfield, Ed.D., says, you're not climbing steps, you're creating your own stairway.

At first, just get used to the variety and possibilities. Jump on for five-minute stints to acclimate your muscles and your mind to how the machine works. Find out what is most comfortable for you in terms of pace and depth of step. Just make sure you never allow the pedals to come all the way up or to hit bottom, as that can jar your joints.

Cedric Bryant, Ph.D., director of sports medicine for StairMaster, suggests you practice stepping up rather than trying to push the pedals down. It's a subtle distinction, but there is a difference.

"We supported a study at Stanford University and found that people who try to push down are more likely to experience numbness or tingling in their feet from too much pressure on the nerves," says Dr. Bryant. "It's like lying on one arm too long and having it fall asleep—uncomfortable but not dangerous, and completely avoidable."

Allow your foot to go through the normal range of motion. Don't stay up on your tippy-toes as you pump the steps. Think about your walking form. Use a heel-to-toe roll and allow plenty of ankle movement. Stand tall, with your head erect. No leaning on the console or the arm rails. Anything more than a balancing touch will reduce the workload.

And don't read, which may put undue tension in your neck, back or shoulders. "Your shoulders and hips should stay pretty level," says Wayne Westcott, Ph.D., strength-training consultant for the YMCA of the USA. "Otherwise you may stress the lower back, hips and knees."

As you get acclimated, you may even be able to swing your arms naturally at your sides.

More Short Workouts Better for Weight Loss

Here's a new factoid to factor into your workout schedule: When it comes to weight loss, three shorter workouts are better than two long ones, according to a new study.

When researchers from San Jacinto College in Pasadena, Texas, compared exercise results for 67 people—about half of whom worked out twice a week for 60 minutes, while the other half worked out three times a week for 40 minutes—the more-frequent movers and shakers lost 3.7 inches from their thigh, bicep, waist and chest measurements after 15 weeks. People working out twice a week trimmed less than half an inch.

"You're going to burn extra calories after your workout ends. The Monday-Wednesday-Friday people are getting three days of extra burn, while the Tuesday-Thursday people are getting only two days of extra burn," explains study leader Michael J. Soileau, Ed.D., health and physical education expert at San Jacinto College.

But if you're trying to improve cardiovascular fitness, Dr. Soileau notes, go for the two longer workouts. The extra workout time per session may coax the cardiovascular system into learning to last longer.

HEALTH FLASH

More Magic Steps to a Healthy Weight

Going up in the world may be the easiest way to get more calorie-burning exercise—even if you climb by taking the stairs at home, in the office or at the mall.

Like a daily coin dropped in a bank, little by little those flights of stairs can help add up to a fitter, trimmer you. In a London subway station, some researchers posted these signs by the escalators: "Stay Healthy, Save Time, Use the Stairs." In the three weeks the signs were up, men's use of the stairs rose from 12 to 20 percent; women's use rose from 5 to 12 percent. So next time you have a choice between stairs and an escalator—like at many shopping malls—remember: "Stay Healthy, Save Time, Use the Stairs." Keep off the "flab-alator!"

Go for the Big Benefits

For optimal weight loss, work out at a pace that allows you to talk but one in which carrying on a conversation would be a little difficult. Long, slow workouts are good fat burners for beginners, but they don't have the corner on the market when it comes to shedding pounds. As you become more fit, higher-intensity workouts can burn calories faster (and total calories burned is what's important for dropping weight).

If you can maintain the pace, you'll burn more calories. And sometimes just a change of activity seems to shock the body into moving toward your weight-loss goal.

At first, you may become breathless quite quickly on the stair-climber, but after three or four sessions, you'll be able to find a reasonable adjustment between depth of step, speed and heart rate. Work up gradually to 30-minute sessions, adding two or three per week to your walking workout. You should be able to judge by the way you feel that you're working harder than your normal walking workout. If it seems too easy, step up the pace or deepen your steps.

Be careful not to take too long or deep a step, which may lead to injury. The depth of the step you take should allow you to maintain good posture as you're exercising. If your hips and shoulders are moving up and down, your step is too deep.

Short, quick steps don't involve enough muscle mass to give you maximum calorie burn, but they are great for warming up and cooling down.

As you work up to longer workouts, use short steps for your warm-up, progress to deeper steps for the high-intensity core of your workout and then cool down with five minutes of shorter steps at the end. Go for high intensity, Dr. Westcott suggests, because the fun factor of a stair-stepper is not very high and you may get bored very quickly, compared with walking. So you may as well burn lots of calories while you're in the stepping mood.

The Science of Intervals

Most stair-climbers allow you to set a course that varies the intensity of your workout, although you can set the high and low parameters. Intervals (short bursts of intense activity followed by a longer rest period) are great for weight loss.

Here's how it works. Instead of maintaining a steady, moderately fast pace, you fluctuate between very fast and recovering at a slower pace.

Studies have shown that most people are able to burn more calories this way because their average speed tends to be a little bit higher than what they could sustain continuously at a moderately difficult pace. And because they get a chance to rest and recover, they don't feel they've worked that much harder.

Stair Gear

Your walking shoes should be fine for stair climbing, as long as they fit well to begin with. That would mean plenty of room around your toes and a snug-enough heel to avoid slippage. Your feet are doing a lot of the work here, and your feet and toes may temporarily swell as you work out, so give them room by buying shoes with an adequately roomy toe box.

Dress in layers. You may need a sweatshirt as you start out in what seems like a frigid gym, but you'll be peeling off those layers lickety-split as your body heats up during the workout. Strip down to a T-shirt or leotard once you get cooking.

You won't have the benefit of a breeze like you would if you were walking outside. And keep a water bottle handy. You're going to work up a sweat, and you could dehydrate fairly quickly. While it's true that the stair-stepper works the muscles of the lower body more than walking does, don't worry about bulging muscles. "You'll get some more toning in that area," says Dr. Bryant, "but most people get more endurance rather than gains in muscle strength."

To ward off shinsplints (especially if you're a regular walker), this exercise can help: Take a five-pound weight, tie a shoestring through the center hole or to both ends if it's a dumbbell, and hang it over your shoe. Sit on a high desk or bench and, using your foot only, raise and lower the weight by bringing your toes up toward your shin. Do this three days a week and it will help keep your ankles strong to withstand the increase in activity, prevent shinsplints and avoid stress fractures in that area. Follow any stair-climber workout with leg stretches.

Avoid Pain in the Knee

If yours are among the millions of wounded knees in the world, you don't have to avoid stair-steppers. Dr. Bryant suggests using a stair-stepper cautiously.

"Go through as full a range of motion as you can without pain," says Dr. Bryant. "If you feel pain, back off immediately."

Stay with shorter steps, and as you strengthen the muscles that support and protect your knees, you can deepen the steps you take, he suggests.

Stair-climbers have been used by physicians to rehabilitate knees after re-constructive surgery. The biomechanics are very similar to climbing real stairs except that you don't expose your joints to high amounts of stress.

Since you're always "going up," you eliminate the most stressful phase of the activity and avoid the excessive body-weight pressure of going down the steps on those all-too-easily-injured joints.

NURTURING YOURSELF

Part **7**

Whenever we get back to nature, it's a soothing experience.

—psychotherapist
Philip Sutton Chard

Female Advantage

For once, something enjoyable is actually good for us. Research shows that a healthy, regular sex life not only can bring women pleasure but also can boost physical and emotional well-being in uniquely female ways.

"Steady, once-a-week, monogamous sex with a man provides wonderful benefits for a woman's physiology and reproductive health," says Winnifred Cutler, Ph.D., president and founder of the Athena Institute for Women's Wellness in Chester Springs, Pennsylvania.

More than a decade of ongoing research conducted by Dr. Cutler at the University of Pennsylvania in Philadelphia and at Stanford University has revealed that a woman's sexual behavior profoundly affects her fertility, hormone levels and the way she ages.

One main reason for these benefits is that estrogen levels are twice as high in women who have weekly sex, compared with women who are celibate or have sporadic sex. "And high estrogen levels bring women a host of health benefits," Dr. Cutler says. Men, whose dominant sex hormone is testosterone, miss out on these specific advantages.

Another factor may simply be the scent of a man: Dr. Cutler has found that glandular secretions given off by men may stimulate chemical changes in a woman that promote physical well-being.

For sex to be most beneficial, it helps if a woman is engaged in an ongoing, loving and nonabusive relationship. The stability of the once-a-week pattern counts, too. "More than once a week is fine," Dr. Cutler says. "But if you miss weeks in between, if you have big feasts interspersed with famines, it seems to throw off the body's hormonal system."

If you need more convincing that time spent in the bedroom is good for your health, read on for a list of possible rewards.

- Higher self-esteem
- More regular menstrual periods
- Higher fertility
- Better resistance to stress
- Clearer skin
- Increased tolerance to pain
- Improved circulation
- Stronger bones
- Fewer menopausal hot flashes

The New Fatigue Fighters

W hy is fatigue one of the top ten complaints that women will report to their doctors this year? Blame it on lifestyle. Women who juggle jobs, families and households often get little sleep and less exercise. Instead of eating nutrition-packed, energy-boosting meals, we graze at salad bars and fast-food drive-throughs, missing out on the essential vitamins and minerals that are needed to maintain energy.

We may intentionally undereat in an attempt to lose weight, undernourishing ourselves in the process. We may feel drained of energy due to pregnancy, childbirth and menopause. Or feel sluggish because we have overeaten and our bodies are busy digesting extra fat.

Call it fatigue, listlessness, tiredness, lethargy or just plain pooped out. It's a small wonder that women are well-represented among the seven million Americans who visit their doctors each year seeking an answer to the question, "Why am I dragging?"

Sometimes, a woman's fatigue has an obvious cause. Anemia, depression, thyroid problems, sleep problems and even being overweight can make you feel overtired. (Once in a while, chronic fatigue is a sign of a serious medical condition, which is why you should consult your doctor if you have prolonged, unexplained fatigue.)

But there are many sneaky causes of fatigue that you would never suspect of being capable of draining your batteries. Here is a rundown of some of these little-noticed energy zappers and how to zap them back—to reclaim some of that boundless energy of youth.

245

Beat Desk-Jockey Syndrome

It seems odd, but just sitting for long periods can wear you out. Intense mental activity is more tiring than most of us appreciate. The very act of directing attention to one thing, such as the company books, means that you must block out other stimuli in the environment, and that uses up incredible amounts of energy.

In addition, women with sedentary jobs—and that is most American women who work—who don't exercise regularly are hit with a double energy-zapping whammy.

The solution? Instead of a coffee break, try an exercise break. "A brisk 10-minute walk causes you to feel more energized and less fatigued for anywhere from 30 to 90 minutes following the walk," says Robert Thayer, Ph.D., professor of psychology at California State University in Long Beach.

Leap Out of the Boredom Rut

Let's say that you're a homemaker getting lots of exercise in short bursts—running laundry up and down the steps or chasing after a busy toddler. Why, then, are you dead tired by midafternoon?

Ask yourself this question: Despite feeling exhausted, would you have enough energy to do something you love, such as move your perennial flower bed or play a game of tennis?

Often, the real cause of fatigue is boredom. Work that is repetitive, boring and unsatisfying may feel fatiguing even if it doesn't cause you to break a sweat.

"Taking regular breaks throughout the week to engage in some enjoyable exercise or other physically demanding but interesting activity should help relieve this fatigue," says Gregory Heath, D.H.Sc., an epidemiologist and exercise physiologist at the Centers for Disease Control and Prevention in Atlanta.

Savor the Sip That Refreshes

Unwatered, your houseplants quickly droop. Similarly, lacking optimal hydration, your body may respond with a sluggish, droopy feeling—although you might not realize why.

"While the consequences of dehydration are very apparent when the body is exercising and working hard, there are also problems associated with constantly walking around slightly dehydrated—as many people do," says E. Wayne Askew, Ph.D., director of the Division of Foods and Nutrition at the University of Utah in Salt Lake City.

Each cell of the body contains countless chemicals, minerals and vitamins, and they function best when they're diluted in just the right amount of fluid.

The body is also dependent on the bloodstream to transport nutrients and other substances from one part of the body to another. And this, too, depends on optimal fluid conditions.

"Although research has focused on the consequences of severe dehydration, it stands to reason that when vital components are in a less-than-optimal fluid concentration, cells are handicapped. Fatigue is a very likely consequence," says Dr. Askew.

So to stay ahead of dehydration, you should drink the equivalent of at least eight eight-ounce glasses of fluids a day (including water, juice and soup, but not alcohol)—enough to replace the fluid lost each day via exhaled breaths, body waste and the skin. You'll need more fluid when you exercise, especially in hot weather.

Go Easy on Weight-Loss Diets

Although you're trying to lose weight the right way—eating healthy meals and exercising regularly—you're still tired. Amazingly, even modest calorie restriction can lead to marginal vitamin levels, of which fatigue may be the only early symptom.

Women's Sleep Deficit Timed

It is no surprise that women get tired. But now, experts have discovered that a woman is more likely to experience sleep deprivation than a man—thanks to a host of factors that threaten the quality of her sleep.

What could be keeping us awake? In part, our many roles as mothers, breadwinners, housekeepers, cooks, volunteers, caretakers and more. Half of all women with small children juggle their family life with jobs outside the home.

But that's not all. Female hormones can also keep us from catching much-needed shut-eye, thanks both to premenstrual syndrome and menopause.

"The average menopausal woman with hot flashes is awakened during the night an average of every eight minutes with hot flashes," says Suzanne Woodward, Ph.D., assistant professor of psychiatry at Wayne State University School of Medicine in Detroit. This can continue for five or more years.

How can you get better sleep? Make sure that your bedroom is quiet, dark and not too hot or cold.

But above all, be aware of the sleep deficit. Catch a short nap of 20 to 30 minutes if you can. And if you have a long drive ahead—be it a commute, vacation or other trip—stop for coffee or to rest, says Dr. Woodward.

HEALTH FLASH

"Consuming less than 1,800 calories per day is a risk factor for low-nutrient intake, simply because nutrient intake is tied to calorie intake," says clinical dietitian Jo Ann Hattner, R.D., of Stanford University Medical Center. She advises dieters eating less than 1,800 calories per day to take a vitamin/mineral supplement.

In addition, chronic dieters can develop fatigue from more serious and complex metabolic abnormalities that mimic a low thyroid condition, says C. Wayne Callaway, M.D., associate clinical professor of medicine at George Washington University in Washington, D.C.

Chronically starved for calories, the body turns down insulin production to spare vital blood sugar for use by the brain. Now short on insulin, the body cannot convert enough of the inactive form of thyroid hormone into the active form it needs. The body also makes less of the hormone norepinephrine. Because norepinephrine and activated thyroid hormone are the two major controls of metabolic rate, metabolism slows down, mimicking a low thyroid condition—of which fatigue is a prominent symptom. And, ironically, this slowdown thwarts weight loss.

The cure is as surprising as the curse: If you're trying to lose weight, eat a little more, says Dr. Callaway, or exercise a little less.

Catch a Few Zzzs

The fatigue that follows a night of just three to four hours of sleep is predictable. But you might not connect your persistent fatigue with chronically shortening your sleep by just an hour or so.

"Many Americans force their bodies to run day after day on five to six hours of sleep, when they really need seven to eight," says sleep expert Mary A. Carskadon, Ph.D., professor of psychiatry and human behavior at Brown University in Providence, Rhode Island.

"After one or two nights of shortened sleep," she says, "they may still feel fine and mistakenly think they can get by this way indefinitely. Little do they know that the sleep debt accumulates. Nor do they realize that as the debt compounds, they are less able to recognize that they are sleep deprived, simply because one consequence of not getting enough sleep is a deficit in cognitive abilities."

You may also be able to fight fatigue with an afternoon catnap, she says. "You can wipe out the midafternoon slump very quickly with a 20- to 30-minute nap," says Dr. Carskadon. "I think napping is undervalued in our society."

Don't Do the Java Jive

As you know, coffee has eye-opening power. But scientists have recently confirmed that the caffeine in your cup can also leave you dragging.

If you have had a splitting headache after skipping your usual caffeine for a day, you can attest to that. But there's also a more subtle sign of withdrawal: the fatigue that comes from following a normal day of caffeine consumption with a lighter intake or even from following a heavier day with a normal amount.

"Fatigue may be the first sign of caffeine withdrawal," says caffeine researcher Roland R. Griffiths, Ph.D., of Johns Hopkins University School of Medicine in Baltimore. "Someone experiencing unexplained fatigue should take a hard look at his caffeine intake."

Surprisingly, as little as one cup of brew a day (or the equivalent amount of caffeine from another beverage) can be addicting. The typical American who consumes about 2½ cups of coffee per day should gradually cut out coffee over a one- to two-week period to avoid withdrawal symptoms.

Schedule Pleasure Breaks

Are you one of countless Americans who has no downtime? Do you go from work to home to your volunteer position or children's activities, leaving no time for your pleasures?

Then you may be on overload, says Reed Moskowitz, M.D., author of *Your Healing Mind.* Overload is not just a result of being extremely active— lots of people are constantly active and don't suffer from it. Overload is being active without ever attending to your own human needs.

Dr. Moskowitz says that many people have become "human doings" instead of human beings. "Absolutely everyone needs true downtime to relax and recover," he notes.

In case it has been so long that you've forgotten what downtime is, it is that wonderful "free period" when you don't have to answer to anyone, when you have no responsibilities. It's that time when you garden, read a mystery, go for a walk or lose yourself in gourmet food preparation.

To convert from a human doing into a human being, prioritize your activities, says Dr. Moskowitz. What eats up your time? While many time-eaters aren't optional, others are. Cut activities that are low priority and reclaim that time for yourself.

Relax, Relax, Relax

"Stress is the number one cause of fatigue in this country," says Dr. Moskowitz. The cascade of physiological reactions kicked off by stress is the same emergency response that protected our prehistoric ancestors from predators.

In this fight-or-flight response the body produces excess adrenaline and other hormones that make the heart beat faster and energize the body. But the extra burst of energy gobbles up incredible amounts of power, which eventually ends up dropping you into a slump of fatigue.

"Being constantly stressed out is like living with one foot on the brake and the other on the accelerator—you're eventually going to strip your gears. Among other things, that translates into fatigue," says Dr. Moskowitz. Stress also triggers other physical responses that compound the fatigue, including tense muscles.

So if you're going to beat fatigue, you have to learn how to tackle stress. The first step, says Dr. Moskowitz, is to develop an awareness of how stress affects you. Observe your physical and emotional states: Do you get tension in your neck? Does your stomach get queasy? Does your back ache? Or do you feel anxious? Upset? Angry? Giddy?

Once you've identified your own stress characteristics, step two is to take action on them. Relaxation techniques like deep breathing, yoga and tai chi can help release excess bodily tension. If you tend to get stuck in a lot of emotional negativity, try a problem-solving approach—using your cognitive capacity to understand and then change the self-defeating perceptions. If need be, consult a qualified mental-health professional, especially one who specializes in stress.

Mobilize to Energize

Logically, doesn't it seem as though we should feel more energetic if we haven't done anything physically taxing? Shouldn't inactivity be like saving up energy? Why, then, do we generally feel full of energy after engaging in physical work or exercise?

"Even though energy is used during exercise, it creates more," says William J. Evans, Ph.D., professor of applied physiology and nutrition and director of the physiological research center at Pennsylvania State University in State College. "That's because the muscles and cardiovascular system are like a car engine. Regular exercise can increase the efficiency and the horse-power of the engine. Thus, whenever you perform any activity, it feels easier."

38

The Perfect De-Stressors

H ere is a welcome surprise for the one in two American women who, in a recent national survey, said that they feel frazzled every day: You can create a personalized relaxation experience whenever and wherever you want.

How? By tuning in to the sights, sounds and even the scents that you love most. But first, it's important to learn a simple, two-step approach to relaxing.

"The first thing that you need to do is break the train of everyday thought that typically induces stress," says Herbert Benson, M.D., president of the Mind/Body Medical Institute at New England Deaconess Hospital and associate professor of medicine at Harvard Medical School, both in Boston. "And one of the most effective ways to do this is through repetition. Repeating a word, a sound, a thought, a breathing exercise or even a religious phrase."

Here is where you can personalize your relaxation time: The secret is that repetition need not simply be static. Water flowing in a creek is both repetitious yet ever-changing. The foundations of music composition are built upon repetition, and yet music also changes from measure to measure. The real trick is to find something simple that your mind can focus on to the exclusion of all other thoughts.

"That's where step two comes in," adds Dr. Benson. "As you focus on your particular technique, other, unbidden thoughts will interrupt that focus. You need to passively disregard them and keep gently bringing your attention back to the repetition."

So what are you waiting for? Find a focus object—be it music, prayer, a babbling brook or your own breathing—and start tuning out the mental static with the following inventive ideas.

Nature's Calming Embrace

How often do you really experience nature? With a six-inch slab of cement between your feet and the earth and an inch-thick insulated windowpane between your climate-controlled office and the wind, the answer is probably not much.

"But we are born of the natural world," says psychotherapist Philip Sutton Chard, author of *The Healing Earth: Nature's Medicine for the Troubled Soul.* "And whenever we get back to nature, it's a soothing experience much like the relaxed sleep that a baby falls into when held close by its mother."

Perhaps because of this, nature can enhance the act of relaxation, providing especially meaningful focal points for both deep, purposeful meditation and spontaneous stress-chasing mini-breaks.

Elemental meditations like these help you connect with nature and with your own relaxation response.

Gaze on wide vistas. "A good view of far-reaching vistas can be relaxing in the winter months because the wide-open space counteracts tense feelings of being closed in," says Mel Bucholtz, director of the Stillness Institute in Lincoln Center, Massachusetts. "Gaze out over the countryside for a few minutes and then try to capture it internally." Close your eyes and picture it; notice how you feel.

Contemplate the ocean. The fact that the surf does have a very rhythmical and repetitive action also means that it is a great focal point to use for relaxation exercises, notes Chard. Try to match your breathing to the waves. Breathe in as the wave comes up to shore. Breathe out as the water recedes. If the waves are running too fast, stagger your breath to match every second or third wave.

Soak up a little sun. "Traditionally, the sun is the symbol of life and energy," notes Chard. But with all the time we spend indoors, especially during the winter, we tend to lose contact with it. "Try sitting in the backyard and imagining yourself as a rock in a field," suggests Bucholtz. "Feel the rocklike weightiness in the base of the spine and then the sun, coming in through the surface of the rock, slowly warming you to the core of your coldness." If the day is too cold, do it indoors, by a picture window with ample sunlight streaming in.

Hear the wind blow. "Listening to the wind provides the same kind of steady comfort that a baby gets lying on its mother's chest and listening to her breathing," says Chard. "A great way to meditate on the wind is by sitting in a field of tall grass so that you can actually see the breeze as well as hear it."

Take in the stars and clouds. "The sky is totally boundless," notes Bucholtz. "Many of our worries and self-important activities are placed in perspective against the limitless sky." Stargazing is particularly good in the winter because there's less humidity in the air, making the constellations seem much sharper.

"But, I find the best time to look at the sky is the hour before sunrise and the hour after sunset," says Derrick Pitts, vice-president and chief astronomer at the Franklin Institute in Philadelphia. "Concentrating on the slow, subtle color changes that occur as the light begins to grow or fade is not only relaxing, but very beautiful."

Quiet Sounds

It's hard to deny that music can inspire, inflame, agitate or irritate every nerve in your body. But music can also produce the most profound states of mental and physical relaxation as well.

"The right music in the hands of a trained music therapist can yield reductions in blood pressure, heart rate and even the levels of stress hormones, such as cortisol, that the body produces," says Cheryl Dileo Maranto, Ph.D., professor of music therapy at Temple University in Philadelphia and

The Sweet Scent of Relaxation

Forget about the roses. The aroma of green apples may be Mother Nature's most powerful tranquilizer, according to new research into connections between scents and anxiety.

"We've been looking at a form of long-term anxiety, called generalized anxiety disorder, hoping to find an odor that might reduce the level of stress," says Alan R. Hirsch, M.D., neurological director of the Smell and Taste Treatment and Research Foundation in Chicago. "So far, green-apple smell seems to be the most effective."

According to Dr. Hirsch, a scent can have a tranquilizing effect on the brain. On another level, a smell can also relax you by bringing back the good old days.

"It's called olfactory-evoked nostalgia, where a scent reduces anxiety by bringing back happy memories from a less-complicated time in your life," he says. Scents that evoke this response vary from person to person, depending on personal experiences. When and where you grew up can provide these additional clues, he adds.

If you were born between 1900 and 1930, you're most likely to feel relaxed when sniffing natural smells like trees, pine needles and hay. If you were born between 1930 and 1980, try artificial smells from childhood, such as Play-Doh, Pez or Sweetarts.

If you grew up in the East, your best relaxing scent could be flowers. In the Midwest, try the smell of farm animals. From the South? Could be simple fresh air. And out West, folks tend to relax to the smell of meat barbecuing, Dr. Hirsch says.

HEALTH FLASH

Soak Stress Away

Does stress have your muscles wound as tightly as your mind? Unravel both in a body-warming bath scented with lavender essence. "Get some lavender flowers and separate one cup of buds," says Richard Bird, director of beauty and massage at the Golden Door spa in San Marcos, California. "Using cheesecloth, tie up the buds into a 'giant tea bag.' Boil some water and, after pouring it into a ceramic or glass bowl or pot, add the tea bag and let the whole thing cool. When you start your bath, tie the tea bag under the faucet so that the water pours over it. Once the bath is filled, add the leftover water from the ceramic bowl." You haven't smelled lavender until you have tried it like this.

president of the World Federation of Music Therapy.

While you may not have access to the same tools and techniques used by the pros, a good stereo and a few tips on choosing the right music can go a long way toward making your next listening experience a mellower one.

Choose music with no lyrics. "Lyrics encourage your brain to sort out the words, to make sense of them," says Dr. Maranto. "It's a cognitive process that could interfere with your attempts to relax."

Choose music that is familiar. "A piece of music you've never heard before is new terrain that your mind will be busy analyzing," notes Dr. Maranto.

Choose music with no emotional baggage. "You want to be careful that the music you choose for peace and relaxation is not connected to a turbulent, unhappy or emotionally charged period of your life," says Dr. Maranto.

Tranquillity Built for Two

Nestling in the arms of the one you love not only warms the heart but soothes the soul.

"Physical contact opens up a whole level of 'mother is home' feelings that hearken back to an infant memory of the initial intimacy, safety and caring we experienced in infancy," says Harold H. Bloomfield, M.D., psychiatrist and co-author of *The Power of 5: Hundreds of 5-Second to 5-Minute Scientific Shortcuts to Ignite Your Energy, Burn Fat, Stop Aging and Revitalize Your Love Life*. "Developing the right kind of touching can actually allow you to produce this 'safe harbor' response with greater and greater efficiency."

Here are a few steps to becoming a master cuddler.

Connect with your eyes. "Eighty percent of the information we take in about one another comes through the eyes," says Dr. Bloomfield. "And typically, when most women complain about not experiencing enough intimacy with their husbands, it's the gentle eye-to-eye contact that they're missing. But if you want to take touching to the limit, eye contact touches the soul."

Make touching the main event. "Both men and women complain that they are only being touched when it's a signal for sex, so touch gets associated with performance anxiety," says Dr. Bloomfield. "Take the anxiety out of it by having sessions that are strictly touching for touch's sake."

Get in sync. Try spooning with the one you love by lying on the couch and wrapping your arms around him from behind. "You'll find that after a while, with your chest pressed against his back, the two of you will start breathing in sync," says Dr. Bloomfield. While it does happen naturally, actually focusing on synchronized breathing is not only very meditative, but it strengthens the bonding process as well.

Don't just hug. "Try different rituals that involve touch," suggests Dr. Bloomfield. "For example, washing each other's hair is wonderfully relaxing—you're touching, you're doing something for each other, plus the scalp is a very sensitive area."

Stroll together. Walking together can be like cuddling—your bodies syncronized as you take time out just to be a couple, says Susan Olson, Ph.D., a clinical psychologist in Seattle, Washington. Try going for a walk and not talking. Just stroll together in silence and touch each other. Hold hands. Or just touch lightly to share something you see.

Or, build intimacy with a memory-improvement game. As you're walking, say something like, "Tell me what you remember from your early childhood about. . . ." Complete the sentence with anything you like. Let the surrounding scenery give you ideas: a bicycle, an elderly person, the color green. It's a great way to get to know someone more intimately and improve memory.

Mirror each other. This is a skill trademarked by couples' therapist and author Harville Hendrix, Ph.D., and in it, one person talks and the other mirrors. They say exactly what the other person says with the same intensity and tone of voice. It helps people know they are understood, and it promotes better communication—and a sense of closeness.

The 60-Second Massage

Break the grip of muscle tension with these one-minute massages from Mark Dixon, massage therapist in Huntington Beach, California.

Palming. Rub your hands together until you create heat from the friction. Press your palms over your eyes, allowing that handmade warmth to sink in.

Cheekbone press. Inhale deeply as you press your fingers into the tops of your cheekbones just below your eyes. Press firmly enough to move the tissue but not to cause pain. Exhale and release. Repeat, moving the fingers in half-inch increments toward your ears.

Forehead release. Place the fingertips of both hands on your forehead so that they are pointing toward each other. Using as much pressure as you find comfortable, move your fingers in straight lines across the forehead to the temples, as if smoothing away tension.

Occiput press. Place your fingers on top of your head toward the back, thumbs at the base of your skull. Starting at the outer edges of the crevices formed by the base of your skull (the occiput), press your thumbs in and up. Apply as much pressure as you find comfortable and slowly work your thumbs up the back of your head.

Scalp relaxer. Place all your fingers and thumbs on your scalp. Applying deep pressure, move the skin around without moving your skull.

39

Sizzling Secrets for More and Better Sex

I t's nine o'clock on a Saturday night, and you and your mate have just seen the perfect romantic comedy. You stroll out of the movie theater hand in hand into an equally perfect, starlit night.

Love—or more accurately, sex—is in the air. But Saturday is restaurant night for the two of you, so you pop into your favorite little Italian place for a quick bowl of pasta.

By the time you get home, it is past midnight and you're searching the medicine cabinet for the antacids. You've barely hit the mattress before you're both down for the count. Unconsciously, you wound up choosing food over sex.

This may be happening a lot in America. If, as a recent survey of sexual behavior found, most couples have sex just six or seven times a month, and most of us are faithful to our one sexual partner, then perhaps a lot of bedroom routines could use a little shaking up.

To change this situation, you don't have to see a sex therapist. Interviews with couples and a few sex experts yielded the following list of everyday habits that can hamper your love life as well as some new, easy-to-acquire practices that can make sex significantly better.

First, Get Steamy

For a lot of people, making out was the best thing about high school. It can also be one of the sweetest elements of a happy adult love life—a truth that Nancy, a 27-year-old Ph.D. candidate, and her boyfriend, Stephen, forgot.

Deluged with work, Nancy felt guilty because she didn't want to have sex as frequently as Stephen did. Even worse, she stopped kissing and touching him as often, worried that he would take any contact as a cue for intercourse. "I was so scared of making him feel rejected if I wasn't in the mood—and he was so afraid of being rejected—that we both became sexually paralyzed."

The solution: Rediscovering "the bases." Nancy and Stephen started making out again with the understanding that they didn't have to "go all the way" every time they got physically affectionate, and that took the will-we-or-won't-we pressure off of sex.

Once they stopped censoring their impulses, "a single kiss or a stray caress could be just that, or the beginning of something more serious," says Nancy. "Now we make out everywhere—in front the TV, in the park, squished in our car." Sometimes these make-out sessions lead to sex; sometimes they wind down into cuddling and sleep.

Renew the Joy of Exploration

In the early stages of a relationship, we spend hours luxuriating over our lover's body, and he returns the favor. You discover that spot at the base of his neck; he finds out that Fergie isn't the only one who loves having her toes sucked.

But as the relationship matures, there is a tendency to focus increasingly on the target zones—breasts and genitals—and to cut directly to the surefire techniques. Renewing your commitment to sexual exploration is one of the best ways to revive your sex life.

"I've always liked to think of sex and my wife as recess," says Nick, a 34-year-old professor, "and our bodies as a playground, made for fun. I consider it my sacred obligation to remind us of that, especially when we both get busy and foreplay starts to suffer."

Pull the Plug on Leno and Letterman

"When Letterman moved to 11:30, he basically took our sex life with him," says Matthew, a 29-year-old editor. Matthew and his partner used to hit the sheets anywhere between 10:00 P.M. and midnight, making love whenever they felt like it. "Letterman came on too late to distract us. But we started tuning in to the new, earlier show, and pretty soon the Top Ten list took the place of sex."

Once Matthew and Nina realized that Dave was the culprit, they kicked him out of their bedroom. "It took discipline because watching had become such a habit," he says.

Television at any hour can have a deadening effect. It's important to miss even *ER* now and then because you're otherwise engaged. Rebecca, a 27-

year-old elementary-school teacher, says she and her husband became prime-time zombies and watched their sex life wilt. The solution? "We imposed a version of that homework rule we had when we were kids. Something like, 'No TV until we've had sex.'"

Solve the Late-Night Dinner Dilemma

When a man unbuckles his belt after a big meal, it's not to unbridle his passion. And women seem to find it especially difficult to feel sexy and digest at the same time.

"My boyfriend and I have very different eating habits," says Monica, a 25-year-old graphic artist. "He doesn't eat much during the day and then has a huge meal late at night. I eat small meals all day and don't eat much after eight o'clock."

Initially, Monica bent to Curtis's schedule. "It was fun chowing down together, but afterward I'd be much more inhibited and lazy in bed because I felt so stuffed." She finally brought up the dinner dilemma. "Curt laughed at first, but he was willing to change in order to make me feel comfortable. And sometimes I'll compromise—we'll order in after making love."

Make the World Go Away

It's nearly impossible to keep the stresses of the work world away from the bedroom when you're struggling to block out the grinding sound of an incoming fax, the blip of a screen saver or the specter of a pile of unpaid bills.

"When I started freelancing from home, I set up my office in our bedroom," says Ethan, a 28-year-old journalist. "And all of a sudden, for the first time in my life, I developed performance anxiety. We'd be in bed and I'd find myself wondering if a source was going to return a phone call or when a fax was going to come in. It made me a total wreck."

Moving career paraphernalia into the living room didn't wipe out the work stress entirely, but it made it easier for Ethan to call an occasional time-out for sex.

As for your answering machine, out of sight isn't out of mind. As long as the machine is within earshot, friends and family will unwittingly trespass on your privacy.

Call Off the Bedroom Summit Conferences

You're lying in bed at the end of a long, hard day, or during that early morning quiet time, or in those warm, glowing moments after making love. It seems like the natural time and place to talk about the things that concern you most.

Don't do it, experts and couples advise. Talking dirty, reading the love poems of Pablo Neruda, whispering words of devotion are all fine, but your bed is no place for certain highly charged topics, including money, domestic responsibilities and your in-laws. "The only heat you want in your bed is the sexual kind," says New York City marriage and family therapist Jane Greer, Ph.D. "You don't want to contaminate the bedroom with heat generated by anger or anxiety, so deal with potentially hot topics in a neutral place and save bed for exclusively pleasurable experiences."

Ironically, the subject that seems perfect for pillow talk—your romantic future—may be the most taboo. "People frequently think the bedroom should be a particularly good setting for relationship talks because it fosters closeness and intimacy," says Dr. Greer. "But you should have that kind of discussion in bed only when you're in total agreement."

Outgrow Baby Talk

Lovers almost always develop a language they use only with one another, and it frequently involves letting that inner child do the talking. While some

Bashful about Condoms?

HEALTH FLASH

Canadian researchers have uncovered mixed feelings among women about carrying condoms—feelings that could ultimately endanger a woman's health.

Researchers at McGill University in Montreal asked 57 women to draw conclusions about "Anne Marie," a fictitious character who confides to her diary that she engaged in sex after a romantic, passionately charged date. In one version, the man provides a condom, while in another, Anne Marie produces one from her purse—"Thank God!" she later tells her diary. In yet a third, the couple has unprotected sex.

Women saw the Anne Marie with a condom as "clearly less nice," while they were far less harsh in judging the "unwise" Anne Marie who had sex without any protection, despite the risks of unwanted pregnancy or sexually transmitted diseases.

Researcher Michaela Hynie, Ph.D., a post-doctoral fellow in psychology at McGill, notes that guilt about sexual desires may keep women from making sure that condoms are on hand or from offering one. That's a mistake, she says. Even if you use another form of contraception to prevent pregnancy, a condom is the best protection from sexually transmitted diseases.

Still feel shy about offering a condom? Consider this: In a later study, Dr. Hynie found that men were not so judgmental when a woman offered a condom, perhaps because they were relieved.

easing of adult control is healthy, couples can run into trouble if they begin to rely on baby talk as a shortcut to intimacy. It may instantly communicate, "I love you, you make me feel secure and nurtured," but baby talk is rarely a turn-on.

Rachel, a 32-year-old investment counselor, says she and her boyfriend, Rick, found baby talk "comforting and easy and familiar." But she realized there was a problem when "we started using that lovey-dovey tone all the time." This sweet affectation eventually sapped their relationship of its adult passion.

"It even changed the way we touched each other," says Rachel. "We'd be in bed and Rick would sort of pat me gently, whisper, 'I wuv you' in my ear, and I would instantly turn off. I felt like a little kid instead of a sexy woman."

When they realized their language of love was the problem, Rick and Rachel reined it in. "Baby talk is still nice when I've had a really bad day or I come down with the flu," she says. "But we definitely keep it away from our sex life."

Energize Your Body

It was by pure accident that Allie, a 29-year-old commercial producer, found out that a mini-workout before bed could pump up desire. A devoted jogger and skier, Allie didn't react well when a knee injury and subsequent surgery put her on the disabled list for nine months. "I was miserable. I complained to everyone," she says, "and my husband caught the worst of it."

Oddly enough, a sexual boost helped them through this difficult time. Allie found that performing her rehabilitation exercises before bed every night got her warmed up in unexpected ways. "I'd grudgingly strap on my weights and do my leg lifts, and afterward I always felt wide-awake and invigorated, a little sweaty in a sexy way," she says. "It actually psyched me up for some more activity before going to sleep."

Building Satisfaction

Sexual habits, good and bad, are cyclical—a good tendency can slip away, a bad one can crop up when life gets hectic or priorities shift.

So before you diagnose a more serious problem—the flame has died, your hormones are out of whack—take a minute to re-evaluate your lifestyle and daily patterns. Think about the circumstances that contributed to great sex and those that led to sex that you can barely remember or would rather forget, then adjust your routine accordingly. Break a bad habit, build a good one and give Letterman something besides Leno to worry about.

Take Five to Make Love Last

Psychologists agree on two central truths about love: First, loving relationships are built, not found. And second, they have little—if anything—to do with luck and, contrary to popular wisdom, have absolutely nothing to do with being "made for each other."

Experts also agree that lasting love—and the deep, often exhilarating shared experiences of intimacy and romance—may be kindled and sustained in innumerable small and varied ways.

You've heard before that "it's the little things" that can make or break a relationship. But chances are, you've never heard about these little suggestions or their power to bring big changes. And this year, when more and more of us are headed for divorce or at least for the marriage counselor's office, aren't they worth a try?

Here are some of them—simple steps that may take only five minutes (or five seconds), that if done consistently and with care can make all the difference in the world, as suggested by the authors of the book *The Power of 5: Hundreds of 5-Second to 5-Minute Scientific Shortcuts to Ignite Your Energy, Burn Fat, Stop Aging and Revitalize Your Love Life*, psychologist Harold H. Bloomfield, M.D., and Robert K. Cooper, Ph.D., a health and fitness instructor certified by the American College of Sports Medicine.

Synchronize Your Love Life

Take five minutes at day's end to get in sync with your lover. There is just no denying it: Intimate relations are tied to a kaleidoscope of biological forces. Researchers have discovered a key relationship between sexual energy and the natural, ongoing influence of two biological cycles—the 24-hour circadian rhythm and the 60- to 90-minute ultradian rhythms. Successful, sexually satisfied couples tend to have overall activity patterns, appetite, need for diversion and sexual rhythms "all occurring in synchrony."

Years ago, at the end of the day in almost any town or village in Europe, America or Asia, you could see couples sitting together in rocking chairs or on a porch swing, gazing at the sunset, talking to each other, reflecting on the day. Without realizing it, says psychologist and chronobiology researcher Ernest Lawrence Rossi, Ph.D., they were synchronizing their circadian and ultradian rhythms and increasing their sexual energy. Today, more and more couples rush home, hurry to prepare dinner, flip through the newspaper, eat quickly and then either collapse for the evening in front of the television or plunge into another round of scheduled activities—nightly errands, exercise sessions, parental duties, catching up on paperwork, preparing reports or paying bills.

What's missing is a transition period—15 or 20 minutes will do—to unplug from the commotion and sit together quietly, without the television on in the background, to tune in to each other's energy rhythms and recover together from the day's pace. Here are some of the ways to increase sexual synchrony.

- Kissing and greeting each other whenever leaving and arriving, thereby using the sensory power of touch to help align your energy cycles.
- Slowing down the pace when seated for the main meal and enjoying each other's dining companionship.
- Going for a shared early-morning or evening stroll.
- Spending time together fixing meals, doing dishes or puttering around the lawn or garden.
- Sitting together quietly, listening to music you both enjoy, sipping a cup of tea or a glass of wine.
- Stretching out on the sofa and holding each other—fully clothed, with nothing unsnapped, unhooked or unzipped—in a "spoon" position, with one person wrapping arms around the other from behind. The warmth and comfort of this sensual embrace strengthens the closeness between you and helps release stress.
- Sharing a warm bath or gentle, rhythmic massage for 15 to 20 minutes prior to sexual intimacy.

In each of these simple actions, powerful verbal and nonverbal cues are helping to synchronize your energy rhythms and renew and increase intimate bonds after time apart.

Laugh Together

Enjoy five-second humor breaks. Every love relationship has its own unique reservoir of humor. Private jokes, shared laughter, ticklish spots on the body, comic faces, favorite funny experiences together. Make it a point to find more moments to ignite this humor each day, to remember some of the comical situations you witnessed or created during the day.

Usually there are lots of humorous little events and situations. Share these with each other. A study by Avner Ziv and Orit Gadish, professors of psychology at Tel Aviv University in Israel, suggests that 70 percent of a married couple's satisfaction may depend in some way on humor—on making each other laugh and feel happy despite life's ups and downs.

Cuddle Close

Share a five-minute snuggle at least once a day. Of all the ways in which people need each other, holding is the most primary, the least evident and the hardest to describe, says Ruthellen Josselson, Ph.D., professor of psychology at Towson State University in Baltimore and author of *The Space between Us: Exploring the Dimensions of Human Relationships*.

"From the first moments of our life to the last, we need to be held—or we fall," says Dr. Josselson. "There are physical and emotional aspects of holding. Holding not only provides care and meaning; it also provides hope."

Gaze into Your Beloved's Eyes

Relate eye-to-eye. One of the most important ways we affirm our connection to loved ones is eye-to-eye. No matter how old you become, you never cease to need unconditional, simple valuing in another's eyes—and in your own eyes. "These looks," says Dr. Josselson, "are far beyond words: Eyes

---

Couples Do Look Alike

Couples look alike more often than they may realize.

In a new study of 20 couples, Jody Meerdink, Ph.D., assistant professor of psychology at Nebraska Wesleyan University in Lincoln, took snapshots of partners in romantic couples, then asked students to match up the photos. Most of the students made correct matches more often than can be explained by chance, basing their matches on facial similarities.

Oddly, the couples themselves often said that they didn't see the similarities. But Dr. Meerdink thinks that perhaps, on an unconscious level, they actually chose each other in part because they look similar. And that can be a positive thing.

"I think some people would tell you that it's a positive sign of bonding," says Dr. Meerdink. "You're naturally more comfortable with that which is familiar to you, and what can be more familiar than your family? Everyone wants to marry someone like dear old dad—or mom—and some of our ideas of attractiveness are dictated to some extent by that."

HEALTH FLASH

speak more profoundly than language the tenor of relatedness. They express, surely and absolutely, how much and in what way we matter to the other."

Be Here, Now

End "unconscious exits." A related way that many of us lose romance and kill intimacy is by making detours in and out of the time we spend together. Beyond eye-to-eye validation, reduce the bothersome exits that drive people apart, such as staying up late, night after night, watching television while our partners are in bed; making long business calls in the evening and on weekends; not paying attention when your partner talks ("tuning out"); or making plans without consulting loved ones first.

Consider bringing this out into the open by writing a simple agreement: "Beginning now, I agree to give our relationship more energy and attention. In particular, I agree to . . ." and then make a brief list of simple changes you could make that your partner would value.

Express Empathy

Strengthen your love with five-second validations. For many of us, some of the best relationship advice is "Worry a bit less about what you think is important—money problems, career track, the annual vacation—and pay more attention to the little things." Begin with the power of validation.

"Letting your spouse know in so many little ways that you understand him or her is one of the most powerful tools for healing your relationship," says John M. Gottman, Ph.D., professor of psychology at the University of Washington in Seattle. "Validation is simply putting yourself in your partner's shoes and imagining his or her emotional state. It's then a simple matter to let your mate know that you understand those feelings and consider them valid, even if you don't share them. Validation is amazingly effective. It's as if you opened a door to welcome your partner."

Appreciate, Too

Grow closer by expressing five seconds to five minutes of appreciation. Once you're making progress with validation, take a look at the power of appreciation. How many times has your day been brightened by one small, unexpected gesture of appreciation or caring?

Unfortunately, many men think they make "points" with their partners when they do big things—like buying a car, replacing the refrigerator, setting up a new stereo or taking the family on a vacation. At the same time, many men assume that little things—opening doors, sharing loving glances, giving hugs or kisses, saying "I love you," sitting close together when watching a movie or television, checking with each other first before making plans, holding hands, saying "You look great," buying flowers or writing thank-you notes—count very little when compared with the "big things."

To help bring this concern to the fore, spend a few minutes doing sentence completions, such as: "I feel valued and loved when you . . . " and "I used to feel valued and loved when you . . . " and "To feel more valued and loved I would like you to. . . ." When you finish, exchange lists—and circle the items that are conflict-free for you and that you would be willing to start doing more of. You can add ideas as they arise and express appreciation to each other for each new caring behavior that results.

Don't keep score—do your caring behaviors as gifts, not obligations, and do them no matter how you feel about your partner or how many caring acts he or she has done for you that day.

Three Little Words—Once More, with Feeling

Use "I love you" as a heartfelt phrase—not a verbal club. In most cases, to say, "I love you" is not to report or express a feeling of intimacy or passion.

"It is an aggressive, creative, socially definitive act," says Robert C. Solomon, Ph.D., professor of psychology and philosophy at the University of Texas at Austin. Dr. Solomon notes in his book *About Love: Reinventing Romance for Our Times* that the expression "I love you" is essentially a plea, sometimes a demand, for a response in kind. Its uses and meanings are nearly as varied, or elusive, as lasting love itself. How you use the expression "I love you" can, by itself, be a significant force in defining and expressing the love in your relationship. The best advice? Initiate the reciprocal romantic exchange—"I love you," "I love you, too"—only when you can mean it heart-to-heart. Find other ways—and alternative expressions—to draw closer to each other and clearly assert your needs.

Good News That Can Jolt Your Marriage

When Ronnie, a homemaker for many years, was accepted into a business school, she and her husband, Eric, were more than thrilled.

"This had been my dream since I was little," says Ronnie, now 35. She couldn't have anticipated that the reality would turn her 12-year marriage into a nightmare.

The fighting started as soon as Ronnie's classes began and the pair's schedules shifted. "Eric would walk through the door at night and grumble that he was coming home to his second job," says Ronnie. "Instead of support, I got complaints about one thing or another that hadn't been done around the house. I couldn't believe it. Why was this happening to us?"

When Good News Shakes Your World

With half of all marriages ending in divorce, knowing how to handle the surprising jolts that can come on the heels of good news is as important as ever.

Like most of us, Ronnie, whose problem eased with time, knew that marriage had its ups and downs. She was aware that certain events—such as the death of a parent or the birth of a child—could bring on relationship low points. But she was stunned to discover that even a welcome shift could cause a sudden, stomach-lurching swoop in a marriage or send the roller-coaster car careening off the tracks.

The issue, say experts, is change, whether it's negative, positive or even apparently neutral, such as another couple's divorce. "Change is inevitable, and it can shake up a relationship," explains Norman Epstein, Ph.D., professor of psychology at the University of Maryland.

The best stabilizer is knowing how to anticipate and deal with the jolts. Here are some common ones and tactics for riding them out.

And Baby Makes Three

Everyone warns you that moving from husband and wife to mom and dad will be, well, different. What they rarely mention is that each subsequent child requires you to make more adjustments—in roles, lifestyle, schedules.

"Anytime there's an addition, it shifts the whole dynamic within the household," explains Susan Heitler, Ph.D., a clinical psychologist in private practice in Denver.

Walking into Each Other's Heart

Beyond dropping pounds or getting fit, walking may work wonders for many couples. Some marriage counselors believe that walking may help soothe a stressed-out relationship through a whole smorgasbord of means.

"Walking outside takes you away from all the distractions that take the fun and romance out of a relationship—like dirty dishes, bills, everyday hassles," says Patricia Love, Ed.D., marriage counselor and co-author of Hot Monogamy.

As a bonus, there's some evidence that when people have their spouses' support in an exercise routine, they're more likely to stick with it. If you're feeling a lack of commitment in either department, you may find that knowing the power of walking together and using these tips to enhance it may add harmony to your home as well as miles to your walking log.

Many couples find it easier to communicate while walking, says Dr. Love. "The male gets to face straight ahead, which is his preferred style of communicating." (Two men will talk facing straight ahead, while two women tend to face each other.) So women may find their husbands more willing to open up on a walk.

"Plus, just the movement of walking tends to release tensions and might get both of you talking more," Dr. Love adds. Walking in public might keep the discussions more mannerly, too, since both parties will be more likely to control angry outbursts, she says.

To get the most benefits from walking together, plan to take at least a short walk every day, suggests clinical psychologist Susan Olson, Ph.D., of Seattle, Washington. Going for a walk doesn't take a lot of planning. It's just a way of saying, "This relationship has some importance to us. So we're going to devote special time to it regularly."

Decide together beforehand what you want the walk to be like. Do you want to air out problems? Enjoy the sunset? Just get a workout?

If, as you're walking, you talk about old times, it may help you remember why you got together in the first place. "Too often in the 1990s culture we have married singles, not married couples," says Dr. Olson. "Walking together helps us to see that it's 'we,' not just 'me.' "

Good Marriage: A Fresh Look

What makes good marriages succeed? Psychologist Judith S. Wallerstein, Ph.D., author of the new book *The Good Marriage: How and Why Love Lasts*, studied 50 married couples over time and identified nine pillars on which any good marital relationship rests.

Her new study—one of the few to look at successful marriages—revealed that for a happy partnership, couples must:

- Separate emotionally from their childhood families.
- Build togetherness and intimacy, while respecting each other's independence.
- Establish a rich and pleasurable sexual experience.
- Embrace the daunting roles of parenthood, if they choose to have a family.
- Work to maintain the strength of the marital bond in the face of life's inevitable adversities.
- Create a safe haven for the expression of differences, anger and conflict.
- Use humor and laughter to keep things in perspective and to avoid boredom and loneliness.
- Provide nurturance and comfort to each other.
- Keep alive the early romantic images of falling in love, while facing the sober realities of change.

"When these nine psychological tasks are done well, and redone when necessary as the partners and circumstances change, the marriage thrives," Dr. Wallerstein says. "Done poorly, the marriage will be weak in some important regard and may be too feeble to withstand the inevitable strains on it."

Studies consistently show that marital satisfaction decreases with the birth of each child. Explains Dr. Heitler: "Children take time and attention away from a marriage." After the second or third child, she says, "the husband or wife or both may wonder, 'Hey, what happened to my time with you? What happened to us?'"

The best stabilizer? Heart-to-heart talks. You see each other, if at all, on the way into or out of a child's bedroom. Now you're supposed to talk?

Yes, yes, yes, say the experts. Ironically, the busier you are, the more indispensable conversation is. So once in a while, ignore the dirty laundry or have someone else tuck in the baby. Talking may not be easy. If he is still fuming because you won't give him Monday nights off to go out with his buddies, if you believe he is shirking his load, a discussion can quickly become a donnybrook.

To avoid that scenario, really listen. Maybe he has a real gripe. Maybe you can help him adapt to your altered family state. And at least half the time, steer conversations away from your disputes. What really works magic is not hashing out problems but just connecting, keeping those two hearts in sync.

Honey, I Got a Promotion

A fat raise. A prestigious promotion. A new job. How could such windfalls be anything but a plus for a marriage?

Well, for starters, a new work situation changes schedules, child care responsibilities and the amount of time that you spend together. And in these downsizing times, job security, yearly raises and frequent promotions can't be assumed—they have to be earned. Competition can be intense, and many employees sense that the rewards they've been given must be justified by harder work and longer hours.

The recommended stabilizer? Seize the other opportunities that change produces.

First, a caveat: If you're the one who has taken on a new position or increased responsibilities, cut back for a while on other activities. Now may not be the time to rejoin your book group.

Then, keep in mind that the Chinese have a sign for crisis that represents danger and opportunity—danger because it means change, opportunity because it can help you grow. A new job for one of you can mean new independence, responsibilities and experiences for both. One woman, who could have fretted when her husband's new job left her alone with their two young children many evenings, instead used part of his raise to hire a babysitter. Two nights a week she headed for a yoga class. Today, a few years later, she's a yoga instructor herself.

Change also provides a chance to remake your relationship. Maybe you were always "the insecure one." Now, landing a new job has boosted your confidence, causing a nice shift in the marital terrain.

New-House Blues

So much money, so many decisions: Where should we live? What can we spend? What do you mean, you hate center-hall colonials?

Buying a house, "sometimes feels like more of a commitment than signing a marriage certificate," says Jeffrey Friedman, Ph.D., a psychologist in San Luis Obispo, California.

Explains Dr. Heitler, "A house is not just a roof over your heads. It has so much impact on your life. It is a strong expression of who you are, of self."

One woman confides that she and her husband had such huge arguments over where they should buy a house—he insisted on the city, she the suburbs—that for three years they were stuck in a tiny one-bedroom apartment with two kids, two dogs and lots of tension. "We were so cramped, so miserable and so stubborn."

Stabilize this situation by remaining flexible. Too often, home buying turns into a test: "If he loves me, he'll agree to the split-level." What is really being tested here, however, is your ability to bend, to open yourself to ideas and possibilities that you may have rejected in the past.

The unfortunate truth that grown-ups must accept is that "we never can get our way completely," says Charles Figley, Ph.D., director of the Psychosocial Stress Research Program at Florida State University in Tallahassee. So make flexibility your byword. Find a way to satisfy both of your needs.

Howard Markman, Ph.D., a psychologist in Denver and co-author of *We Can Work It Out*, recalls one classic negotiation between a husband and wife who could have gone into battle over whether to buy a house (he thought they should own something) or continue renting an apartment (she knew they both hated yard work). After much discussion, they came up with a third alternative: a town house.

AGE-DEFYING BEAUTY SECRETS

Part **8**

Protect your skin now— your future good looks and health depend on it.
—dermatologist Jouni Uitto, M.D., Ph.D.

Female Advantage

None of us can stop the aging process. Fortunately, though, women have an edge over men when it comes to aging gracefully.

"In general, women seem to take a greater interest in their appearances than men do. They are more informed about the hazards of the sun, more likely to protect their skin and more likely to use cosmetic products to reverse aging," says dermatologist Wilma F. Bergfeld, M.D., head of clinical research in the Department of Dermatology at the Cleveland Clinic Foundation and author of *Women Doctors' Guide to Skin Care*. Still, even the most looks-conscious woman may ignore certain age-prone spots that can add years to her appearance. Here's a head-to-toe body map of five frequently overlooked age spots in women, with tips for rejuvenation from Dr. Bergfeld.

▶ Crinkly neck. V-neck blouses, bathing suits and sleeveless tops may look sexy, but they leave the upper chest and neck exposed to the sun's damaging rays. As a result, skin becomes wrinkled and blotchy.

Quick fix: Shield neck and chest with sunscreen with a sun protection factor (SPF) of 15. Wear shirts that cover the chest and hats that shade your neck from the sun.

▶ Flabby upper arms. With age and inactivity, women's upper arms become crepey and wobbly.

Quick fix: Bust flab with a one-two combo of diet (to lose weight) and upper-arm exercises (to tone muscles).

▶ Elephant-skin elbows. Elbows really take a beating: Constant leaning, bumping, and chafing from clothing leads to tough, dry, scaly skin.

Quick fix: Gently scrub elbows with a loofah brush every time you bathe, to abrade rough skin.

▶ Weathered hands. The ultra-thin skin that covers the backs of hands is especially prone to dryness, sun damage, wrinkling and brown age spots.

Quick fix: Ask your doctor for a prescription of Renova, a cream formula of tretinoin (the active ingredient in Retin-A). Renova is specifically designed to reverse the signs of aging; it also bleaches brown spots.

▶ Sun-fried feet. The tops of the feet are often neglected when it comes to slathering on sunscreen, so the skin becomes dry, thin and wrinkled.

Quick fix: Drench feet with moisturizers containing alpha hydroxy acids, to slough off dead skin cells, baring new smooth, fresh skin.

The Year's 20 Top Natural Beauty Solutions

L ooking your best is no accident. It's the natural result of a healthy lifestyle that includes eating wholesome foods, getting enough sleep, being active and treating your body's special needs simply and naturally.

But not all natural beauty solutions are equally worthwhile. To bring you the year's best, we've sorted through dozens and tossed out the questionable (such as scrubbing away body hair with a pumice stone) and the singularly unappealing (smearing one's own ear wax onto chapped lips). What's left behind? Simply the most gentle, effective and soothing options to enhance your well-being and good looks, from head to toe.

Smooth, Radiant Skin

Moisturize, correct oily skin, smooth rough spots and more, with natural ingredients.

Make the ultimate moisturizer. To keep your skin moist and supple, apply a body moisturizer after every bath or shower to seal in moisture. Some of the best natural emollients are cocoa butter and oils such as almond, apricot kernel, sesame and olive.

Try an oil bath. This practice of reversing the bath-and-moisturizer routine is borrowed from African and Indian cultures. Smooth an oil—shea butter is traditionally African, sesame oil is typically Indian—all over your body and relax on a towel for a half-hour or so. Then, with a loofah or a rough washcloth, gently scrub the oil away in a bath or shower. Sitting in the bath may be your best bet, to avoid the possibility of slipping with oily feet.

Create a fruity skin smoother. Do you have problems with extra-dry skin like those little red bumps on the backs of your arms and legs? Called keratosis pilaris, they're a harmless condition caused by an excessive buildup of skin cells around hair follicles.

You can smooth these bumps with an exfoliator granular scrub or loofah. Follow up with a dose of an extra-rich moisturizer such as natural shea butter.

To really zap those patches, add the power of alpha hydroxy acids (AHAs), which exfoliate through natural chemical action. Apply some sour milk, which contains lactic acid, or use the fruit acids present in fresh papaya or strawberries (grind the fruit in a food processor and add a bit of honey to form a paste). Leave the milk or fruit paste on your skin for ten minutes, then gently scrub it off in a warm shower and finish with a moisturizer. The AHAs will gently dissolve layers of dead skin and reveal the fresh new skin beneath.

Cool sunburn with oats and cukes. By now, everybody knows that one of the simplest ways to ensure skin health is to stay out of the sun. But what should you do if you do get a sunburn? Try applying a soothing poultice of grated cucumber to the red areas (cucumber can help heal burned or chapped skin). Or soak in a lukewarm bath with a cup of rolled oats tied into a small cheesecloth bag; the oats will soothe and soften your skin.

Lighten with lemon. If years of past sun abuse have left you with visible sun damage—so-called age spots or freckles—you can lighten the discolored areas with a daily dab of pineapple or lemon juice, which acts as a mild bleach. Be careful not to rub (the juice can be irritating and can't be expected to take away these marks in only one session). Follow up with moisturizer.

More Tips for a Glowing Complexion

Work wonders with your face—unclog pores, erase oily shine and shrink under-eye puffiness with surprising ingredients such as chamomile, honey and brewer's yeast.

Soothe puffy eyes. For a surefire solution to can't-quite-wake-up eyes, grate a few teaspoons of fresh cucumber and put it onto two cotton pads. Or, use two chamomile tea bags, steeped and cooled. Rest with your eyes closed beneath the pads or tea bags for 15 to 20 minutes. Both help reduce swelling in the delicate area beneath your eyes.

Reduce the shine. Bothered by a shiny nose or forehead? Oil glands are generally more plentiful in these areas than on the cheeks, creating the dreaded four-o'clock shine. To fight it, wipe your face with a homemade toner made with one peeled cucumber, one teaspoon witch hazel and one teaspoon rose water, whipped together in a blender or food processor. Throughout the day, you also can dust your face with a little loose powder or silky, fine-ground arrowroot powder to take away the shine.

Cleanse with yogurt and honey. Even if you've left your teens far behind, you may be susceptible to adult acne and pimples. Dermatologists say that people in their thirties can get even more pimples than the pre-prom set.

Every day, clean your face with a yogurt-and-honey wash (add a few table-spoons of organic honey to a cup of natural yogurt). Honey is a gentle cleanser and skin conditioner, and yogurt helps to smooth the skin as it cleans and exfoliates. To treat individual pimples, dab them with a bit of tea tree oil (but use caution, tea tree oil causes rash in some people) or with fresh garlic juice (better on evenings spent alone). Both are antibacterial agents and will speed the healing of blemishes.

Unclog pores with peppermint and papaya. Blackheads, those blocked pores that often appear on the nose, chin and forehead, can be tough to get rid of, and dermatologists agree that it's best to avoid trying to do so by

When Natural *Isn't* Better

Green tea, chamomile, fruit acids, grape seed extract, vitamins C and E—lately, the ingredients in many cosmetics are sounding more like edibles from a health food store.

Unlike make-at-home beauty products that use natural ingredients like oils and fruits—and are fun to concoct, usually gentle and often offer simple solutions to everyday hair and skin problems—commercial products with whole-some-sounding ingredients don't necessarily deliver more than traditional formulas with synthetic ingredients.

"There isn't much evidence that 'natural' products are better," says Barry I. Resnik, M.D., clinical instructor of dermatology at the University of Miami School of Medicine.

Every woman's skin and hair is slightly different—it's possible that yours may derive some benefit from a partic-ular ingredient, natural or otherwise.

But some ingredients—like vitamin C, often added to moisturizers and cleansers, and vitamin E, found in hair-styling products and deodorants—may do less than the label would lead you to believe. While these vitamins can be potent antioxidants inside your body, helping lower the risk of heart disease and other illnesses, applying them to skin and hair probably has reduced effect on how young your hair or skin looks, Dr. Resnik notes.

And other natural ingredients should be used cautiously. "Tea tree oil, also called TC3 or melaleuca on labels, is a potent 'contact sensitizer'—it can cause rashes in some people with repeated exposure," he says.

The bottom line? If you like natural products, use them—but stop if irritation develops.

HEALTH FLASH

squeezing. To help unclog blocked pores without damaging your skin, try a refreshing peppermint steam.

Boil a pan of water and remove from heat. Add a handful of fresh peppermint leaves, two tablespoons dried peppermint or a few drops of peppermint oil to the hot water. Drape a towel over your head and let the steam bathe your face—and unblock your pores—for a few minutes. Next, gently rub your face with the inside of a fresh papaya skin—it will slough away old, dead skin cells while conditioning your skin with vitamins A and C.

A Fresh Mouth

To keep your breath fresh and your mouth healthy, try incorporating these safe and easy solutions into your hygiene routine.

Brush with cinnamon. For a change of pace from your usual toothpaste, try mixing a batch of homemade cinnamon tooth powder by blending one teaspoon ground cinnamon with two teaspoons baking soda. Or, use a bit of natural sea salt instead.

Freshen your breath with herbs. For a natural way to keep your breath smelling clean and appealing, add one of these remedies to your morning brushing routine. Rinse your mouth with diluted peppermint oil (add a drop or two to a glass of water). Or, try munching on some fresh parsley leaves or anise seeds.

You also can make a fragrant, breath-sweetening lavender gargle by steeping a handful of fresh lavender flowers (or one tablespoon dried lavender) in a cup of boiling water for ten minutes; strain and gargle. Other herbs that make great breath-freshening gargles are allspice, clove and eucalyptus. Use one tablespoon of the herb per cup of water.

Vibrant Hair

Keep your crowning glory at its natural best with easy-to-make hair-care preparations.

For dandruff control, apply jojoba. Dandruff, which is characterized by an excessive sloughing of the scalp's skin cells, can be caused by stress, dietary imbalances and—surprise—overuse of harsh commercial dandruff shampoos. For an effective natural dandruff remedy, try massaging your scalp with some warm vegetable oil before shampooing.

The oil will help soften and loosen dandruff flakes. Jojoba oil works especially well; it penetrates the scalp to deliver extra moisture without making your hair oily. You can add a few drops each of rosemary and eucalyptus oil for added sensory and curative powers (both have stimulant and astringent properties).

Tame the frizzies with rosemary. Here's a tip for managing frizzy or very thick hair. Rub a few drops of rosemary oil between your palms and apply the oil to your hair. It will condition your hair and weigh it down slightly, making it easier to control.

Boost body with a nettle rinse. If your tresses tend to be flat, an herbal rinse made with stinging nettles can boost volume (the nettles are slightly astringent). Mix four tablespoons of the dried herb with a cup of water and simmer for 30 minutes (or simmer for 30 minutes and allow the mixture to steep overnight). Strain, cool and apply to clean, conditioned hair. Your hair will be noticeably fuller.

Nourish dry hair naturally. If your hair has a tendency to be dry or brittle, try this Native American solution. Wash it with pounded yucca root mixed with enough water to make a soapy paste. Yucca root lathers just like soap or shampoo and will leave your hair lustrous.

Banish oil with this essential shampoo. If oily hair is a problem for you, try a homemade essential oil shampoo (mix ten drops of juniper or cypress oil with a cup of mild, unscented shampoo). The oils act as astringents, counteracting an oily scalp and stimulating the scalp and the senses.

Enhance your natural hair color. If you're finding your hair color less than inspiring, try giving it a natural color and shine boost with an herbal shampoo. Simmer the appropriate herbs for your hair color in a half-cup of water for ten minutes, then strain, cool and add to a half-cup of mild shampoo.

Use two tablespoons dried chamomile flowers if you're blond or one black tea bag, one tablespoon dried rosemary and one tablespoon dried sage for darker hair.

Note: The longer you steep the herbs, the deeper the color will be. Give your hair a final rinse of warm water mixed with a few tablespoons of apple cider vinegar if you have darker hair or lemon juice if your hair is blond. This will smooth the hair's cuticles, making it sleek and shiny.

All the Rest

Don't neglect your extremities. These all-natural remedies pamper your elbows, fingernails and more.

Relax in a soothing soak. To smooth and soothe dry, rough skin and nails, soak your hands in a bit of warm vegetable or castor oil and follow with this healing massage. Mix two boiled, mashed potatoes with equal amounts of rose water and milk (enough to make a paste) and add two drops of glycerin. Rub on your hands for several minutes, then rinse.

The texture of the mashed potatoes feels like, well . . . mashed potatoes, but trust us: Your hands will feel great afterward. If potatoes don't appeal to you, substitute a cup of cooked oatmeal.

Revitalize dry nails with almond oil. Do your fingernails tend to split? Dry nails can be revived with a soothing almond oil soak. For an extra measure of moisturizing and healing, you can add a few drops of healing sandalwood oil. If your nails are too soft, apply a bit of vitamin E (from a capsule) every day. Both of these remedies will do wonders for dry, ragged cuticles, too.

Soften rough skin. Often forgotten underneath heavy layers of winter clothing, your feet, hands, knees and elbows can end up with thickened, dry skin. You can soften these patches by rubbing them with the inside of a fresh avocado peel. Its slightly abrasive texture will smooth the bumps away. And the emollient avocado oil, which contains vitamins A, D and E, will moisturize and condition the skin. (The inside of a fresh papaya skin will have the same effect.)

How Will You Look Ten Years from Now?

Think about getting older and your skin is a shoo-in on your list of worries—wrinkles, blotchiness, dryness, the seemingly inevitable hallmarks of passing years.

Some prevention strategies—stay out of the sun, don't smoke, eat a well-balanced diet—we've heard about for years. But for the first time, researchers can offer products and treatments that stop the skin-aging clock or, for those who didn't pay attention when they should have, turn it back.

As dermatologic researchers learn more about the aging process, they now realize that when it comes to your skin, biology alone plays a relatively small role. How healthy your skin looks now and how youthful it will look decades from now depend largely on how well you take care of it.

Your Twenties

This is count-your-blessings time. Although some women are still recovering from adolescence, and a few problems hit this age-group particularly, the majority of women in their twenties aren't yet seeing much deterioration.

Acne

This is probably the most common complaint of women in their twenties, says Michael G. Mancuso, M.D., senior clinical instructor at Case Western Reserve University School of Medicine in Cleveland. It usually stops by mid-decade, but many also get acne from oral contraceptives.

Where it shows up: Generally, on the face, neck, chest and back.

What to do about it: For milder cases, drugstore remedies such as benzoyl peroxide and salicylic acid may be enough. Dermatologists may prescribe antibiotics or tretinoin (Retin-A) or its oral counterpart, isotretinoin (Accutane), which is very effective. But because of its link to birth defects, you should never use it if you're pregnant or trying to conceive.

Melasma

Pregnancy or birth control pills can trigger melasma, or "mask of pregnancy"—a pattern of darkened skin that results from hormones and sun exposure combined.

Where it shows up: Over the forehead, down the sides of the face onto the cheeks and over the nose.

What to do about it: It usually goes away on its own, especially if it results from pregnancy, says Neil Fenske, M.D., professor and director of dermatology and cutaneous surgery at the University of South Florida College of Medicine in Tampa. But if the melasma is related to taking the Pill, dermatologists may prescribe creams that will lighten it, provided you stay out of the sun.

Moles

Your body continues to produce these throughout your twenties and thirties, says Dr. Mancuso.

Where they show up: Anywhere.

What to do about them: To rule out melanoma, a dermatologist should check any new or existing mole that is asymmetrical, has uneven color or irregular borders, is larger in diameter than a pencil eraser, has uneven elevation or that bleeds or oozes. Moles can be removed by cutting.

Skin Tags

These tiny flesh-colored growths may start to appear now, or perhaps not until your thirties; they are especially likely after pregnancy.

Where they show up: On the neck, under breasts, around eyes, under armpits.

What to do about them: They're benign, but if you want them removed for cosmetic reasons, a doctor can easily snip a tag or burn it off with an electric needle.

Photoaging

If you're extraordinarily sun sensitive or have had unusually heavy ultraviolet exposure (you work outdoors or have been a slavish sun worshiper), you may see sun damage, including some wrinkling, drying, freckling or blotchy pigment, slight sagging, precancerous spots or, very rarely, skin cancer.

Where it shows up: On the most heavily exposed areas, usually the face and the backs of hands and the V-shaped area of the neck and chest.

What to do about it: Start getting smart about the sun now and you'll not only minimize additional damage but also repair some of what has already been wrought. That means using a broad-spectrum sunblock with a sun protection factor (SPF) of at least 15 and staying out of midday rays altogether, covering up with a hat and, as much as possible, long sleeves and long pants. Also have a dermatologist check any suspicious growths.

Your Thirties

For most women, this is the decade of first wrinkles, first telltale traces of sunning not wisely but too well. Other, nonaging-related problems may crop up in these years, too.

Acne

Although they're not sure why, some doctors are noticing a tremendous increase in first-time acne in women ages 35 to 40. "Is it part of photoaging?" asks Dr. Mancuso. "Or is it because of all the different cosmetics

---

More Adult Women Have Acne

Blame it on heredity or blame it on hormones. Either way, more and more women in their thirties and forties seem to be coming down with adult acne, dermatologists note.

"We're beginning to think that inflammatory acne could be a lot like hay fever—it's an inherited, inappropriate sensitivity to a benign thing," says Guy Webster, M.D., Ph.D., associate professor of dermatology at Jefferson Medical College of Thomas Jefferson University in Philadelphia. In this case, you're oversensitive to the harmless bacteria in the tiny hair follicles on your face.

Another theory has to do with hormones. At different stages of your life, as various hormones change, they may either stimulate or improve acne. Hormone replacement therapy, however, seems to have no effect on acne.

When you're looking to get rid of an angry, red pimple and prevent more from popping up, remember these rules: Never squeeze. Wash gently. Look for makeup and moisturizers that say on the label that they're oil-free, or nonacnegenic or noncomedogenic (will not cause comedones, commonly known as blackheads or whiteheads). Try a benzoyl peroxide lotion or alpha hydroxy acids with a minimum concentration of 8 percent (available most often by prescription) to prevent new comedones from forming.

And if pimples tend to be large and inflamed, see your dermatologist about antibiotics and other prescription-only anti-acne medications.

HEALTH FLASH

women use now? Or does it have something to do with hormonal factors related to postponing childbearing?"

Where it shows up: Face, neck, chest, back and, in the case of acne cysts, along the jawline.

What to do about it: Treatment is the same as for younger women, but if your skin is starting to feel dry, you may want to use one of the new mild or moisturizing formulations.

Contact Allergies

Rashes or irritation become common as women "see wrinkles or other things they don't like and get into gooping stuff on," says Dr. Fenske. You can react to a new product or to one that you've been using a long time, because increased usage promotes sensitivity.

Where they show up: Primarily on the face, where cosmetics are used most; nail polish can cause rashes to appear on the eyelids because you rub your eyes.

What to do about them: Stop using any suspect product. If you can't track down the cause, see a dermatologist, who may do a patch test and also prescribe a cortisone cream. To help track a possible allergy, add only one new product at a time to your cosmetic repertoire and use it at least a month before adding another.

Fat Shifts

Fat may have started to shift in your twenties, but the shift becomes noticeable now. Fat changes position because of a genetically programmed rearrangement just under the skin, which makes the surface bumpier and more uneven, explains Jouni Uitto, M.D., Ph.D., chair of the Department of Dermatology at Thomas Jefferson University in Philadelphia. Toward the end of the decade, you may also notice that major fat deposits on your body are shifting locale.

Where they show up: Irregularities in fat distribution can appear on the face and almost anywhere that skin has a lot of natural cushioning—thighs, buttocks and the backs of your arms. Larger-scale shifts show up (as you're probably all too aware) as extra padding on your hips, thighs, buttocks and stomach.

What to do about them: Losing weight may help, but you'll probably just get skinnier in other areas, such as your face and chest, where you probably want to hold on to whatever fat you have. Exercise can tone the muscles and skin, which gives you a smoother look.

Cherry Angiomas

These benign blood vessel growths look like tiny red bumps.

Where they show up: On the face, neck and chest.

What to do about them: They're harmless, but if you'd like to attack angiomas for cosmetic reasons, a dermatologist can remove them through freezing, electroburning or cutting, or with a laser.

Seborrheic Keratoses

A consequence of natural aging, these waxy pencil eraser–size brown growths start turning up in the late thirties and early forties.

Where they show up: On the face, chest and back.

What to do about them: If their appearance bothers you, you can have a dermatologist remove them.

"Broken" Capillaries

These fine red lines or flat spidery spots are actually dilated (not necessarily broken) tiny blood vessels.

Where they show up: On the face, particularly around the nose, cheeks and sometimes the chin.

What to do about them: Avoid sun and alcohol, which may aggravate them. A dermatologist can erase individual red lines with an electric needle or laser.

Innate Aging

Many genetically programmed slowdowns, including breakdown of elastic fibers, started in the twenties but, except for some fine wrinkles, the consequences are not too visible yet.

Where it shows up: Everywhere. Intrinsic aging affects skin over the entire body.

What to do about it: Moisturizers temporarily improve the appearance.

Photoaging

Unless you have dark skin or have been a lifelong sun avoider, you'll start paying the piper for sun exposure now.

Where it shows up: Hands and face provide prime territory. Legs are prone to quarter-inch squarish white spots, hands and arms to tiny hemorrhages that leave little white star-shaped scars where they heal.

On the neck and chest, you may see striated beaded lines—V-shaped rows of oil glands (enlarged by the sun), which stand out all the more because the skin surrounding them has been thinned by sun exposure, reports Dr. Fenske.

What to do about it: Stop the sun-aging clock by becoming serious about sun protection. You may also want to try antiphotoaging products: Tretinoin (Retin-A), for instance, stimulates the turnover of skin cells; alpha hydroxy acids work as mild peels that make complexions smoother; and antioxidants protect cells from further damage.

Some moisturizers containing liposome deliver lost lipids to the subsurface, says Dr. Uitto, which helps to diminish many of the fine wrinkles from sun damage.

Your Forties

Aging—from advancing years as well as from too much sun—moves center stage this decade, along with a few other skin risks.

Seborrhea

This greasy, scaly skin condition typically appears early in the decade.

Where it shows up: Especially around the nose and scalp, where it creates dandrufflike problems.

What to do about it: An over-the-counter dandruff shampoo may be enough for mild scalp flaking; for more stubborn cases, see a dermatologist, who may prescribe a stronger shampoo or cortisone lotion.

Moles

Moles start to decrease in your forties, a disappearing act that continues the rest of your life.

Where they show up: They don't show up much anymore, which is why you need to be especially suspicious of any new growths, says Dr. Mancuso.

What to do about them: Have a dermatologist check any new mole, especially if it has unusual characteristics (as described in "Your Twenties" on page 280).

Fat Loss

As fat gets deposited on the lower torso and upper legs, it decreases in other areas.

Where it shows up: You'll notice this decrease primarily in the face and neck but also on the arms and upper torso.

What to do about it: Gaining weight will help compensate those diminished areas, but the weight will show in the rest of your body, too.

Varicose Veins or Spider Veins

The tendency to develop these thin or thick squiggly purple lines or red or purplish stars is primarily genetic. But they're further provoked by years of sun exposure, pregnancy, occupations that call for a lot of standing and a slowed-down circulatory system (blood pools in the veins because your body doesn't pump it back toward the heart as efficiently as before).

Where they show up: Anywhere on the legs, but often they appear on the upper thighs.

What to do about them: Wear special support hose (available in sheer weights and stylish colors) and keep your feet elevated as much as possible to relieve discomfort and help prevent more vein damage. Also, surgery or injections can usually banish them. But frequent walking is one of the best treatment-prevention strategies. Working the leg muscles assists the upward blood-pumping action.

Innate Aging

This is the decade in which little fine wrinkles, thinning skin layers and some uneven pigmentation becomes noticeable. Aging suddenly accelerates because your skin can no longer repair the degradation of elastic fibers. Also, as oil production and cell turnover slow down, skin becomes drier.

Where it shows up: All over. To get a better sense of what's innate and what's photoaged, compare unexposed skin (such as that on your breasts) with skin on your face or hands.

What to do about it: Moisturizers help compensate for dryness, and photoaging remedies may counteract some of the visible effects of innate aging.

Photoaging

Almost every white woman shows signs of sun damage by her mid-forties, says Sheldon Pinnell, M.D., chief of dermatology at Duke University in Durham, North Carolina.

And by the end of the decade, many women will be getting a lot of age spots, cherry angiomas and flat liver spots on the backs of the hands. In addition to these, be prepared, says Dr. Uitto, for more wrinkling, sagging, a loss of elasticity and tone, blotchiness and possibly some deep furrows. Look, too, for actinic keratoses—scaly red lesions caused by overexposure to the sun—that are common at this age.

Where it shows up: Face and hands usually lead the way, but expect almost any place that has had regular sun exposure—legs, arms, chest, neck—to show some changes.

What to do about it: In addition to the prevention strategies and repair potions discussed previously, you may want to consider a heavier-duty fix. To erase fine wrinkles, freshen tone and blend uneven pigment, possibilities include a series of light, glycolic acid peels; a stronger chemical peel or—popular these days—a laser peel.

Injections of collagen or fat temporarily fill in deeper lines (make sure that you consult a reputable doctor and that you consider all the risks). The newest technique is injecting botulism toxin, which temporarily paralyzes frown muscles and smooths between-the-brow furrows.

Sleep: Nature's New Beauty Secret

For women seduced by the fast lane and ravaged by stress, getting a good night's sleep has become something that we can only dream about.

Once, we just said we were tired. But now, sleep deprivation has a new, almost uncanny cachet. In fact, there's even a new name for it—insufficient sleep syndrome—which means, according to Michael Stevenson, Ph.D., director of the North Valley Sleep Disorder Center in Mission Hill, California, "not allowing yourself an adequate amount of time to get enough sleep so that you feel viable and alert during the daytime."

Not surprising, insufficient sleep syndrome is most common among women ages 20 to 40, who are juggling family and career and end up doing most of the child care and domestic duties. This year, as in any given year, probably 50 percent of the population is not getting enough sleep, notes Dr. Stevenson, and one-third of the population will experience some kind of insomnia.

"Most likely, people who claim that they need only five to six hours are building up a 'sleep debt.' There are people who do that all week, then catch up all at once on the weekend," he says.

Why Snoozing Is a Beauty Necessity

You know who you are: The puffy, swollen-eyed ranks of the chronically sleep deprived who nod to one another from beneath hardened layers of smudge-proof undereye cover-up.

You exchange tips on whether Visine beats out Murine in the redness-relief category and debate how often yellowed, coffee-stained teeth need to be cleaned, while you're slugging down megadoses of caffeine. Even women whose looks earn them their living don't get their beauty sleep these days, which would be between seven and eight hours per night for most adults.

"I've made up more than my share of models coming off the red-eye," says makeup artist Bobbi Brown. "The irony is that the more beautiful and in the limelight you are, the less you sleep. That's why those women are always running off to a spa."

It's not a myth that beauty sleep supplies the body with a literal time-out—a time to rest, restore, moisturize, clean the skin and take yourself out of offices, restaurants, subways and other potentially polluted environments.

"During the day," says Patricia Wexler, M.D., a New York City dermatologist affiliated with Beth Israel Medical Center, "your adrenaline is rushing, your blood pressure goes up, you tend to get dehydrated, your oil secretion goes up and pores enlarge. Beauty sleep is, literally, time that you give yourself to beautify."

And chronic sleep deprivation, according to Dr. Wexler, can do just the opposite: cause puffy, sallow and lackluster skin; hair loss and nail breakage—not to mention dark circles around the eyes. It can also affect your cognitive abilities (scattering your attention and hindering your memory retention) and your personality (making you more susceptible to emotional situations that ordinarily wouldn't bother you).

For those of us who try to catch up on our sleep on the weekends, here's the bad news: "Sleep deprivation is just another sign of stress on the body," says Dr. Wexler. "When people are chronically sleep-deprived and then try to catch up all at once, they can look even puffier because of their prolonged recumbent position and fluid retention." And catching up on your sleep all at once is not a healthy practice to follow, according to Dr. Stevenson—you should get it when you need it.

Pick-Me-Ups for the Fatigued

If you wake up with puffiness under the eyes, Dr. Wexler says, apply ice compresses. Warmth causes swelling, whereas cold is a vasoconstrictor—causing blood vessels to shrink, reducing puffiness.

Ice-cold, wet tea bags work well, and they contain caffeine—a diuretic that draws fluid out of the area. Or try a bag of frozen peas, which will conform more comfortably to the under-eye area than, say, a bag of frozen broccoli. But don't overdo it; you may be sensitive to broken capillaries around the eye area. Just a few splashes from a sinkful of ice cubes and cold water will do the trick. Stay away from alcohol and salt, which cause fluid retention, but you needn't resist the overwhelming urge to indulge in the occasional double espresso.

The New Art of Camouflage

In the 1950s, concealers came in one basic consistency—Spackle—and one color. But anything seemed better than dark circles. It still does.

Happily, concealers have improved. Walk down the cosmetics aisle this year and you'll find dozens to choose from. But which is best for you? And how should you apply it? When 15 women tried out 12 new concealers for *Prevention* magazine, they uncovered some selection guidelines that may save your "not-quite-right" makeup drawer from overflowing.

First, however, let's be clear that you can be healthier than Jane Fonda and still have undereye circles. Causes range from thin skin to allergies to fatigue.

"People who have circles as children were just born with more prominent vascular structures than people without circles," says Ly-Le Tran, M.D., assistant vice-president of corporate scientific affairs for L'Oréal, the cosmetics company. "And for most people, the blood vessels under the eye area become even more noticeable as they get a little bit older, because they have a reduced number of skin layers in that area."

Here are some guidelines for choosing and applying a concealer, gleaned from the experience of the 15 women who tested a dozen different brands.

▶ Choose a color that matches your skin tone, but one shade lighter. Going too light makes circles stand out instead of hiding them.
▶ The oilier your skin, the lighter in weight your concealer should be. Women with dry to normal skin got good results with a range of concealers—from the heaviest to the sheerest.
▶ Use a damp sponge makeup wedge or your fingertip to apply and blend the edges of your concealer underneath your eyes. Apply from the inner corner of your eye to a point about halfway across at the center of your eye. Blend by patting the margins down into the cheek.
▶ Experiment with applying your foundation first, then patting the concealer over top. Many makeup artists do this.

HEALTH FLASH

Beauty expert Dorit Baxter, of the Dorit Baxter Day Spa in New York City, suggests exercise and a steam bath to get the circulation going. Try massaging your face, says Baxter, who recommends light tapping or circling, with creamy fingers, from your inner eye to the outer corners of your eye and then back around, about 20 times.

Or take a few minutes for a soothing facial like the Anti-Stress Mask from Annemarie Borlind. With its carrots, ginkgo and menthyl lactate, the mask relaxes and energizes you and your skin.

When the body is sleep-deprived, drinking water is a big help because your skin may be dehydrated. Choose hydrating makeup, says Brown, who recommends moisturizing in the morning and using a foundation with a creamy base, or a tinted moisturizer. Resist the impulse to pile on makeup—in fact, wear less, especially around the eyes.

When you're tired, Brown says, your skin looks one shade paler. What you need to do is warm up the skin and brighten the face—with a bronzer perhaps—to give it a glow. Yellow powder, along with a concealer one or two shades lighter than the skin, helps mute undereye circles.

You may want to wear your blush a little brighter to make your cheeks pop out so that the dark circles won't be as noticeable. Stay away from orange- and yellow-based lipsticks. When you're tired, seek out rose tones.

The poet Adrienne Rich says, "A thinking woman sleeps with monsters." If that's your destiny, you might just consider it another thing to lose sleep over. Maybe you can, at least, learn to take a quick nap. But most of all remember this: Walk softly and carry a big undereye concealer stick.

45

The Inside Story on Thick, Lustrous Hair

R apunzel, Rapunzel, let down your hair!" the prince hollered. Rapunzel, in the Brothers Grimm fairy tale, promptly did as she was told. From the top of the tower, she unwound her crowning glory.

Right there, it's obvious that Rapunzel was no modern woman. Today, a woman might have to shampoo, condition, plug in the hair dryer and the curling iron, apply styling gel or mousse, comb and spray before letting the world glimpse her tresses.

And if Rapunzel were a baby boomer, even that routine might not be enough. This year, experts say that the cover-the-gray trend among women in their forties and fifties is growing even larger.

And if she had to shop for hair-care products first, the process could take a very long time. These days, the variety of special hair-care products on store shelves has become even more overwhelming—there's a goop, gel, mousse, color tint or moisturizer for everyone's unique needs. With them, you can fine-tune your hair, getting the curl, control, bounce, hue or texture that you desire. But do we need all those spritzes and deep conditioners, the hot-oil treatments and cooling shampoos?

Experts say yes. Each product is right for someone. But the key to getting the most out of them is to understand what a product can and cannot do, use it correctly and not expect miracles.

So when a glimpse of your hair in the mirror gives you that "Oh, no!" feeling, it's probably time to do something about it. Fortunately, there's a lot that can be done.

Raising the Dead

Hair is just hard, dead protein. Even so, a healthy head of hair looks vibrantly alive, says Diana Bihova, M.D., clinical assistant professor of dermatology at New York University Medical Center in New York City. "That's the interesting thing. It's smooth. It shines. You almost want to touch it."

Special Treatment for Scalps

To womenfolk in the Wild West, getting scalped was a whole lot worse than just a bad hair day.

While scalpings have gone out with the flintlock, the irony is that we're still losing a sizable portion of our tightly stretched scalps, flake by flake, day by day.

Two kinds of common skin problems can accelerate that shedding process. One is an inflammation called seborrheic dermatitis. It's better known as problem dandruff, which is different from regular dandruff.

"True dandruff is common and harmless," notes Jerome Shupack, M.D., professor of clinical dermatology at New York University Medical Center in New York City. Seborrheic dermatitis, on the other hand, is a real problem that won't go away without special treatment.

Psoriasis is the other dead-skin problem that can make your scalp flake. If you have psoriasis, it's even more likely than seborrheic dermatitis to show up on other parts of your body—often in the form of red, itchy or scaly patches.

"Psoriasis makes a thicker type of crust than seborrheic dermatitis," says Dr. Shupack. "If you try to scrape it off, it bleeds."

You'll probably want to have a doctor check out psoriasis if you suspect that you have it. But dandruff and mild seborrheic dermatitis don't necessarily require any special medical attention. Here's how to nix unwanted flakes at home.

Lather up. Any shampoo will wash away dead skin cells, says Dr. Shupack. "If you shampoo every day, you'll mechanically remove the scales."

Do something special. If regular shampoos don't do the trick, use a dandruff shampoo twice a week and use regular shampoo the other days to control normal scaling, suggests Dr. Shupack.

But dandruff shampoos may be harsh and can damage hair—especially fine hair—and they can discolor blond, white or gray hair, cautions Diana Bihova, M.D., clinical assistant professor of dermatology at New York University Medical Center in New York City. Use a hair conditioner to prevent any dryness or damage.

Rotate shampoos. Even when a dandruff shampoo clears up flaking without a hitch, you'll probably find that the flakes will start falling again after a few months. Switch shampoos about three times a year, Dr. Bihova suggests. "Each kind of shampoo works differently. You have to find the right one that works for you at any particular time through a process of trial and error."

More Women Are Coloring Their Hair

More and more women are covering their gray hair—most likely because there's more gray hair out there. As baby boomers head into their forties and fifties, nearly one-half of all women are now choosing to change the natural tint of their tresses.

Why? In part, the answer lies in the fact that there are so many coloring options now—with new products landing on the market seemingly every few months. "There are more choices," says John Corbett, Ph.D., vice-president of scientific and technical affairs at Clairol in Stamford, Connecticut.

Not ready to commit to a permanent new look? You can choose a semipermanent rinse that will last through 6 to 12 shampooings—about two weeks if you wash your hair daily. Or go with a *demi*permanent color, which lasts longer than semipermanent shades but is gentler on the hair than the stronger chemical processes found in permanent color processes.

"A lot of growth in the market has been in these areas," Dr. Corbett says. "They're great for coloring gray—especially hair just beginning to gray."

Color-enhancing shampoos, which add a color boost lasting through less than six ordinary shampooings, are another option. "They're marketed to those who like red and gold shades and can be used between permanent colors to perk up the color," says Dr. Corbett.

What if your hair is beyond the beginning-to-gray phase? "Hair that's 40 percent gray or more needs permanent color," Dr. Corbett says. The advantage of permanent color is that you can go darker or lighter (with semipermanent processes, you can only go darker). And, for better or for worse, it won't wash out.

The outer layer of each hair is made up of overlapping shingles of keratin cells called the cuticle. When our hair is clean, and when we don't torture it with perms and dyes, those shingles lie flat and reflect light—so hair is shiny. Dirt and damage from hair dyes or permanents can rough up those shingles. That's when our hair looks dull or lifeless.

For healthier, gleaming tresses, gentle washing and gentle conditioning are the keys. That's why shampoos get so much attention in the hair-coddling world. Here's what experts say about using them.

Brush up your technique. The first step to a good shampoo is a good brushing. "This loosens excess grooming products, dirt and natural oil as well as stimulates your scalp," says Damien Miano, top hairstylist and co-owner of New York City's Miano/Viél Salon and Spa. Begin by brushing just the ends of your hair to detangle it. Then gradually work your brush in toward your scalp. If you brush in one stroke from the scalp out to the ends, the force of brushing can damage the oldest part of your hair—especially if you have long hair—and cause split ends.

Don't brush too long or too strong. "You'll traumatize the hair if you brush it 100 times, like the old adage says," warns Dr. Bihova.

Select a smart one. Shampoos are becoming more and more select, with many new products targeted to treat specific hair types. For example, blonds with fine hair can pick thickening shampoos to add body. The label may say "thickening," "volumizing," "remoisturizing" or "body-building." Other shampoos are custom-made for processed hair that's been dyed, bleached or permed.

Hair isn't predictable, and you can't go entirely by the label. Even baby shampoos aren't as gentle as they're touted to be, says Marty Sawaya, M.D., Ph.D., assistant professor of dermatology at the University of Florida Health Science Center in Gainesville.

So how do you test them out? Dr. Bihova recommends that you audition shampoos. Buy sample sizes until you find ones that you like.

Do the old switcheroo. "Don't get stuck with one shampoo; keep switching them often," says Dr. Bihova. "This is especially important for people with scalp problems like dandruff, psoriasis or dermatitis." You'll know that it's time to switch when the shampoo is less effective than it was when you first started using it. This doesn't mean that you have to buy a new brand every week. "Keep two main brands around and interchange them. For normal hair, switching gets rid of buildup."

Wash out a myth. The old saw that washing your hair every day dries it out is untrue, says Philip Kingsley, owner and founder of Trichological Centers in London and New York City and author of *Hair*. "If you get the correct shampoo, it does just the opposite. And it's a misconception that daily washing dulls your hair. It makes those cuticles lie down flat and tight and shiny."

The more frequently you wash your hair, the less shampoo you'll need at each washing, experts say. A nickel-size dab is the maximum amount for a daily shampoo, and one application will do the job.

Condition hair into shape. After shampooing, work in a conditioner. Many conditioners are targeted for your hair type just like shampoos are. Use a lightweight conditioner on fine, thin hair and a heavier conditioner on coarser or curly hair, Kingsley advises. Using a heavy conditioner on fine hair could make it limp and greasy, and a light conditioner on heavy or curly hair won't condition sufficiently.

If your hair is chemically treated or damaged, look for a product called deep conditioner to apply once or twice a week. Some deep conditioners are applied before you shampoo, allowed to set, then shampooed out. Others are leave-in versions. You can work them into your wet hair after you shampoo.

Gentle Strategies for Tender Tresses

What the weather's like, what you wash with and even how you style your tresses can make the difference between hair that's a crowning glory and plain old dull, frizzy tresses.

Summer's sunburns can easily give you flakes in your flip. So protect your part with sunscreen.

In the winter, the dryness of the air, the gradual slowdown in the consumption of fluids and even the added stress the cold months put on some people can equal a flaky scalp. Winter wisdom from Philip Kingsley, owner of the Philip Kingsley Trichological Centers in New York and London—and author of the book *Hair*—is to keep drinking fluids and wash your hair as often as you do in the summer. (By the way, *trichology* is simply the study of hair.)

Massage your scalp now and then, too. It may help stimulate circulation in your scalp, which may benefit the hair follicles, says Kingsley. If you're going to indulge, use proper technique. Always massage your head gently, and use only the pads of your fingertips. Do one section at a time and move from front to back. Better yet, get someone to do it for you.

If your scalp leans toward the dry side, use mild shampoos and use conditioners. If it's very dry, try this treatment recommended by Diana Bihova, M.D., clinical assistant professor of dermatology at New York University Medical Center in New York City: Mix a little of your bath oil with water, apply it directly to the scalp and leave it on for an hour. (Wrap it in a towel or turban.) Then shampoo it off.

No matter what your hair type, don't use a detergent shampoo every time you wash—it's too harsh. Interchange shampoos that strip or medicate the hair and scalp with milder ones. And don't forget to rinse well, especially after swimming.

When styling your locks, hold your hair dryer at least ten inches from your scalp when it's on a high setting. Held closer, it can dry out your scalp. And don't brush hard or use a brush that has sharp bristles. Scratches can leave your scalp open to infection.

As for how much you should use, that's a matter of trial and error, according to Kingsley.

The Thin, Gray Line

Most women don't change their hair as dramatically as Madonna does. One-third of American women do color their hair, however, especially as they start to go gray.

If you're happy with gray hair, there's no reason to dye it. But hair dyes can not only add color; they can also fluff and roughen hair cuticles, which makes thin hair appear fuller. That can be an advantage. Even luxuriant hair can start thinning around the time you're age 40—or earlier. So there may be a time when you want to try dye. (But remember, while dye can make your tresses appear fuller, the coloring also damages your hair.)

Once you've decided to color your hair, what's the best way? It helps to consult a good hair pro. Not only can she tell whether you should color your hair but she can also actually look at your hair and tell you the percentage of gray in it. That number can help you make some decisions.

Credits

"Saying No to Hysterectomy: The Controversy Continues" on page 16 was adapted from "The Operation Every Woman Should Question" by Lynn Payer, which was originally published in *McCall's*. Copyright © 1995 by Gruner & Jahr USA Publishing. Reprinted with permission of *McCall's*.

"The New Prescription for Passion" on page 22 was adapted from "Prescription for Passion" by Rick Weiss, which originally appeared in *HEALTH*. Copyright © 1995. Reprinted with permission of *HEALTH*.

"The Healing Power of Phytomins" on page 52 was excerpted with permission from "Reinventing the Vegetable" by Lambeth Hochwald, which originally appeared in the March/April 1996 issue of *Natural Health*. For more information, write to *Natural Health* at P.O. Box 7440, Red Oak, IA 51591-0440.

"Olestra: Olé or Oh No?" on page 67 was adapted from "Fat-Free Foods: Are They a Shortcut to Health?" by Mary Ann Howkins, which originally appeared in the March 1996 issue of *Glamour*. Copyright © 1996 by Condé Nast Publications Inc. Permission courtesy of *Glamour*.

"Alternative Healing: New Options for Women" on page 79 was reprinted from *Nature's Cures*. Copyright © 1996 by Michael Castleman. Permission granted by Rodale Press, Inc.

"The Mind-Body Connection: Stronger Than Ever" on page 86 was adapted from *Healing Mind, Healthy Woman* by Alice D. Domar, Ph.D., and Henry Dreher. Copyright © 1996 by Alice D. Domar, Ph.D., and Henry Dreher. Reprinted with permission of Henry Holt and Co., Inc.

"Uncommon Relief from the Common Cold" on page 92 was adapted from "Uncommon Remedies for the Common Cold" by Ilene Springer, which originally appeared in *Ladies' Home Journal*. Copyright © 1995 by Meredith Corporation. All rights reserved. Reprinted with permission of *Ladies' Home Journal* magazine.

"New Thinking That Outsmarts the Blues" on page 98 was reprinted from *Nature's Cures*. Copyright © 1996 by Michael Castleman. Permission granted by Rodale Press, Inc.

"Get Heart Smart" on page 116 was adapted from "Heart Disease: Who's at Risk?" by Grace Bennett, which originally appeared in *McCall's*. Copyright © 1995 by Gruner & Jahr USA Publishing. Reprinted with permission of *McCall's*.

"Take Control of Your Checkup" on page 130 was adapted from "Brave New Check-Up" by Carolyn Hagan, which originally appeared in *Mademoiselle*. Copyright © 1995 by Condé Nast Publications Inc. Permission courtesy of *Mademoiselle*.

"The New Obesity Drugs: Are They Right for You?" on page 182 was adapted from "Will the New Diet Drugs Work for You?" by Katharine Grieder, which originally appeared in *Mademoiselle*. Copyright © 1995 by Condé Nast Publications Inc. Permission courtesy of *Mademoiselle*.

"The Seven-Meals-a-Day Diet" on page 192 was reprinted from *Low-Fat Living*. Copyright © 1996 by Robert K. Cooper, Ph.D., and Leslie L. Cooper. Permission granted by Rodale Press, Inc.

"A Routine to Shed a Size" on page 206 was reprinted from *Low-Fat Living*. Copyright © 1996 by Robert K. Cooper, Ph.D., and Leslie L. Cooper. Permission granted by Rodale Press, Inc.

"Sizzling Secrets for More and Better Sex" on page 256 was adapted from "12 Little Changes for More and Better Sex" by Jane Zucker, which originally appeared in *Glamour*. Copyright © 1996 by Jane Zucker. Reprinted with permission.

"Good News That Can Jolt Your Marriage" on page 266 was adapted from "Even Good News Can Shake Up Your Marriage" by Ester Davidowitz, which originally appeared in *Redbook*. Copyright © 1995 by Ester Davidowitz. Reprinted with permission.

"Good Marriage: A Fresh Look" on page 268 was adapted from "Tackle Nine Psychological Tasks to Maintain a Good Marriage," which originally appeared in *Executive Health's Good Health Report*. Copyright © 1995 by *Executive Health's Good Health Report*. Reprinted by permission.

"The Year's 20 Top Natural Beauty Solutions" on page 273 was excerpted with permission from "25 Natural Beauty Solutions" by Martha Schindler, *Natural Health*, March/April 1996. For more information, write to *Natural Health* at P.O. Box 7440, Red Oak, IA 51591-0440.

"How Will You Look Ten Years from Now?" on page 279 was adapted from "How Good Will You Look in 10 Years?" by Catherine Clifford, which originally appeared in *Redbook*. Copyright © 1995 by Catherine Clifford. Reprinted with permission.

"Sleep: Nature's New Beauty Secret" on page 286 was adapted from "Beauty Sleep" by Rona Berg, which originally appeared in *SELF*. Copyright © 1995 by Rona Berg. Reprinted with permission.

Index

A

Abdominal exercises, 208–13, 227–32, **227, 228, 229, 230, 231, 232**
  abdominal roll-ups, 210–11, **210**
  exhalation roll-ups, 211, **211**
  reverse trunk rotations, 212–13, **212**
  transpyramid breathing exercise, 209–10
  Abdominal fat
  dangers of, <u>170</u>
  high blood pressure and, <u>226</u>
  hip fat versus, <u>170</u>
Abdominal roll-ups, for abdominal toning, 210–11, **210**
Accutane (Rx), for acne, 280
Acne
  adult, causes of, <u>281</u>
  natural remedies for, 275
  in thirties, 281–82
  in twenties, 279–80
Actinic keratoses, from sun exposure, 285
Activity level, of women, <u>200</u>
Acupuncture, for natural healing, 92, 93, 95
Adipex-P (Rx), for weight loss, 183

AFP test, for prenatal screening, 37, 38–40, <u>40</u>
Age spots
  in forties, 285
  lightening, 274
Aging, quick fixes for, <u>272</u>
Alcoholic beverages
  cancer risk from, 151
  headaches from, 157, 159, 161
  hot flashes from, 7
Alendronate (Rx), for osteoporosis, 114, 115
Allergies, contact, causes of, 282
Allyl sulfides, disease prevention from, 55
Almond oil, for dry nails, 278
Aloe vera, for burns, 79, 81–82
Alpha-carotene, disease prevention from, 55
Alpha-fetoprotein (AFP) test, for prenatal screening, 37, 38–40, <u>40</u>
Alpha hydroxy acids, for relieving
  keratosis pilaris, 274
  photoaging, 283
  sunburned feet, <u>272</u>
Alternative healing
  with cognitive therapy, 98–105
  for colds, 92–97

with herbal medicine, 79–85, 94–95, 96–97
with mini-relaxations, 87–91
popularity of, among women, <u>78</u>
Amniocentesis, for prenatal screening, 37, <u>40</u>
risk of complications from, 38
Androgens, for reducing
breast pain from hormone replacement therapy, 33
depression and anxiety from hormone replacement therapy, 35
headaches from hormone replacement therapy, 34
Anger
heart attacks and, <u>120</u>
overeating from, 191
Angiomas, cherry, 282–83
in forties, 285
Anthocyanins, disease prevention from, 55
Antibiotic, goldenseal as, 84
Antidepressants, 99
Antioxidants, for photoaging, 283
Anti-Stress Mask, as facial, 289
Anxiety
cognitive therapy for, 98–105
from hormone replacement therapy, 34–35
relieving
with music, 102
with scents, 253
Appetite suppressants
over-the-counter, 185
prescription, 183
Apples, green, tranquilizing scent of, <u>253</u>
Appreciation, in love relationships, 264 65
Arm curls, for muscle toning, 218, **218**
Arms, upper
flabby, <u>272</u>
muscle-toning for, 218–19
Arthritis
causes of, 152–53
estrogen and, <u>108</u>
increased incidence of, <u>154</u>
prevention of, 153
relieving pain of, 154–56
Artificial sweeteners
headaches from, 160
hunger from, 195–96
Aspartame, headaches from, 160
Aspirin, for reducing heart attack risk, <u>120</u>, 122
Asthma attacks, ginkgo for, 83

Astroglide, for vaginal dryness, 7
Atypical endometrial hyperplasia, hysterectomy for, 21
Avocado, for dry skin, 278

B

Baby talk, sex and, 259–60
Back
lower, muscle-toning for, 213–14
upper, muscle-toning for, 215–17, 231
Back-of-the-upper-arm extensions, for muscle toning, 219, **219**
Bathing, relaxation from, <u>254</u>
Bath oil, for skin care, 273
Benzoyl peroxide, for acne, 279–80
Beta-carotene
disease prevention from, 55
for lung cancer prevention, 139
Biofeedback, for learning Kegel exercises, 164–66
Birth control
emergency, <u>15</u>
methods *(see individual methods)*
myths about, 9–15
Birth control pills
blood sugar levels and, 141
for emergency contraception, <u>15</u>
for endometriosis, 21
melasma from, 280
migraines from, 158
myths about, 9, 12–14
for short-term protection, 10
smoking and, 135
Birth of children, marriage affected by, 267–69
Blackheads, unclogging, 275–76
Bleeding
heavy menstrual, hysterectomy for, 19
from hormone replacement therapy, 31–32, 33
during pregnancy, smoking and, 135
Bloating, as side effect of progestin, 30–31
Body fat, abdominal versus hip, <u>170</u>
Bone density, effect of testosterone on, 25
Bone-density tests, 109, 110–11, <u>112</u>, 113, 114, 115
Bone loss. *See* Osteoporosis
Bones, estrogen and, <u>108</u>
Boredom, fatigue from, 246
Botulism toxin injections, for wrinkles, 285
BRCA1 gene, breast cancer and, <u>125</u>

Breakfast
cereal for, 71–76
nutritional benefits of, *73*, *75*
Breakthrough bleeding, from hormone
replacement therapy, 31–32
Breast cancer
dietary fat and, 151
estrogen and, *108*
preventing with
diet, 147
fiber, 149–150
soy products, 60
vegetables, 54
risk from
hormone replacement therapy,
122
the Pill, 13
Breast cancer gene, *125*
Breast care, 123–29
Breast exams
clinical, 123–26, 131–32
by female versus male doctors, 128
timetable for, *126*
Breastfeeding, smoking and, 135–36
Breast pain, from hormone replacement
therapy, 33–34
Breast self-exams, 126–27
Breath fresheners, natural, 276
Breathing
for controlling hot flashes, 7
for mini-relaxations, 87–90
"Broken" capillaries, 283
Burns, aloe vera for, 79, 81–82
Butter, saturated fat in, 64
Buttocks, muscle toning for, 223
Buying a house, marriage affected by,
269–70

C

Caffeine
breast pain from, 34
calcium absorption blocked by, *156*
hot flashes from, 7
Caffeine withdrawal
fatigue from, 248–49
headaches from, 160
Calcium
daily requirement for, 112, 113, *156*
depleted by sodium, *114*
menopausal requirement for, *8*, *34*
for preventing
cancer, 148
headaches, 161
Calf raises, standing, for lower leg
muscle-toning, 224, **224**

Calories
in cereal, 72
in low-fat foods, *47*, *69*
Cancer. *See also specific types*
foods for preventing, 146–51
Cane, for hip pain, 156
Capillaries, "broken," 283
Capsaicin
for congestion, 95
disease prevention from, 55
Carbohydrates, diabetes and, 142–43
Carnosol, disease prevention from, 55
Carotenoids, blocked by olestra, 67–68
Cereal
calories in, 72
combining brands of, *74*
fat in, 72–73
fiber in, 74, 75
fortified, 75–76
as ideal breakfast food, 71–76
serving size of, 72
sodium in, 73–74
sugar in, 75
Certified nurse-midwives, *37*
Cervical cancer
increased incidence of, *132*
smoking and, 136
Cervical cap, for birth control, 15
Cervicography machine, for Pap smears,
131
Chamomile
as medicinal herb, 82
for puffy eyes, 274
Cheekbone press, for relieving muscle
tension, *255*
Cheese, headaches from, 158, 159, 160
Chemical peels, for wrinkles, 285
Cherry angiomas, 282–83
in forties, 285
Chest, strengthening, 215–17, 230–31
230
Chest and shoulder raises, for muscle
toning, 216, **216**
Chest crosses, for muscle toning, 217,
217
Childhood obesity, heart disease risk
from, 118
Children, marriage affected by, 267–69
Chlamydia, testing for, 132
Chocolate
fat-free, 197–98
headaches from, 157, 160
reduced-fat, *189*
Cholesterol
HDL (*see* HDL cholesterol)
high, low-fat diet for, 48
LDL (*see* LDL cholesterol)

lowering, with soy products, 60
saturated fat and, 63
trans-fatty acids and, 63, 64
Chorionic villus sampling, for prenatal
screening, 37, 40
risk of complications from, 38
Cinnamon
antimicrobial properties of, 80
for fresh breath, 276
Circles, undereye, concealer for, 288
Cognitive therapy, for overcoming
distorted thinking, 98–105
Colds
incidence of, in women, 94
natural healing of, 92–97
Collagen injections, for wrinkles, 285
Colon cancer
dietary fat and, 151
hormone replacement therapy and, 30
preventing with
diet, 147
fiber, 149–150
folate, 148
Color-enhancing shampoo, 292
Concealers, choosing and applying, 288
Conditioners, hair, 293–94
Condoms
for birth control, 10, 15
reluctance to carry, 259
Cones, for pelvic-floor exercises, 165
Congestion, natural healing of, 95–96
Constipation, pelvic-floor weakness from,
167
Contact allergies, causes of, 282
Contraception. See Birth control
Copper-T 380A IUD, 14–15
Cosmetics. See also Makeup
natural ingredients in, 275
Coughing, natural healing of, 96–97
Couples, resemblances between, 263
Cravings, food. See Food cravings
Cross-training, for preventing knee pain,
155
Crunches, for abdominal toning, 227–28,
227, 228
Cucumber, for relieving
oily skin, 274
puffy eyes, 274
sunburn, 274
Cuddling, importance of, 263
Cytobrush, for Pap smears, 131

D

Dalkon Shield IUD, 14
Danazol (Rx), for endometriosis, 21

Dandruff, 291
jojoba oil for, 276–77
Dandruff shampoo, 291
Deep breathing, for mini-relaxations,
87–90
Dehydration
fatigue from, 246–47
with sleep deprivation, 289
Depo-Provera, for birth control, 10, 11,
12
Depression
cognitive therapy for, 98–105
from hormone replacement therapy,
34–35
from quitting smoking, 136
St.-John's-wort for, 81
testosterone and, 26–27
Desserts, diabetes and, 145
DEXA, for measuring bone density,
110–11, 112
Dexfenfluramine (Rx)
risks of, 184
for weight loss, 183, 184
Diabetes
abdominal fat and, 170
deaths from, 143
drinking fluids for, 144
eating to control, 142–45
risk factors for, 140, 141–42
triglycerides and, 121
undiagnosed, 141
Diaphragm
for birth control, 10, 15
for uterine prolapse, 20
Diary, food/mood, for curbing emotional
eating, 188, 191
Diet
for cancer prevention, 148–51
longevity and, 194
low-fat (see Low-fat diet)
for menopause, 4, 6
for perimenopause, 8
Dieting. See Weight loss
Diet pills
over-the-counter, 185
prescription, 183–85,
184
Distorted thinking
steps for undoing, 101–4
ten forms of, 99–101
Diuretics, for fluid retention,
31
Dowager's hump, 110
Down syndrome, prenatal screening for,
37, 38–39, 41
Dried fruit, sugar in, 195
Drinking. See Alcoholic beverages

Dry hair
    treatment of, <u>294</u>
    yucca root for, 277
Dry hands
    quick fix for, <u>272</u>
    soak for, 277–78
Dry nails, natural remedies for, 278
Dry skin
    avocado for, 278
    treatment of, 274
Dual Energy X-ray Absorptiometry, for
        measuring bone density, 110–11,
        <u>112</u>
Dyes, hair, <u>292</u>, 294

E

Eating
    for cancer prevention, 146–51
    emotional, 186–91
    longevity and, <u>2</u>
Eating habits, changing, for weight loss,
        178–79
Echinacea, for treating colds, 94–95
Echocardiography, exercise, for detecting
        heart disease, 117
Ectopic pregnancy, <u>11</u>
    the Pill and, 13
Elbows, dry, quick fix for, <u>272</u>
Emergency contraception, <u>15</u>
Emotional eating, 186–91
Emphysema, from smoking, 135
Endometrial cancer
    abnormal bleeding from, 32
    progestin and, 29–30
Endometrial hyperplasia, hysterectomy
        for, 21
Endometrial resection, for heavy
        menstrual bleeding, 19
Endometriosis, hysterectomy for, 21
Essential oil shampoo, for oily hair, 277
Estrogen. *See also* Hormone replacement
        therapy
    doses of, in hormone replacement
        therapy, 29
    effects of
        breakthrough bleeding, 31
        breast pain, 33
    health benefits of, <u>108</u>
    in perimenopause, 3–4
    in the Pill, 13
    for preventing
        heart disease, 122
        osteoporosis, 114, 115
    sex for increasing levels of, <u>244</u>
    vaginal dryness and, 7

Estrogen cream, topical, for vaginal dry-
        ness, 7–8
Estrogen patch, for preventing
    headaches, 34
    nausea, 35
Evening primrose oil, for vaginal dryness,
        7
Exercise echocardiography, for detecting
        heart disease, 117
Exercise(s)
    abdominal (*see* Abdominal exercises)
    for arthritis pain, 154–55, 156
    energy from, 246, 250
    frequency and duration of, <u>239</u>
    habitual, 233–36
    high-impact aerobic, pelvic-floor
        weakness from, 167
    Kegel, 8, 163–67, <u>165</u>
    longevity and, <u>2</u>
    for menopausal women, 4–6, <u>34</u>
    for preventing
        arthritis, 153
        heart disease, 121, 122
        osteoporosis, 5–6
        overeating, 203
    resistance (*see* Resistance training;
        Strength training)
    sexual desire from, 260
    stretching, 156
    walking as (*see* Walking)
    for weight loss, 177–78, 180–81
Exhalation roll-ups, for abdominal
        toning, 211, **211**
Eye contact, with loved one, 263–64
Eye puffiness
    compresses for, 287
    soothing, 274

F

Facials, for revitalizing skin, 289
Fat, body, abdominal versus hip, <u>170</u>
Fat, dietary
    calculating daily allotment of, 49
    cancer and, 150, 151
    in cereal, 72–73
    how much to limit, 47–48
    saturated
        cholesterol increase from, 63
        limiting, in diet, 49, 122
    sources of, 46
    types of, 48–49
Fat-free products, pitfalls of, 68–70, <u>69</u>
Fatigue, causes of, 245–50
Fat injections, for wrinkles, 285
Fat loss, in forties, 284

Fat shifts, causes of, 282
Fat substitutes, 67–70, 196
Feet, sunburned, quick fix for, 272
Fenfluramine (Rx)
    memory loss from, 184
    for weight loss, 183
Fertility
    in older women, 10
    smoking and, 135
Feverfew, for migraines, 82–83, 97, 161
Fiber
    for cancer prevention, 149–50
    in cereal, 74, 75
    diabetes and, 143–44
    soluble versus insoluble, 74
Fibroids, hysterectomy for, 17, 18–19
Flat hair, stinging nettles for, 277
Flavonoids, for cancer prevention, 147
Fluid retention, as side effect of
        progestin, 30–31
Fluids
    for congestion, 96
    for diabetes, 144
    for preventing fatigue, 246–47
Fluoxetine (Rx), for weight loss, 183
Folate, for cancer prevention, 148
Folate deficiency, heart disease risk from,
        121
Folic acid
    in cereal, 75
    preconception requirement for, 39
Food cravings
    from hormone replacement therapy, 31
    reasons for, 44
    reduced-fat chocolate for, 189
Food/mood diary, for curbing emotional
        eating, 188, 191
Foods
    for cancer prevention, 146–51
    filling, for weight loss, 171–75, 174
    hot, hot flashes from, 7
Food variety, longevity and, 194
Forehead release, for relieving muscle
        tension, 255
Fosamax (Rx), for osteoporosis, 114, 115
Fractures, hip, from osteoporosis, 110
Freckles, lightening, 274
Frizzy hair, rosemary oil for, 277
Fruit, dried, sugar in, 195
Fruit juice, sugar in, 195
Fruits, for cancer prevention, 146–49

G

Garlic, as medicinal herb, 83
Garlic juice, for pimples, 275

Genistein, disease prevention from, 56
Ginger, as medicinal herb, 83
Gingerol, disease prevention from, 56
Ginkgo, as medicinal herb, 83–84
Ginseng, as medicinal herb, 84
Glycolic acid peels, for wrinkles, 285
Glycyrrhizin, disease prevention from, 56
Gn-RH agonists (Rx), for endometriosis,
        21
Goldenseal, antibiotic properties of,
        84
Gonorrhea, testing for, 132
Gray hair, coloring, 292, 294
Green apples, tranquilizing scent of,
        253
Gum disease, estrogen and, 108
Gynecological exam, 130–33

H

Hair
    dry
        treatment of, 294
        yucca root for, 277
    oily, essential oil shampoo for, 277
Hair care, 290–94
    natural, 276–77
Hair color, enhancing, with herbal
        shampoo, 277
Hair coloring, 292, 294
Hair conditioners, 293–94
Hands
    arthritis in, 153, 155
    dry, 272, 277–78
HDL cholesterol
    abdominal fat and, 170
    activity level and, 200
    effect of testosterone on, 25
    exercise and, 122
    heart disease risk and, 120, 200
    low-fat diet and, 48
    Mediterranean diet and, 144
    trans-fatty acids and, 63
Headaches
    feverfew for, 82–83
    foods causing, 157–61
    from hormone replacement therapy,
        34
Heart attacks, anger and, 120
Heart disease
    abdominal fat and, 170
    cholesterol level and, 63, 64, 120, 200
    estrogen and, 4, 108
    overlooked, in women, 116–17
    preventing, with lifestyle changes,
        119

Heart disease *(continued)*
  reducing risk of
    with lifestyle changes, 121–22
    with soy products, 60
  risk factors for
    childhood obesity, 118
    cholesterol, 120
    short stature, 119
    triglycerides, 120–21
    weight gain, 117
  from smoking, 135
  testosterone and, <u>24</u>, 25
  trans-fatty acids and, <u>65</u>
Heat, for arthritis pain, 154
Heberden's nodes, 153
Height, heart disease risk and, 119
Herbal shampoo, for enhancing hair
    color, 277
Herbs
  breath-freshening, 276
  medicinal, for natural healing, 79–85,
    94–95, 96–97
High blood pressure, abdominal fat and,
    <u>170</u>, <u>226</u>
High-density lipoprotein (HDL)
    cholesterol. *See* HDL cholesterol
Hip fat, versus abdominal fat, <u>170</u>
Hip flexors, abdominal toning and, 229,
    229
Hip fractures, from osteoporosis, 110
Hip pain, cane for relieving, 156
Hip raises, for buttock muscle-toning,
    223, **223**
Hips, arthritis in, 153
Histamine, headaches from, 159
Honey, for acne, 275
Horehound, for coughs, 96
Hormone replacement therapy
  after oophorectomy, <u>20</u>
  benefits of, 6–7
  continuous regimen of, 32, 33, 34
  customizing, 28–35
  cyclic regimen of, 32, 33, 34
  longevity and, <u>2</u>
  for preventing heart disease, 122
  side effects of
    bloating, 30–31
    breast pain, 33–34
    depression and anxiety, 34–35
    food cravings, 31
    headaches, 34
    nausea, 35
    periods, 33
    unpredictable bleeding or spotting,
      31–32
    weight gain, 31
  testosterone in, 22–27

Hormones. *See also specific hormones*
  acne and, <u>281</u>
  migraines from, 158
Hot flashes
  controlling, 7
  in perimenopause, 4
  sleep deprivation from, <u>247</u>
Hot foods, hot flashes from, 7
House buying, marriage affected by,
    269–70
Household tasks, increased activity from,
    200
Humor, in love relationships, 262–63
Hydrogenation, trans-fatty acids from,
    64
Hysterectomy
  alternatives to, 16–21
  doctors prescribing, <u>18</u>
  questions to ask about, <u>20</u>

I

Ice, for arthritis pain, 154
Imipramine (Rx), for depression,
    81
Incontinence
  stress, 8, 162–67
  urinary, smoking and, 136
Indoles, for cancer prevention, 56,
    147
Infections
  urinary tract, 8
  vaginal, 8
Infertility, from smoking, 135
Injury, arthritis from, 153
Innate aging, of skin, 283, 285
Insufficient sleep syndrome, 286. *See also*
    Sleep deprivation
Insulin resistance, abdominal fat and,
    <u>170</u>
Intermittent claudication, ginkgo for, 84
Intrauterine device. *See* IUD
Iron, in cereal, 76
Iron supplements, for relieving anemia,
    19
Isoflavones
  for cancer prevention, 147
  in soybeans, 59
Isothiocyanates, for cancer prevention,
    147
Isotretinoin (Rx), for acne, 280
IUD
  diabetes and, 141
  for emergency contraception, <u>15</u>
  for long-term protection, 10, 11
  myths about, 9–10, 14–15

J

Job changes, marriage affected by, 269
Jojoba oil, for dandruff, 276–77
Juice
    phytomins in, <u>57</u>
    sugar in, 195
Juvenile-onset diabetes, 141

K

Kegel exercises, for stress incontinence, 8,
    163–67, <u>165</u>
Keratoses
    actinic, from sun exposure, 285
    seborrheic, 283
Keratosis pilaris, treatment of, 274
Knee bends, modified, for thigh and but-
    tock muscle-toning, 220, **220**
Knee pain
    preventing, <u>155</u>
    stair climbing and, 241–42
Knees, arthritis in, 153, <u>155</u>
Knee-to-chest lift, single, for lower back
    muscle-toning, 213, **213**
K-Y Jelly, for vaginal dryness, 7

L

Laser peels, for wrinkles, 285
Lavender essence, bathing in, <u>254</u>
Laxative, senna as, 80
LDL cholesterol
    exercise and, 122
    heart attack risk and, 120
    reducing with
        corn oil products, 66
        Mediterranean diet, 144
        strength training, 207
        trans-fatty acids and, 63
Left ventricular hypertrophy, from over-
    weight, 118
Leg extensions, seated, for thigh and but-
    tock muscle-toning, 221, **221**
Leg raises
    for preventing arthritis pain, 155
    standing side, for thigh and buttock
        muscle-toning, 222, **222**
Legs
    lower, muscle-toning for, 224, **224**
    thighs, muscle-toning for, 220–22
Lemon juice, for age spots, 274
Leptin, obesity and, <u>172</u>
Libido, decreased, in menopause, 22, 24,
    25, 26, 27, <u>27</u>

Licorice, for coughs, 96
Life expectancy, of women, <u>2</u>
Lifting, proper technique for, 167
Limonenes, disease prevention from, 56
Liposome, for photoaging, 283
Liver spots, in forties, 285
Longevity
    food variety and, <u>194</u>
    weight loss for, <u>235</u>
    of women, <u>2</u>
Love relationships, improving, 261–65
Low birth weight, smoking and, 135,
    137
Low-density lipoprotein (LDL)
        cholesterol. *See* LDL cholesterol
Lower back muscle-toning, 213–14
Lower back stretches, seated, for lower
        back muscle-toning, 214, **214**
Lower legs, muscle-toning for, 224, **224**
Low-fat diet, 45–51
    benefits of, 45, 46, 47
    calories and, <u>47</u>, <u>69</u>
    for cancer prevention, 150, 151
    how to follow, 49–51
    for menopausal women, <u>34</u>
    for preventing heart disease, 6, 122
    for weight loss, 179
Low-fat foods, pitfalls of, <u>69</u>, 69–70
Lubricants, for vaginal dryness, 7
Lunchmeat, headaches from, 157, 159,
    160
Lung cancer, from smoking, 135, <u>137</u>
Lutein, disease prevention from, 56
Lycopene, disease prevention from, 56
Lymph nodes, examining, for signs of
    breast cancer, 124–25

M

Makeup
    concealers, <u>288</u>
    for hiding fatigue, 289
Mammograms, <u>126</u>, 127
Margarine
    choosing, 64–66
    trans-fatty acids in, 63–64
Marriage
    improving, 261–65
    life changes affecting, 266–70
    successful, keys to, <u>268</u>
Mask of pregnancy, 280
Massage
    face, 288–89
    for muscle tension, <u>255</u>
    neck, <u>159</u>
    scalp, <u>294</u>

Meal size, in Three-Plus-Four Eating Plan, 192–93
Meats, cured, headaches from, 157, 159, 160
Medical history, longevity and, 2
Medicinal herbs, for natural healing, 79–85, 94–95, 96–97
Mediterranean diet, for diabetes, 144
Medroxyprogesterone acetate (Rx), periods from, 33
Megestrol acetate (Rx), in hormone replacement therapy, 33
Melaleuca, 275
Melanoma, ruling out, 280
Melasma, in pregnancy, 280
Memory, estrogen and, 108
Menopause. *See also* Perimenopause
  bone density during, 113–14
  natural remedies for, 27
  prelude to, 3
  preparing for, 4–5
  sleep deprivation during, 247
  smoking and, 136
  strength training after, 207
  testosterone for, 22–27
Menstruation
  heavy, hysterectomy for, 19
  migraines from, 158
Miacalcin (Rx), for osteoporosis, 114
Micronized progesterone, in hormone replacement therapy, 31, 32, 33–34
Midwives, certified nurse-, 37
Migraines
  feverfew for, 82–83, 97
  foods causing, 157–61
Mind-body connection, 86–91
Mini-relaxations, for stress relief, 87–91
Mint, as medicinal herb, 84–85
Miscarriage, smoking and, 135
Moisturizers
  for skin care, 273
  for vaginal dryness, 7
Moles, 280, 284
Monosodium glutamate, headaches from, 159–60
Monoterpenes, for cancer prevention, 57, 148
Monounsaturated oils, benefits of, 49
Mori-Nu Silken Tofu, 60, 61
Motion sickness, ginger for, 83
MSG, headaches from, 159–60
Muscle toning. *See* Resistance training; Strength training
Music, for relaxation, 102, 253–54
Myomectomy, for fibroids, 19

N

Nails, dry, natural remedies for, 278
Nasal calcitonin (Rx), for osteoporosis, 114
Natural cosmetics, commercial, 275
Natural healing
  with cognitive therapy, 98–105
  for colds, 92–97
  with herbal medicine, 79–85, 94–95, 96–97
  for menopause symptoms, 27
  with mini-relaxations, 87–91
  popularity of, among women, 78
Nausea, from hormone replacement therapy, 35
Neck, wrinkled, quick fix for, 272
Neck massager, homemade, 159
Negative thinking
  steps for undoing, 101–4
  ten forms of, 99–101
Nettles, for flat hair, 277
Neural tube defects, prenatal screening for, 38, 39
Nicotine, calcium absorption blocked by, 156
Nicotine gum, for quitting smoking, 137–38
Nicotine patch, for quitting smoking, 122, 137, 138
Night sweats, in perimenopause, 4
Nitrates, headaches from, 159, 160
Nitrites, headaches from, 159, 160
Nonsteroidal anti-inflammatory drugs (NSAIDs), for heavy menstrual bleeding, 19
Norethindrone acetate (Rx), in hormone replacement therapy, 31, 33
Norethindrone (Rx), in hormone replacement therapy, 31, 33
Norgestrel (Rx), in hormone replacement therapy, 31, 33
Norplant, 10, 11, 12
NSAIDs, for heavy menstrual bleeding, 19
Nutlettes, as soy cereal, 61
Nutraceuticals, for disease prevention, 52

O

Oats, for sunburn, 274
Obesity. *See also* Overweight
  childhood, heart disease risk from, 118
  diet pills for, 183–85
  preventing, 46

Obesity gene, 172, 182–83
Occiput press, for relieving muscle tension, 255
Oily hair, essential oil shampoo for, 277
Oily skin, homemade toner for, 274
Olean, in fat-free foods, 68
Olestra
  benefits of, 68
  side effects of, 67–68
Omega-3 fatty acids, importance of, 49
Omega-6 fatty acids, importance of, 49
Oophorectomy, effects of, 20
Oral contraceptives. *See* Birth control pills
Oral micronized progesterone, for hormone replacement therapy, 31, 32, 33–34
Organosulfur compounds, for cancer prevention, 147
Orgasms, for vaginal dryness, 8
Osteoarthritis, 152
Osteoporosis
  development of, 110
  estrogen and, 4, 108
  preventing with
    resistance exercise, 5–6
    soy products, 60
    weight-bearing exercise, 5
  risk factors for, 112–15
  testing for, 109, 110–11, 112, 113, 114, 115
Ovarian cancer
  estrogen and, 108
  the Pill and, 13
  ultrasound for detecting, 17
Ovaries, removing, in hysterectomy, 20
Overeating, exercise for preventing, 203
Overload, fatigue from, 249
Overweight. *See also* Obesity
  arthritis and, 152–53
  cancer risk from, 150
  left ventricular hypertrophy from, 118
  low-fat diet for, 48
  pelvic-floor weakness from, 167

P

Pain
  arthritis, 154–56
  breast, 33–34
  hip, 156
  knee, 155, 241–42
Palming, for relieving muscle tension, 255

Papaya
  for blackheads, 276
  for dry skin, 278
Pap tests
  accuracy of, 132–33
  decline in number performed, 132
  state-of-the-art tools for, 131
ParaGard IUD, 14–15
Patch test, for natural beauty treatments, 276
Pelvic-floor exercises, for stress incontinence, 163–67, 165
Pelvic-muscle contraction, for preventing stress incontinence, 166
Pelvic tilt
  for abdominal toning, 228–29, **228**, **229**
  for lower back muscle-toning, 214, **214**
Peppermint
  for blackheads, 275–76
  as medicinal herb, 84, 85
Perimenopause, 3–8. *See also* Menopause
  diet for, 8
  self-care for, 5
  symptoms of, 4, 5
Perineometer, for learning pelvic-floor exercises, 165
Periods
  heavy, hysterectomy for, 19
  from hormone replacement therapy, 33
Pessary, for uterine prolapse, 20
Phenethyl isothiocyanates, disease prevention from, 57
Phentermine (Rx)
  memory loss from, 184
  for weight loss, 183, 185
Photoaging
  in forties, 285
  in thirties, 283
  in twenties, 280–81
Phytic acid, disease prevention from, 57
Phytochemicals
  for disease prevention, 53–55
  types of, 55–57
Phytomins
  for disease prevention, 52–57
  in juice, 57
Pill, the. *See* Birth control pills
Pimples, natural remedies for, 275
Pineapple juice, for age spots, 274
Polyphenol catechins, disease prevention from, 57
Polyphenols, disease prevention from, 57
Polyunsaturated oils, benefits of, 49
Pondimin (Rx), for weight loss, 183

Posture, for flattening abdomen, 226
Potatoes, as satiating food, 172, 173, 174,
        174
Potbellies, flattening, 208–13, 225–32
Pre-cancer, hysterectomy for, 21
Pregnancy
    after-40, prenatal testing during,
        36–42
    melasma from, 280
    smoking during, 135, 137
    tubal, 11
        the Pill and, 13
Prenatal testing, 36–42
Progestasert IUD, 15
Progesterone, micronized, in hormone
        replacement therapy, 31, 32,
        33–34
Progestin (Rx). *See also* Hormone
        replacement therapy
    for breakthrough bleeding, 32
    effects of
        breast pain, 33
        depression and anxiety, 35
        fluid retention, 30–31
        periods, 33
    sensitivity to, 29, 32
Prolapse, uterine, hysterectomy for,
        19–20
Prostate cancer, dietary fat and, 151
Prozac (Rx), for weight loss, 183
Psoriasis, 291
Puffy eyes
    compresses for, 287
    soothing, 274
Purple coneflower, for treating colds,
        94–95
Push-ups, modified, for muscle toning,
        215, 215

R

Rashes, causes of, 282
Rectal cancer, dietary prevention of,
        147
Redux (Rx), for weight loss, 183, 184
Red wine, headaches from, 157, 159,
        161
Relationships, improving, 261–65
Relaxation
    for stress relief, 250
    techniques for, 251–55
        bathing, 254
        experiencing nature, 252–53
        massage, 255
        mini-relaxations, 87–91
        music, 102, 253–54

repetition, 251
scents, 253
touching, 254–55
Renova (Rx), for dry hands, 272
Replens, for vaginal dryness, 7
Resistance training. *See also* Strength
        training
    metabolism increased by, 31
    for osteoporosis prevention, 5–6
Retin-A (Rx)
    for acne, 280
    for photoaging, 283
Reverse trunk rotations, for abdominal
        toning, 212–13, 212
Rosemary oil, for frizzy hair, 277

S

Salicylic acid, for acne, 280
Salt. *See* Sodium
Salt restriction, for fluid retention, 31
Saltwater, for sore throat, 97
Saponins, disease prevention from, 57
Saturated fat
    cholesterol increase from, 63
    limiting, in diet, 49, 122
Scalp massage, 294
Scalp relaxer, for relieving muscle tension,
        255
Scents, relaxation from, 253
Seborrhea, 284
Seborrheic dermatitis, 291
Seborrheic keratoses, 283
Selenium, for cancer prevention,
        149
Senna, as laxative, 80
Serotonin
    appetite suppressed by, 183
    artificial sweeteners and, 195
Sex
    health benefits of, 244
    improving, 256–60
Sex counseling, for decreased sex drive,
        27
Sex drive, decreased, in menopause, 22,
        24, 25, 26, 27, 27
Sexual habits, analyzing, 260
Sexually transmitted diseases, discussing,
        during checkup, 131
Sexual synchrony, increasing, 261–62
Shampoos
    choosing, 293
    color-enhancing, 292
    dandruff, 291
    natural, 277
    switching, 291, 293, 294

Shea butter, for skin care, 273, 274
Shinsplints, preventing, 241
Shoes
    for preventing knee pain, 155
    for using stair-climbers, 241
Short stature, heart disease risk from, 119
Shoulders, strengthening, 215–17, 230, **230**
Skin
    dry
        avocado for, 278
        treatment of, 274
    oily, homemade toner for, 274
Skin care, natural, 273–76
Skin damage. *See also* Photoaging
    from smoking, 136
Skin problems. *See also specific skin problems*
    in forties, 284–85
    in thirties, 281–83
    in twenties, 279–81
Skin tags, 280
Sleep, mood affected by, 100
Sleep deprivation
    causes of, 247
    effects of, 286–89
    fatigue from, 248
Slippery elm bark
    for coughs, 96–97
    as medicinal herb, 85
Smoking
    effects of, 135–36
    light, risks of, 137
    longevity and, 2
    pelvic-floor weakness from, 167
    the Pill and, 13
    quitting, 134, 136–39
        for preventing heart disease, 121–22
        withdrawal symptoms from, 136, 138, 139
Snacking
    diabetes and, 143
    guidelines for, 193–98
Snacks, low-fat, 196–97
Sodium
    calcium depleted by, 114
    in cereal, 73–74
    diabetes and, 144–45
Sodium fluoride, for osteoporosis, 114
Sore throat, saltwater for, 97
Soy
    examples of one serving of, 62
    health benefits of, 58–62
Soy milk, 59–60
Soy-protein beverages, 61–62
Spearmint, as medicinal herb, 84, 85

Speculoscope, for Pap smears, 131
Spider veins, 284
Spina bifida
    folic acid for preventing, 75
    prenatal screening for, 37, 38, 39
Spiru-Tein soy protein powder, 61–62
Splints, for arthritis pain, 155
Spotting, from hormone replacement therapy, 31–32
St.-John's-wort, for depression, 81
Stair-climbers, for weight loss, 237–42
Stair climbing, arthritis pain from, 155
Steam, for congestion, 96
Sterilization
    as birth control method, 9, 10–12
    pregnancy after, 11
Stop-smoking programs, 137
Straight-leg raises, for preventing arthritis pain, 155
Strength training
    benefits of, 207
    guidelines for starting, 208
    for older women, 207
    for osteoporosis prevention, 5–6
    for toning
        buttocks, 223
        chest, 215–17
        lower back, 213–14
        lower legs, 224
        shoulders, 215–17
        thighs, 220–22
        upper arms, 218–19
        upper back, 215–17
Stress
    fatigue from, 249–50
    methods for relieving, 88
    mini-relaxations for, 87–91
    physical effects of, 86, 88
Stress incontinence, 162–67
    Kegel exercises for, 8, 163–67, 165
Stretching, for arthritis pain, 156
Sudden infant death syndrome, smoking and, 135, 137
Sugar, in cereal, 75
Sulforaphane, disease prevention from, 57
Sunblock, for preventing photoaging, 281
Sunburn, treatment of, 272, 274
Sun damage
    in forties, 285
    in thirties, 283
    in twenties, 280–81
Support system, for weight loss, 177, 191
Sweet beans, as soy source, 61

T

Take Care High Protein Beverage Powder, soy protein in, 61, 62

TC3. *See* Tea tree oil

Tea bags, for puffy eyes, 287

Tea tree oil
    for pimples, 275
    rashes from, 275, <u>275</u>

Television, sex life affected by, 257–58

Testosterone
    heart disease and, <u>24</u>, 25
    for menopausal women, 22–27

Testosterone implants, <u>26</u>

Testosterone pills, <u>26</u>

Testosterone shots, <u>26</u>

Textured soy protein, sloppy joes made from, 61

Thallium treadmill test, for detecting heart disease, 117

Theaflavin, disease prevention from, 57

Therapy, cognitive, for overcoming distorted thinking, 98–105

Thighs, muscle toning for, 220–22

Three-Plus-Four Eating Plan, 193–98

Thyroid, effect of dieting on, 248

Tofranil (Rx), for depression, <u>81</u>

Tofu, recipes using, 60–61

Tooth loss, estrogen and, <u>108</u>

Touching, relaxation from, 254–55

Trans-fatty acids, health risks from, 63–66

Transpyramid breathing exercise, for abdominal toning, 209–10

Tretinoin (Rx)
    for acne, 280
    for dry hands, <u>272</u>
    for photoaging, 283

Triglycerides
    abdominal fat and, <u>170</u>
    heart attack risk and, 120–21

Triple screen, for prenatal screening, <u>40</u>

Triterpenoids, disease prevention from, 56

Tubal ligation
    as birth control method, 10–12, <u>11</u>
    pregnancy after, <u>11</u>

Tubal pregnancy, <u>11</u>
    the Pill and, 13

Tyramine, headaches from, 158–59, 160, 161

U

Ultrasound, for prenatal screening, <u>40</u>

Undereye circles, concealer for, <u>288</u>

Upper arms
    flabby, quick fix for, <u>272</u>
    muscle-toning, 218–19

Upper back, strengthening, 215–17, 231, **231**

Urinary incontinence, smoking and, 136

Urinary tract infections, after menopause, 8

Urination, frequent, Kegel exercises for, 8

Uterine prolapse, hysterectomy for, 19–20

V

Vaginal dryness, in menopause, 7–8

Vaginal infections, after menopause, 8

Valerian, tranquilizing properties of, 85

Validation, in love relationships, 264

Varicose veins, 284

Vegetables, for cancer prevention, 146–49

Veins
    spider, 284
    varicose, 284

Vitamin C, for colds, 95

Vitamin D
    for headache prevention, 161
    for healthy bones, <u>111</u>, 112

Vitamin E
    for dry nails, 278
    for vaginal dryness, 7

Vitamin E cream, for nose irritation, 97

W

Waist-to-hip ratio, diabetes risk and, 142

Walking
    for couples, <u>267</u>
    for diabetes control, 145
    for weight loss, 180, 201–5, 237–38

Weight control, for preventing
    arthritis, 153
    cancer, 150
    heart disease, 121
    knee pain, <u>155</u>

Weight gain
    heart disease risk from, 117
    from hormone replacement therapy, 31
    from quitting smoking, <u>138</u>, 139

Weight loss
    for arthritis, 152–53
    elements for success in, 176–77
    emotional eating and, 186–91

fatigue and, 247–48
longevity and, 235
techniques for, 177–81
    diet pills, 183–85
    eating filling foods, 171–75, 174
    exercise, 177–78, 180–81
    food routine, 181
    low-fat diet, 46
    low-fat eating, 179
    new eating habits, 178–79
    portion control, 179–80
    self-motivation, 178
    stair-climbers, 237–42
    support system, 177
    Three-Plus-Four Eating Plan for,
        192–98
    walking, 180, 201–5, 237–38
Wine, red, headaches from, 157, 159, 161

Withdrawal symptoms, from quitting
    smoking, 136, 138, 139
Work, effect on
    marriage, 269
    sex life, 258
Wrinkled neck, quick fix for, 272
Wrinkles, in forties, 285

Y

Yogurt, for acne, 275
Yucca root, for dry hair, 277

Z

Zeaxanthin, disease prevention from,
    56